Folklore and the Internet

Vernacular Expression in a Digital World

Folklore and the Internet

Vernacular Expression in a Digital World

Edited by
Trevor J. Blank

Utah State University Press
Logan, Utah

Utah State University Press
Logan, Utah 84322-7800
USUPress.org

ISBN: 978-0-87421-750-6 (paper)
ISBN: 978-0-87421-751-3 (e-book)

Manufactured in the United States of America

Printed on acid-free, recycled paper

Library of Congress Cataloging-in-Publication Data

Folklore and the internet : vernacular expression in a digital world / edited by
Trevor J. Blank.
    p. cm.
  Includes bibliographical references and index.
  ISBN 978-0-87421-750-6 (pbk. : alk. paper) -- ISBN 978-0-87421-751-3 (e-book)
  1. Folklore and the Internet. 2. Folklore--Computer network resources. 3. Digital
communications. I. Blank, Trevor J.
  GR44.E43F65 2009
  398.02854678--dc22
                                    2009026813

To Charley Camp, friend and mentor

Contents

Acknowledgments

First and foremost, thanks are due to the incredible staff at the Utah State University Press for their unwavering support, enthusiasm, and dedication to this project from its inception. I am indebted, in particular, to John Alley, executive editor of the Utah State University Press, for his ongoing correspondence, guidance, and suggestions throughout the project's lifespan.

I wish to also thank the American Folklore Society (AFS), which hosted early versions of several essays contained in this book at annual conferences as well as on AFS discussion forums. As the most prominent folklore organization in America, the society has been a tremendous partner in testing out ideas, sharing information amongst scholars, and garnering support for the project. I am also thankful for the camaraderie and sharing of ideas that have taken place at the annual meetings of the Hoosier Folklore Society, Pioneer America Society: Association for the Preservation of Artifacts and Landscapes, and the Western States Folklore Society, whose conferences have greatly contributed to the growing awareness of the possibilities for the collaborative study of folklore and the Internet in recent years.

Numerous people have provided stimulating discussion and postulations, often suggesting helpful approaches to managing the book project and its content. I am especially grateful to Donald Allport Bird, Simon Bronner, John Dorst, Bill Ellis, Gregory Hansen, Robert Glenn Howard, Lydia Fish, Jay Mechling, Elizabeth Tucker, and William Westerman for their insights. And particularly to Charley Camp, to whom this book is dedicated; I am most appreciative of his nurturing mentorship, friendship, and encouragement in influencing my decision to join the folklore discipline. He is both a scholar and a gentleman, and I am indebted to him for all of his support over the years.

Of course, many colleagues, friends, and family offered incredible amounts of support throughout the book's production. To my parents, Bruce and Anita, and my sister Natalie, I am grateful for the chats that have helped to get my mind off of the never-ending piles of papers that inhabit my living space. I am also fortunate to have worked with my esteemed colleagues at the Department of American Studies, University of Maryland, Baltimore County; in particular I would like to thank Warren Belasco, Kathy Bryan, Jason Loviglio, and Ed Orser for their mentorship and friendship. At Indiana University's Folklore Institute a special thanks are in order for my colleagues Inta Carpenter, Henry Glassie, Jason Baird Jackson, Jon Kay, John McDowell, and Pravina Shukla; in the department of History, Ellen Dwyer, Matt Guterl, Ed Linenthal, and Eric Sandweiss; and in the School of Education, Dionne Danns, Andrea Walton, and Donald Warren. The staff at *Folklore Forum*, especially Curtis Ashton, Kate Schramm, Kristiana Willsey, and Ed Wolf are owed a thank-you for their encouragement and work on the important volume 37 of the journal, which was the special issue dedicated to the Internet. I am also indebted to my friends Ronald L. Baker, Dawn Bowen, Ginny Buckner, Rebekah Burchfield, Susan Eckelmann, Gary Alan Fine, Katherine Forgacs, Laura Garcia-Houser, Angelina Sanfilippo, Rebecca Geitz, Aaron Glatt, Ryan Gray, John Heflin, Angela Johnson, Artimus Keiffer, Jimmy Kerner, Mike "Cleg" Kapp, Kara Lairson, Justin Levy, Mark Liechty, Dane McConnell, Nan McEntire, Lynwood Montell, Mark Montgomery, Selina Morales, Chris Mulé, Dorothy Noyes, Chris Post, Scott Roper, Jim Seaver, Wayne Smith, Michael Stuckey, Michael Symonds, Sabra Weber, Priscilla Wysong, Rebecca Yingling, and Adam Zolkover for their support, suggestions, and friendship.

Last, but certainly not least, all of the contributors to this volume are due tremendous credit for their diligence in meeting our tight deadlines, revisions, and production goals. All were true professionals and have made this experience very rewarding.

Introduction

Toward a Conceptual Framework for the Study of Folklore and the Internet

Trevor J. Blank

In his essay "Toward a Definition of Folklore in Context," Dan Ben-Amos asserts: "If the initial assumption of folklore research is based on the disappearance of its subject matter, there is no way to prevent the science from following the same road" (1971, 14). In similar fashion, Alan Dundes began his presidential plenary address to the American Folklore Society in 2004 with a grim outlook on the future of the discipline by contending that the "state of folkloristics at the beginning of the twenty-first century is depressingly worrisome" (2005, 385). Such alarm-sounding statements merit our attention, but the fact remains that this has been a recurring assertion within this academic discipline for some time (Oring 1998). Richard Dorson lamented in 1972 that in "a few more years, there will be no more folklore, and *ergo*, no need for any folklorists" (41); but as Dorson "responded by looking elsewhere and [subsequently] found folklore in the media and a folk in the city" (Kirshenblatt-Gimblett 1998, 302), we too must respond by looking elsewhere when such feelings of impending doom surface in folklore scholarship.

Folklore is a self-conscious discipline, and speculation on the future of folkloristics—the academic study of folklore—has been pessimistic at best. In a similar vein, Richard Bauman and Charles L. Briggs note that tradition "has been reportedly on the verge of dying for more than three centuries, [yet] . . . continues to provide useful means of producing and legitimizing new modernist projects, sets of legislators, and schemes of social inequality" (Bauman and Briggs 2003, 306). Despite all of the doom and gloom, folklore "continues to be alive and well in the modern world, due in part to increased transmission via e-mail and the Internet" (Dundes 2005, 406). It is time that folklorists look to the Internet, not only to expand our scholastic horizons but also to carry our discipline into the digital age.

The formulation of the World Wide Web network has its roots in the Cold War tensions of the mid-twentieth century. The earliest incarnations were spawned in the form of the U.S. Department of Defense's Advanced Research Projects Agency Network (ARPANET), created mainly in response to the Soviet Union's launching of Sputnik. Beginning in 1958, ARPANET served the military and academic researchers as a means of communication and as a command tool for defense operations. E-mail technology was created in 1970, and by the 1980s people were interacting online through bulletin boards (discussion groups), MUDs (multiuser dungeons), and the WELL (Whole Earth 'Lectronic Link), a social network composed of Internet users from across the globe; later, Internet Relay Chat (IRC) followed (Hafner and Lyon 1998).[1]

The modern Internet emerged with the creation of the World Wide Web in 1989 by English computer scientist Timothy Berners-Lee. The development of HyperText Markup Language (HTML) and web browser technology allowed the Internet to expand from an exclusive academic forum into the worldwide phenomenon it is today. In 1992, the Internet was opened to the public domain.

> At the beginning of the 1990s there took place a fundamental trans-formation of the Internet . . . as the web became the center of the Internet and web browsers became the most common way of access-ing it, transformations in the communication processes established over the Internet also took place due to the specific characteristic of the web and its browsers. The web introduced new ways of commu-nicating over the Internet, facilitated the use of the net, leading to its popularization, and, to a great extent, also facilitated and promoted its commercialization (Bermejo, 2007, 73).

As the Internet developed as a communications facilitator, folklore emerged as recognizably on it as it did in "the real world." From the earliest moments of the modern Internet's existence, folklore was a cen-tral component of the domain, moderating the intersection of computer professionals with hackers, newfangled lingo, and the dispersal of sto-ries, pranks, and legends (Jennings 1990).[2] Bruce McClelland notes that as a result, "the boundary between the actual and the virtual began to become blurred" (2000, 182). Established academics recognized both the power presented by the burgeoning of Internet folklore and the importance carried by studying it: "Right now, all we have on the Net is folklore, like the Netiquette that old-timers try to teach the flood of new arrivals, and debates about freedom of expression versus nurturance of community . . . A science of Net behavior is not going to reshape the way people behave on-line, but knowledge of the dynamics of how people do behave is an important social feedback loop to install if the Net is to be self-governing at any scale" (Rheingold 2000, 64).[3] But while folklore emerged on the Internet, folklorists generally did not follow it.

When the World Wide Web took off in the 1990s, the allied disciplines of anthropology, sociology, and communication studies began paying careful attention to various sociocultural dimensions of the Internet, but amid this dialogue only a small handful of thoughtful folkloristic articles on the burgeoning Internet culture appeared (Baym 1993; Dorst 1990; Howard 1997; Kirshenblatt-Gimblett 1995, 1996; Roush 1997). With few exceptions, folklorists have generally neglected the Internet as a venue for academic inquiry for nearly two decades, and a large portion of the existing literature on folklore and the Internet has been penned by armchair folklorists—scholars untrained in the vocabulary and methodologies of the discipline— through the lens of social science, communication, and literature degrees. Each year, the American Folklore Society's annual meeting boasts more papers and panels on folklore and the Internet than the year before, yet these papers have not found their way to a culminating publication. One of the first and only specialized folkloristic examinations of the Internet took place on the electronic pages of the graduate-student-run *Folklore Forum* of Indiana University,[4] which published a special issue on the topic in spring 2007 (volume 37, no. 1); the issue featured only *two* original articles on the topic (Blank 2007; Foote 2007).[5]

To seek out folkloristic literature about the Internet is to spend numerous hours piecing together data strewn about aimlessly, spanning many years and multiple publications. *Folklore Forum* notwithstanding, no comprehensive work that details the folkloristic approach to the study of the Internet has been produced to date. It is my hope that this book will help to fill that void. In a discipline seemingly obsessed with a fear of its own demise, the Internet provides a limitless frontier for contemporary scholastic possibilities. If it is currency we seek, then we needn't look further. "It is here, in the heat of a nascent technology," writes Kirshenblatt-Gimblett, "that we can contemplate what folklore's contemporary subject might be," adding that "electronic communication offers an opportunity to rethink folklore's disciplinary givens and to envision a fully contemporary subject. It is not a matter of finding folklore analogues between the paperless office and the paperwork empire. The differences are consequential" (1995, 72–73).

So why have folklorists taken so long to systematically study the impact of the Internet? The exact reasons that folklorists as a group have predominantly ignored the Internet and technologically based folklore are uncertain. Folklore theory holds that folkloric expression is reflective and serves as a "mirror" of societal and cultural values; folklorists should therefore use this mirror to analyze society and culture. This ought to encourage a scholarly examination of the Internet, due to this format's status as a major agent of communication (especially over the last decade). Still, folklorists of the late twentieth century have not budged. This lack of motivation in studying the use of folklore in burgeoning technology could conceivably rest within the ideologies bestowed upon folklore trainees prior the advent of the Internet and computerlore. Perhaps Richard Dorson's fears regarding the permeance of "fakelore" made the unverifiability of technologically based folklore a skeptical topic among new and old folklorists alike. Maybe it has been folklorists' favoritism toward the study of vanishing cultures and traditions, or "old-timey stuff" (as Henry Glassie used to call it in his graduate lectures).[6]

Or, perchance, could it be that no one scholar (or group of scholars) has stepped forward to guide the discipline into studying this field? There has been plenty of internal chatter about the Internet at folklore meetings, and the occasional journal article, but folklorists have not engaged in a greater dialogue with allied disciplines. Once folklorists liberate themselves from their self-imposed boundaries of scholastic inquiry, they will be able to complement or challenge the concepts put forth by scholars in fields such as sociology, communications, and popular-culture studies.

As Simon Bronner (2002) notes, the Internet is often thought of as mass culture par excellence, but it is hard to miss its qualities as a system of and a storehouse for folklore.[7] Still, the inherent intangibility of the Internet's interface may have made some ethnographers hesitant to engage the format. After all, Ben-Amos' classic definition of folklore assertively emphasizes that "folklore communication takes place in a situation in which people confront each other face to face and relate to each other directly" (1971, 12–13), yet he also declares that folklore "is the action that happens at [the time of the communicative event]" and, as such, "is an artistic action" (10). This is confusing when carried over into an Internet context. Clearly, communicative events take place, but the lack of face-to-face interactions contradicts the instinctual efforts of the ethnographer. These are only a few of the potential reasons why folklorists have neglected the Internet as a venue for scholastic inquiry.

It is important to note that not *all* folklorists turned a blind eye to the possibilities of studying folklore and technology.[8] Alan Dundes, one of folklore's greatest thinkers, knew that technology was a friend of the folklorist, not a foe. He wrote (as Bronner reminds us in chapter 1) that "technology isn't stamping out folklore; rather it is becoming a vital factor in the transmission of folklore and it is providing an exciting source of inspiration for the generation of new folklore" (1980, 17). Unfortunately, it appears that the majority of folklore scholars have missed this statement. While folk processes will exist so long as humans communicate and create, the academic discipline of folklore continues to be at risk of disappearing into other fields, either by way of assimilation or by a change in terminological boundaries. There has been internal bickering over the term "folklore" itself and its applicability as an ideological label for what folklorists study (Bendix 1998; Kirshenblatt-Gimblett 1998; Oring 1998). Regina Bendix notes that the field of folklore resists "semantic imprisonment" and thrives "on interdisciplinarity of method and thought" (1998, 237). So there is still confusion as to what exactly constitutes folklore, and presumably the debate will continue so long as there are constituents to argue about it.

For the purposes of this book, it is important to define what, specifically, constitutes "folklore," particularly in an Internet context, in order to better frame the ideological underpinnings by which the authors and editor operate. Folklorists must be careful to carve out their niche in the scholarly dialogue so as not to confuse their approaches with those of anthropology or sociology. Not every issue involving electronic communication is necessarily a folklore issue, and we must equally examine the modifying terms that fall under the umbrella of "folklore" in an Internet context. What comprises vernacular expression? What do tradition, belief, legend, performance, and narrative mean in an Internet context? How does the Internet complicate notions of folk group, of audience, and of the dynamic, reflexive character of performance? As a mediatory agent, how does the Internet affect expression, engender unique folkloric material (and thus become a distinctive folk product itself), and reconfigure the nature of communication as a form of cultural maintenance and definition?

McClelland simplifies folklore by describing it as "communicative behavior whose primary characteristics . . . are that . . . it doesn't 'belong' to an individual or group . . . and in the modern context therefore transcends issues of intellectual property; and [that] . . . it is transmitted spontaneously, from one individual (or group of individuals) to another under certain conditions, frequently without regard for remuneration or return benefit. As it is transmitted, it often undergoes modification, according to the inclination of the retransmitter" (2000, 184). This description weighs communication and transmission more heavily as essential components than do traditional notions of folklore, which celebrate the role of creativity and aesthetics. Nonetheless, folklore isn't limited to orality. Kirshenblatt-Gimblett notes that "folklore as a discipline has tended to conceive the everyday in largely aesthetic terms" (1998, 308), pointing to Ben-Amos' definition of folklore as "artistic communication in small groups" (1971, 13) and the American Folklife Center's characterization as "community life and values, artfully expressed in myriad forms and interactions" (Hufford 1991, 1).[9] Elliott Oring puts it succinctly by saying that folklore "is about people—individuals and communities—and their aesthetic expression" (1998, 335). A reliance on *aesthetics* seems to place a stronger emphasis on tangibility as a measurement of what constitutes folklore than the terms *communication* and *transmission* might allow. Furthermore, it leaves room for prejudice—what one person may find beautiful or important conversely may seem ugly or frivolous to another. This is problematic.

We mustn't be afraid to challenge the boundaries of the folklore discipline. For too long we have regurgitated folkloristic studies or have been subsumed by other disciplines' methodologies. I propose a combination of the aforementioned definitions, as they all present limitations to the study of folklore on the Internet and oftentimes to other subdivisions of folkloristic inquiry. For this book, and hopefully beyond it, folklore should be considered to be the outward expression of creativity—in myriad forms and interactions—by individuals and their communities. The debate then falls to what constitutes *creativity* or even what constitutes *community*. *That* should be the job of the folklorist to argue cogently one way or another.[10] The resulting analytical construct, formed by the scholar in reaction to the character of folklore, is where a folklorist is needed for interpretation and indeed is qualified to comment.

It may be noted that *tradition* is curiously absent from this definition. As Simon Bronner notes, Dan Ben-Amos worried that tradition "prevented the folklorist's subject from expanding to emergent performances in mass culture" (Bronner 2002, 30). I share this concern.[11] Robert Glenn Howard reminds us that "what is essential about folkloric expression is not a 'traditional' origin. Instead, it is . . . 'continuities and consistencies' that allow a specific community to perceive such expression as traditional, local, or community generated" (2008a, 201).[12] A caveat worth mentioning is that my definition risks being conceived of as too broad, a longstanding problem in separating folklore from allied disciplines. However, I submit that folklore is empowered by its diversity; this definition is purposefully inclusive to capitalize on that strength of the discipline.[13]

If my definition may stand, then what merits folkloristic study? William Wells Newell believed that "technology, specifically print, produces the social distinction between high and low that generates folklore," and further posited that "genuine folklore" is lore that escapes print (1883, v). But we mustn't forget that print promoted folklore and allowed folklorists to "constitute the oral in relation to a distinctive technology of detachment and extension" (Kirshenblatt-Gimblett 1998, 309). The Internet is the new "print" technology, duplicating our materials from the physical field and transferring them (though not necessarily always altering them) into an electronic vernacular. The result is similar to the way that printed versions of folklore originally stimulated oral tradition in the past.[14] The Internet does not diminish the potency of folklore; instead, it acts as a folkloric conduit. "Electronic messages are neither a playscript nor a transcript . . . They *are* the event," writes Kirshenblatt-Gimblett (1995, 74; emphasis in original).

Benedict Anderson (1991) argues that technology can bring the vernacular into sight, thus facilitating community culture and promoting nationalism—traditional byproducts and correlates of folklore. The Internet has altered established notions of social identity, which has made stigmatizing constraints such as gender and race less relevant than they are in the physical world (McClelland 2000, 182). One must then ask, has this been a positive thing? I believe it has been. Due to its inclusivity, the Internet has helped to re-facilitate the spread of folklore through electronic conduits. Robert Thompson points out that "we have really returned here, in spite of the centralization of technology, to the old-fashioned definition of what folk culture used to be . . . We have these jokes and stories that will never see the printed page that exist only as glowing dots of phosphorous. It's not word-of-mouth folk culture but word-of-modem culture" (Grimes 1992, C14, quoted in Kirshenblatt-Gimblett 1996, 50).[15]

With regard to the burgeoning "telectronic age," John Dorst, in 1990, worried that "our discursive practices as folklorists do not equip us very well to deal with these unprecedented and complex conditions of cultural production" (189). This may have been true twenty years ago, but the Internet has fundamentally changed the world we live in today and has been absorbed into the everyday life of folklorists of all generations.

It is not a foreign commodity; it is a tool of cultural production that we utilize on a daily basis. As Howard notes, Dorst recognized "the capacity for network communication to blend vernacular and institutional modes of communication in ways that frustrated distinctions between 'folk' and mass media" (Howard 2008a, 192). This blending has been problematic for ethnographers, as the Internet's "field" is sometimes construed as foreign to them. It is difficult to find one's bearings at times. Nevertheless, the cyberfield is increasingly engaging humans despite its liminal state.

While the remoteness of the Internet may seem unappealing to the folklorist, Regina Bendix reminds us that "the field has never confined itself to 'remoteness,' and that its most interesting and least dogmatic thinkers have always found the ubiquity of expressive culture (across time, space, class) most intriguing" (1998, 243). Folklore continues on the Internet whether we examine it or not,[16] so it is practical to study folklore in an Internet context. We must rethink the topics that have previously captured our interests and contemplate their Internet correlates. Perhaps some folklorists fear that the Internet will undermine the credibility of their work or negatively impact the content of their research, but it should be noted that "new technologies do not necessarily displace, replace, or eliminate earlier ones. They alter the relations among them and incorporate one another—with far-reaching effects" (Kirshenblatt-Gimblett 1998, 310). In the fraction of a second it takes for the human brain to send a command to the index finger, a single transmission of text can be distributed to potentially thousands, even millions of people. Internet users are frequently participating in many interesting folkloric activities online. Chain letters, "end of the Internet" websites, and forwarded humor are all ubiquitous. The Internet's proclivity for pseudonymous interaction and the ease with which texts can be transmitted make it the ideal location, instead of oral and journalistic venues, for the resurfacing of narrative texts.

So let's look at online narratives for a moment. By nature, e-mail hoaxes and forwarded humor cannot exist without the Internet, as they are exclusive to this venue. Through the microcosm of topical humor, Bill Ellis notes that "traditionally, folklore has been seen as a localized phenomenon . . . While previous collections from before 1987 stressed oral tradition, the anonymity of frequently forwarded messages has quickly made this the preferred mode of circulating topical humor," further adding that the "increased internationalism of email conduits now makes it normal, even commonplace, to exchange impressions and reactions across continental and even linguistic barriers . . . Comparing the content and form of [topical humor] to previous oral-based collections may reveal some significant ways in which the Internet has impacted the folk process" (2001, section 4). In this regard, Daryl Cumber Dance holds that due to its contemporary accessibility, "techlore" has supplanted the paperwork empire as one of the most popular new forms of folklore: "With the advent of E-mail, pieces that were formerly copied and circulated are now sent with one click of the mouse to a long list of one's associates—who often send them on to other groups of acquaintances" (Dance 2002, 647). With topical humor, Liisi Laineste adds that "collecting jokes on the Internet is becoming . . . unavoidable" (2003, 93). In a research setting, then, the text becomes both a primary and a secondary document, depending on the researcher's inclinations for its use.

In the pre-Internet age, one may have seen chain letters or text sprites in the form of letters sent pyramid scheme-like to random addresses or as a component of computerlore or Xeroxlore (Dundes 1965a; Dundes and Pagter 1975, 1987, 1996; Fox 1983). The Internet provides an anonymous medium for web users to quickly disseminate information, which often leads to a more authentic performance of the user's true self (Bargh, McKenna, and Fitzsimons 2002). In this sense, the Internet is an ideal channel for the transmission of folk narratives, due to its anonymity and efficiency in the speedy dissemination of ideas. For researchers, the electronic transmissions of narratives provide a greater paper trail to test out theorizations on the role of conduits in narrative transference. In their oral context, legends are richly evocative of society's fears, hopes, anxieties, and prejudices, and folklorists decode these narratives to reveal and analyze the cultural attitudes expressed within. The Internet provides a new opportunity for us to study legends and their subsidiaries, such as chain letters and e-mail hoaxes. While orally transmitted legends convey societal fears and prejudices in coded language, electronically transmitted narratives express these sentiments more abrasively, due to the sender's anonymity (Bargh, McKenna, and Fitzsimons 2002; Blank 2007; Eichhorn 2001; Fernback 2003; Kibby 2005).

Folk groups are readily identifiable on the Internet, as evidenced by chat forums, blogs, online political activity, fan web pages, and a plethora of other interrelated concepts. New traditions are being forged in online communities, and web lingo—emerging in such forms as net-derived lingo (see netlingo.com), wiki-based Internet vocabulary databases like urbandictionary.com, or the communal folk wisdom of online discussion groups—demonstrates the uniqueness of Internet expression.[17] Of course, these assertions are complicated by a lack of empirical data and physical connectivity between the researcher and his informant. As

Barbara Kirshenblatt-Gimblett has contemplated, "What do terms like *group* or *community* mean when strangers at computer terminals at the far ends of the world type messages to each other? . . . The electronic vernacular is neither speech nor writing as we have known it, but something in between, and increasingly, with the convergence of technologies, it is multimedia" (1998, 284; emphasis in original).

The digital world is paradoxically familiar, due to its governing social dynamics, and simultaneously foreign, due to its virtual format. The ethnographer faces many challenges that must be taken into consideration with the Internet. Milton Shatzer and Thomas Lindlof contend that ethnographers "cannot make adequate sense out of communication" without the ability to observe nonverbal behavioral cues, noting that e-mail and other online communications bypass the social pecking orders imposed in group interaction, such as eye contact, seating arrangements, and characteristics such as "gender, race, expertise, or organizational position" (1998, 178).[18] Coming from the perspective of folklore studies, I disagree. It is foolish to become fixated solely on the subconscious or nonverbal processes of communication. Is cyberethnography illegitimate because it equalizes the social statuses of its users? By ignoring cyberethnographic data, aren't we discounting a very important social dynamic that is taking place? We should be interested in how people express themselves, in whatever manner that occurs. Admonishing cyberethnography for its lack of physicality limits the scope of the researcher's analysis and is narrow-minded. While an expression may appear differently in the online world than it does in the physical world, there is room for analysis on the distinguishing characteristics between the two.

Internet scholar Denise Carter mentions that ethically, "cyberethnography is similar to conventional ethnography because the four main moral obligations of dealing with human subject research are the same: the principle of non-maleficence, the protection of anonymity, the confidentiality of data, and the obtaining of informed consent" (2005, 152). Moreover, communication "in the absence of face-to-face interaction and at a distance is as old as the circulation of objects . . . and the transmission of signals" (Kirshenblatt-Gimblett 1996, 21). As I have suggested before, the "lure of the foreignness of the field may be [a reason why we resist] the Internet as an appropriate place to conduct fieldwork. After all . . . conducting fieldwork 'in the field' is a tradition of the folklore discipline itself. However, as times change, our profession must progress accordingly" (Blank 2007, 21). It is undeniable that the psychological identification of place has been forged in the online format. With this in mind, I have posited that the Internet's "field" cannot be separated from the traditional field to which folklorists are accustomed. While there are fundamental differences between the two—specifically, that the former is virtual and the latter, physical—they are bound by common themes.[19] Both have folk groups, customs, lingo and dialects, neighborhoods, crimes, relationships, games, discussion groups, displays of emotion, banking, commerce, and various other forms of communication and education (Blank 2007).

It is important to realize that just because the Internet is virtual, or "doesn't exist" as McClelland (2000) contends, it still has an inherent base in the real world. The fact remains that there is a human behind everything that takes place online, and this is where the folklorist's field-work on the Internet should begin. We must ask ourselves, how do we interact with the computer as ethnographers and as participants? Who are the folk in cyberspace (the cyberfolk, if you will)? What makes them different from the traditional folk? What are the constraints or exigencies that dictate how they carry themselves in an Internet context? When we begin to answer these questions, we can then make a case for what constitutes vernacular expression and how these expressions evince creativity or traditional components. Howard says that norms and forms can be properly termed *vernacular* when they "signal local or 'home born' qualities of a particular human communication." He further asserts that vernacularity "can only emerge into meaning by being seen as distinct from the mass, the official, and the institutional" and argues that "there is a class of online discourse that is properly termed 'vernacular' because it invokes characteristics that are recognized as distinct from those recognized as 'institutional,'"[20] adding that while "this conception might frustrate our desires to rigidly locate discrete documents that are amateur or professional, traditional or mass mediated, its flexibility provides the theoretical language necessary for speaking about the inextricably intertwined nature of public and private, personal and commercial, individual and group in the communications that new technologies have made possible" (2008a, 194–95).[21] The vernacular comes to have meaning when it is alien to some institution (Glassie 1999; Howard 2005). Scholars may look at the same things, and draw the same conclusions, but they report their findings in their own discipline's terminology. Folklore is too important for that. We *are* the folk—as participants, as scholars, and as citizens. Our insight is needed.

Richard Bauman discusses the traditional concept of the homogeneous folk society as imposing a set of blinders on folklorists, skewing their attention away from conditions under which differences of identity gave shape to the social use of folklore (1972; 1983; 1992). I believe that institutional hegemony runs the risk of imposing similar blinders on the scope of folkloristic inquiry. As scholars, we mustn't neglect technology and mass culture. "Mass culture uses folk culture," writes Kirshenblatt-Gimblett, and "folk culture mutates in a world of technology" (1998, 307).[22] She further notes that "the very technologies that threaten to displace oral traditions are also the instruments for preserving them" (1995, 70). The Internet is changing the game for folklorists and allied scholars; moreover, it is fundamentally changing culture and the way we should think about it (Putnam 2000). "The electronic inscription and reproduction of folklore forms merely epitomizes and makes especially visible the wholesale transformation of social and material relations that characterizes our historical moment" (Dorst 1990, 183).

The Internet has shifted the social constructions of community, often taking on its own unique characteristics and modes of expressions. Participatory media, notes Howard, offer "powerful new channels through which the vernacular can express its alterity" (2008a, 192). Creativity is at the center of folkloristic inquiry, and the manifestations of online identity formation, artistic expression, folk religion, and the social dynamics of community construction are all important venues for analysis.[23] However, as Howard also notes, "there is no 'pure' or finally 'authentic' vernacular. Instead, the vernacular needs the institutional from which to distinguish itself . . . no pure vernacularity exists, only degrees of hybridity" (2008a, 203; see also Howard 1997, 2001, 2005; Lawless 1998). Christine Hine addresses this point: "Ethnography of the [I]nternet can, then, usefully be about mobility between contexts of production and use, and between online and offline, and it can creatively deploy forms of engagement to look at how these sites are socially constructed and at the same time are social conduits" (2009, 11). For Richard Bauman, "members of particular groups or social categories may exchange folklore with each other on the basis of shared identity, or with others, on the basis of differential identity" (1972, 38). Couldn't this extrapolation be applied to a folkloristic study of the Internet? It may be easy to find a text on a venue like the Internet, but the context may be difficult to ascertain. This is a challenge that folklorists can and must overcome as semiotics and the other cultural processes filtered through the Internet demand our attention (Mechling 1993).

In building off of these ruminations, *Folklore and the Internet* hopes to widen the dialogue about the Internet as both an ethnographic field and an area of folkloristic inquiry. This book is about the intersection of folklore—in all of its multifaceted incarnations—and the Internet.

More importantly, the volume attempts to use a folkloristic perspective to critically examine and contribute to the literature on the sociocultural and performative nature of the Internet. Many of the topics traditionally explored by folklorists—such as humor, expression, tradition, narrative transmission, commemoration, religion, and ritual—have taken on new or modified lives in the digital world. The new essays comprising this book will explore the depth and flexibility of the Internet as a viable site of ethnography and scholarship, in addition to its relevance as a host for identity and communal expression and as a purveyor of various narratives and beliefs, ranging from topical humor to apocalyptic hyperbole.

In chapter 1, Simon J. Bronner raises the question of whether the Internet fosters distinctive cultural practices that could be called traditional. This is a major concern for folklorists, who have noted the blending of oral and electronic transmissions. Can Internet folklore be separated as distinct? If so, what differences permeate? Utilizing a comparative case study in the folklore generated around the publically televised suicide of Pennsylvania's State Treasurer R. Budd Dwyer in 1987, Bronner revisits his own documentation of orally transmitted jokes among college students. The footage of Dwyer's death still circulates widely on the Internet twenty years later and has resulted in new folkloric responses, either expressing the event comically—in discussion threads with joking proverbial comparisons—or as tragic narratives that describe the footage as "haunting" and therefore relate it to the stresses of modern life. Bronner finds these expressive reactions to the footage to be commentaries not just on unnatural death, but also, since it was a publicly televised event, on the Internet itself. He ties this case study to concepts about the Internet of "mythic proportions" and to their implications for the way that people think about virtual traditions in a computer, or Petabyte, age. In so doing, Bronner distinguishes between a folk and an elite Internet, with the former characterized by user-generated material and cultural tropes. These include youth-orientation; expressions of the Internet's visual character; the use of initialisms and responsive threads; themes that generate beliefs and narratives related to death, sex, security, and identity; and a tendency toward scatology. Throughout his chapter, Bronner shows the differences in how analog and digital ways of thinking affect the conceptualization of tradition on the Internet, noting that the folk Internet is analytical in its structure, rather than relational.

If we can discern the qualities of the folk Internet, what else bears attention? Folk narratives have often been a subject of great interest among folklorists, since they convey societal fears, hopes, expectations, and celebrations. Elizabeth Tucker examines the relationship between

websites' renditions of missing women's stories and legends about the
ghosts of murdered women in chapter 2. Besides offering warnings,
legends reflect society's fears, especially about women's vulnerability
to danger. Tucker examines two websites about young partygoers who
disappeared, as well as one website about a group of missing women
from the street culture of Vancouver, Canada. The international attention
paid to the disappearance of Natalee Holloway stimulated exchanges
on these websites in which true, false, and dubious reports of Holloway
sightings displayed legend dialectics in action. On the most active websites dedicated to missing women, the objective is clearly to safeguard
those women who still live. Here, the guardians of the living are not
ghosts, but caring women who exchange narratives in order to protect
younger women from fatal mistakes. Through these websites, Tucker
demonstrates that legend dialectics, already well-studied in relation to
oral narratives, also apply to websites about women who have mysteriously vanished. In so doing, she helps to establish the validity of the
Internet in examining narrative forms.

In chapter 3, Lynne S. McNeill investigates the ways in which the
Internet facilitates the creation and propagation of folklore through the
lens of "End of the Internet" websites. As a textually based folk form
devoid of the intricacies of Web 2.0 (such as interactivity and social networking), McNeill believes that these sites exemplify the possibilities
the study of folklore can have in an Internet context. She explores the
idea of "digital natives"—the generation born into communication technologies—and how the general acceptance of this concept implies that
there is a distinct culture on the Internet to which one can be native (or
nonnative) and in which individuals can function. McNeill holds that
it makes perfect sense that folklore would emerge on the Internet in a
normal and even expected way; this locus is simply another conduit of
person-to-person communication and, as such, should encourage folkloric transmission just as efficiently as other folk forms. For McNeill,
electronic venues such as Facebook and texting devices reconceptualize
face-to-face communication and thus operate in the same spirit. These
are important expositions to contemplate as we argue for the validity of
Internet studies, which rests on vernacular principles such as nativity
and distinguishable expressive traits.

Electronic mail has become a robust medium for the transmission of
jokes, especially topical jokes. Unlike oral joke-telling, the "telling" of an
e-mailed joke typically entails forwarding an unaltered text at whatever
moment one happens to receive it, without regard for either what the
recipients are doing at that moment or how they will respond when they

read it. In chapter 4, Russell Frank examines the folkloristic mechanics of these transmissions. The content of these forwarded e-mail messages challenges canonical folkloristic ideas about the importance of performance and social context, as well as the roles of individual creativity and audience response in textual variation. Though the influence of social context is weaker on forwards than it is on orally told jokes, the impact of cultural context appears to be much stronger. Just as the Internet lends itself to reporting news as soon as it happens, it also is prone to registering instantaneous responses to the news—including jokes. In this regard, Frank believes that forwarded jokes may be the most reliable guide we have to which news events, public figures, and joke types have captured the public's imagination at any given moment. He therefore examines several joke types in an Internet context, including riddle jokes, story jokes, and digitally altered photographs.

In chapter 5, William Westerman considers the creation and authorship of the online encyclopedia known as Wikipedia. A product of the "open-source" movement in computer programming and a *wiki*, or editable online text, Wikipedia is by definition self-governing and ever-changing, and thus is an illustration of the folkloric process. This chapter considers the sociology of how knowledge is created and disseminated by a community of several thousand writers and editors who have voluntarily taken up the task of creating the world's largest encyclopedia. Westerman argues that Wikipedia's community of editors and writers is a folk community that has established rules concerning what counts as reliable knowledge and sources and how various points of view can be incorporated to come up with a text that is ultimately impartial. He examines the process through which a nascent community defines its own epistemology and its own rules about neutrality and bias in scholarship. Drawing on folklore scholarship concerning the concept of the group, the philosophical field of social epistemology that has been defined by Steve Fuller (2002), and the extensive archival pages of Wikipedia itself, Westerman posits that knowledge communities, like all folk groups, have to deal with the question of bias in what they produce. What is unique to this occupational folk group of writers and editors, however, is that authority is self-regulating, and they emphasize distributing knowledge as a form of disseminating power.

Rituals, folk belief, and religion are all respected components of folkloristic inquiry, but few scholars have written on the subject in an Internet context as prolifically as Robert Glenn Howard (1997, 2000, 2001, 2005, 2008a, 2008b). He further explores this area of study in chapter 6, which documents the power of what he has previously dubbed a

vernacular web of online expression (Howard 2008a, 2008b). According to
Howard, vernacular webs are emergent communication performances
that come into being as individuals navigate through online discourse.
One such web is the one enacted by conservative Christians who believe
they are engaged in an ongoing war against demonic spirits. Out of
a perceived need to share strategies for combating these evil spirits,
many educated and skilled Internet users see themselves as crusaders
in a world led astray by the homosexual-rights movement, government
conspiracies against Christians, New Age spirituality, and other belief
systems (Howard 1997, 2000; Wojcik 1997). In this struggle, the Internet
serves as an active battleground and as an example of a powerful vernacular web. Howard notes how the beliefs of these individuals have an
influence that stretches from those individual believers, through popular press books, to online expression, and, ultimately, to their effects on
the lives of those who do not believe.

Building on the themes of folk belief and ritual in an Internet context, Robert Dobler's chapter 7 examines the dynamics of the transition
of spontaneous shrines into the virtual world of the Internet. Social networking sites like MySpace have emerged as mediators of the adolescent
experience for an entire generation of American youth, creating online
spaces in which teenagers negotiate identity and grapple with daily life.
As such, events imbued with tragedy and grief cause the MySpace forum
to transcend the boundaries of cyberspace and adopt characteristics of
the physical world's response to grief via rituals. Dobler notes that the
MySpace sites of the deceased often take on the characteristics of a spontaneous shrine, functioning as a virtual site of spiritual communion and
creating a bridge between the living and the dead. Mourners frequently
continue to visit the sites of their deceased friends, often leaving pres-
ent-tense comments, echoing the poignant and striking characteristics
frequently found on the notes and flowers offered at roadside crosses.
Through cyberethnography, Dobler also observes divergent patterns
between genders in their grieving rituals on MySpace and categorizes
their distinctive traits. In so doing, he demonstrates how the Internet
provides an innovative means of examining the processes behind the
creation of spontaneous shrines, allowing folklorists to observe the
workings of vernacular memorialization in alternative ways as traditional forms are adapted to the new digital mode of experience.

Lastly, Gregory Hansen explores "Public Folklore in Cyberspace" in
chapter 8. This piece examines how folklorists use the Internet to edu-
cate nonspecialized audiences about folklore within various regions of
America. Hansen probes public folklore's scope by establishing the major

goals and orientations used within folklife programming in the public and private sectors. He follows this with a typology of presentation modes used in the websites of public folklorists who work in a range of local, state, regional, and national agencies. His analysis of these various categories draws a correlation between web design and the five modes of documentary video production and filmmaking identified by Bill Nichols and developed by Sharon Sherman. Using these modes, Hansen demonstrates how websites include the elements of exposition, observation, interaction, reflexivity, and performativity as predominant orientations within the design of various sites. As an appendix, he includes an extensive annotated webography of sites relevant to public folklore.

To use a metaphor of material culture, the collection of essays in this book is a quilt. Individually, as "patches," they present a distinct viewpoint and unique insight into their respective areas of study, but collectively they represent a blanket of new ideas for the folklore discipline. All of these chapters see the Internet as an important analytic venue for folklorists and examine the possibilities for future research through case studies of narratives, religion, and education in an online context. While *Folklore and the Internet* doesn't have complete answers to all of the questions posed in this introduction, or to the myriad questions naturally imposed by the study of folklore, the chapters in this book seek to both highlight and digest these relevant issues as a thematic contemplation on the academic study of folklore and the Internet. Not all of the authors agree with one another's viewpoints or approaches. The Internet is new territory for the folklore discipline, and while we might be late to the dialogue, our perspectives and methodologies should not only broaden the scope of Internet studies, but provide important insights into the processes of everyday life in the modern technological world. Barbara Kirshenblatt-Gimblett notes that the folklore discipline "is struggling to find a truly contemporary subject, one that is not just *in* the present, but truly *of* the present" (1995, 70; emphasis in original). Here it is.

We hope these essays demonstrate the validity of folkloric study and the Internet as a compatible duo; encourage new dialogues and contributions from scholars in the fields of folklore and allied disciplines; and engage readers seeking new insights into the Internet from a folkloristic perspective. In addition, we encourage feedback, dissent, and all of the pleasantries in between regarding our cause and hope that readers will take the dialogue begun in this book and continue it into the public—and virtual—domain.

Notes

1. There have been some thoughtful writings on the history of the Internet. See Okin (2005) or, for a brief treatment, Bermejo (2007, 57–73). While *Folklore and the Internet* is interested in a folkloristic approach to Internet studies, a few works from allied scholars bear further examination for broad overviews of computer-mediated studies: Healy (1997); Krawczyk-Wasilewska (2006); Kuntsman (2004); Silver, Massanari, and Jones (2006); Weber and Dixon (2007); and Wood and Smith (2005).

2. Jennings's *The Devouring Fungus* (1990) may have been one of the first attempts to examine the folkloric aspects of the shifting currents in technology from the computer/Xeroxlore age to the possibilities presented by the interconnectivity of the Internet. If nothing else, it's an interesting timepiece about changes in folkloric transmission at the end of the 1980s, particularly since it examines "tales from the computer age" only a few years before the modern Internet exploded onto the scene. See also Sproull and Kiesler 1992.

3. This originally appeared in an electronic version in 1993. See also Shea (1994) for a further treatment of the phenomenon that Rheingold is referencing.

4. Full access to past and new issues of *Folklore Forum* is available at http://folkloreforum.net. Archived issues can be found at https://scholarworks.iu.edu/dspace/handle/2022/1168

5. This isn't a criticism so much as it is a disappointment for the lack of interest in the subject matter from seasoned folklore veterans and graduate students. In soliciting entries for this book, it was particularly difficult to find contributors whose primary research interests revolved around the intersection of folklore and the Internet, but many people had a secondary or peripheral interest in the subject matter. Hopefully this will change soon!

6. My thanks to Libby Tucker for sharing her memories of this.

7. Bronner's assertion was expanded upon via personal communication with the author in September 2008.

8. As cited earlier, several scholars have made a name for themselves examining folklore and technology, such as John Dorst, Robert Glenn Howard, and Barbara Kirshenblatt-Gimblett, among a handful of others.

9. See also Marvin (1995).

10. For example, I often ask myself, does a locale require "tradition" in order be considered a "community"? This is a question that could be further examined in great detail by folklorists.

11. See Ben-Amos (1972) for further contemplations on the limitations posed by the inclusion of "tradition" in defining folklore.

12. See also Baym (1993) and especially Georges and Jones (1995), where the idea of "continuities and consistencies" originates. Additionally, see Howard (2008a).

13. My thanks to Robert Glenn Howard for his assistance in clarifying this point.

14. For an example of how sixteenth-century folksong collectors' performances benefited from, and were not diminished by, print, see Kirshenblatt-Gimblett (1998, 309–10).

15. That said, in chapter 1 of this volume Simon J. Bronner argues that there are distinguishable "folk" and "elite" cultures on the Internet.

16. Arjun Appadurai (1986) explores this concept in greater detail.

17. For example, urbandictionary.com is interesting because it presents slang and linguistic culture not only from the Internet, but also from the physical world. It can thus be seen as a facilitator in the relationship between the offline and online world. This should be of particular interest to folklorists who study topical humor, word play, and verbal dueling, as this venue is moderated by anonymous contributors from across the globe and features a combination of narrative lore found in multiple cultural venues.

18. Jan Roush astutely synthesizes some of the main ethical and practical considerations folklorists face in utilizing the Internet for conducting field-work: "Does fieldwork . . . have to be conducted in face-to-face interviews in order to be defined as fieldwork, or is any medium sufficient? . . . How does an effaced interview conducted through electronic mail or real-time Chat groups alter the performance, the context of the collecting? Further, since Internet access is for now limited to a privileged few participants, how representative of vernacular culture is this type of fieldwork? . . . [W]hat assurances does the collector have that the informants are actually who they say they are, an issue particularly crucial in collecting certain types of lore like gender lore? . . . How does the collector obtain valid consent forms? Further, if consent forms are transmitted through say, the medium of e-mail, can this collected information legally be archived?" (1997, 45). These are all valid questions to ponder, and I encourage folklorists to contemplate them further.

19. I believe this assertion is supported by other scholars in allied disciplines. Citing over three years of ethnographic research, Denise Carter reported that her informants found their online community "just another place to meet friends" and that "many of the friendships formed . . . are routinely being moved offline." Consequently, Carter concludes, "the basic tenets of online friendship appear to be impossible to separate from the traditional everyday concept of friendship itself" (2005, 164). This supports my belief that the authenticity of the data collected online is as valid as data collected in person (Blank 2007). Of course, the question remains as to whether the Internet increases a person's likelihood to interact as a non-authentic self, but as Christine Hine so precisely stated: "The point for the ethnographer is not to bring some external criterion for judging whether it is safe to believe what informants say, but rather to come to understand how it is that infor-mants judge authenticity" (2000, 49). For a thorough discussion of authentic-ity as it relates to folklore studies, see Bendix (1997).

20. This assertion is supported by the arguments presented by Simon J. Bronner in chapter 1 of this volume.

21. For a review of the origins of the term "vernacular," see Howard (2005, 327–28).

22. See also Bronner ([1986] 2004); Dégh (1994); and Kirshenblatt-Gimblett (1983) for a deeper discussion of mass culture and its influence on and interaction with aspects of folklore. Howard (2008a, 200–01) also reviews the literature on folklore and the mass media quite appropriately and effectively.

23. John McDowell has utilized the Internet as a medium in his F351 folklore classes at Indiana University ("The Folklore of Student Life"). Through

archival data and student fieldwork, he has pieced together an impressive website that displays a sample of Indiana University folklore from the past and present. I encourage readers to visit it at http://www.indiana. edu/~f351jmcd/. I think that this site is yet another demonstration of how we can think of the Internet not only as a tool for folkloristic inquiry, but as a comrade in the presentation of our work and methods. For a thoughtful report on the concerns folklorists may have with these types of digital media, see Underberg (2006).

Chapter 1

Digitizing and Virtualizing Folklore

SIMON J. BRONNER

One popular sense of tradition signals a human, even naturalistic connection. In this view, tradition is down home, out in the fields, back in the woods, where socializing, ritualizing, and storytelling occur unencumbered by machines or corporations. Hearing *tradition* uttered often raises images of family huddled around the dinner table at holidays or the neighborhood gang getting together for play, and it might be imaginatively set in opposition to the socially alienating quality of modernity dominated by technology. The rhetoric of tradition cited in folkloristic annals is not that far off from these characterizations, although it may broaden to a variety of settings—urban as well as rural, industrial as well as agricultural—and include folk transmission via a host of technologies, from printing press to photocopier (Bendix 1997; Bronner 1998). Still, analytical uses of tradition typically evoke a community's *naturally* authentic customs or face-to-face expressive encounters, in contrast to the artificiality of technology. The folklorist's *tradition* signifies cultural production of earthy artistic expressions, from homey proverbs to hand-wrought pots, which are said to be *folk* because they attach culturally to groups and repeat and vary. To be sure, the joke of the day or the latest rumor on the Internet may be pegged as lore or urban legend, but it is hard to shake the image of folk connections made around the campfire rather than through FireWire.

With the explosion of the Internet as the way that people communicate with one another, is tradition still relevant? After all, texting a joke to an unseen recipient is a far cry from gesturing and making eye contact with huddled buddies in the usual familiar place. In this chapter,

I examine, ethnographically and psychologically, the modernistic tendency to construct various cultural divisions, or binaries, to separate reality from fantasy or imagination. Such binaries include natural and artificial, public and private, analog and digital, group and network, relational and analytical, and especially folk and official. Although folklorists have previously noted that various communication technologies that emerged in the twentieth century, such as the telephone and photocopier, have altered the way that lore, as well as information, is spread, I find that the Internet, more so than other media, has unsettled many of the prior cultural binaries, which is evident especially in the rise of what I call the transgressive folk web. The Internet has become an essential tool of everyday life; it is also distinguished by being envisioned as a separate location or space in which traditions arise and are constituted.

A description often applied to cyberspace and natural space is that each is free and open, in the sense of unrestricted; each invites involvement on common ground, where participants can formulate social guidelines to organize themselves. From the perspective of the user, the Internet is a free medium that opens access to information. A formidable Internet social movement advocates for "open-source culture," in which collectivity, rather than acquisitive individualism, dominates and the communal spirit is manifested by making creative works, including software, that are entitled to copyright protection generally available to the masses (Truscello 2003). Unstructured in this ideal cyber-collective, the Internet could appear as one big open mess were it not for organizational tools that are left to users to put into place, thereby showing their orderliness in creating an *information system*. Practices that specially tag the organization of information and so become metaphors for vitality on the Internet are searching, surfing, and marking. The thrill of the dynamo-proportion search engine driving the conspicuous consumption of information is downright intoxicating, until the sobering realization hits that one has some serious sorting and sifting to do with the results to enable an effective virtual office. Structuring one's knowledge allows, like a grammar of language, the individual to communicate and think together with others.

In the gathering on the digital commons, though, Internet users can only approximate meeting, so when users talk of virtual reality much of its meaning is wrapped up in making a connection that is social as well as electronic, and that is where tradition comes in (Kirshenblatt-Gimblett 1995; Rheingold 2001; Swiss 2004; Žižek 2001). Perhaps most exciting, and troublesome at the same time, is that seated at screens, people negotiate the isolation of one-person/one-hard-drive material culture with a Wi-Fi social breakthrough that allows, as never before, conversations between anywhere and the deep recesses of homes and offices. Examining the web landscape with touch screens on the go or mouse pads in cubicles, users recognize a fundamental difference between sites identified as official or corporate, which control content and broadcast information to a passive viewing audience, and those that allow posting, "live" chat, and free exchange. For many users, the latter constitutes the folk universe of cyberspace, in contrast to its elite realm. The folk realm is not located in a socioeconomic sector or particular nationality but instead represents a participatory process that some posters refer to as the democratic or open web.

Does where you are from matter anymore then? For folklorists, who are perennial commentators on the formation of cultural identity through the production of tradition in place, this context for transmission means rethinking business, or analysis, as usual (see Jackson 2001; Kirshenblatt-Gimblett 1995; Oring 1994). Although folklorists have an advantage among the scholarly pack who look critically at the Internet in having created a niche for themselves as specialists on vernacular expression through various forms of transmission, the engineered or mediated inter- and hyper-textual, visual assemblage that characterizes much of Internet communication provides challenges of identification and interpretation based on the discreteness of extracted artifacts of tradition (see Bronner 2006; Ketner 1976).

Now hold the phone. The traditional, or folk, web is not just a place for simulating storytelling around the kitchen table or bull sessions in the dorm room. Noting that much of folklore research was premised on the social intimacy or familiarity of people engaging in face-to-face oral communication, folklorist Barbara Kirshenblatt-Gimblett argues that rather than transposing pre-modern orality into the new media, folklorists need to start fresh, with the premise that "computer mediated communication, at least in its present form is *between* speech and writing. Listers on X-CULT-X dub this kind of talk putation, and speak of puting or putating. The words on the screen neither precede nor follow speech, though they often feel more like talking than writing. Electronic messages are neither a playscript nor a transcript, particularly in the interactive chat programs. They *are* the event" (1995, 74). She describes the kind of Internet vein mined by folklorists for textual humor, but many websites complicate the matter with visual imagery, often in motion, that is layered, embedded, and juxtaposed with other messages into a multimedia assemblage.[1] A folkloric term that could describe tralatitious Internet praxis, between reading and writing, assembling and visualizing, is the process of relating (and the interactive mode of responding). Carrying a sense of doing more than scribing or sending information, it connotes reaching someone by relating narrative and belief, signifies the connection and assemblage in relating different sources to one another, and considers precedents in relation to the present.

Although it is tempting to see Internet communicative frames as more conversations from which one can extract tradition as rhetorical strategies, if not artifacts, surely something different is occurring when one is using a keyboard for "telling" a joke, yet it is a far cry from pecking out reports on the keys of a mechanical typewriter in a previous epoch. The computer monitor also has transformed from its previous incarnation as a television set in a couch-potato-filled living room of the past. What happens when keyboard and screen conjugate, and out of the union is born a vernacular communication form that by tapping on keys imitates the ease of conversation? What happens when producer and consumer merge in a single interactive medium as *prosumers*, who can readily create as well as consume the message, or product (Toffler 1980)? Is it not a symbolic breakthrough when instead of bowing to sacred icons, people can freely move them around on the screen, create their own avatar (drawing on Hindu mythology of the descent of a deity to earth), and in ordinary, secular life use a cursor like a cleric handling a pointer on sacred parchment scrolls or evoke with a hand symbol that locates a hyperlink the revered *yad*, or hand, in Jewish Torah readings? Maybe the big question, or byte, is whether beyond offering unprecedented access to materials of folklore amassed outside it, in the field, the Internet *facilitates, mediates,* or *produces* tradition on a computer screen. Do some or all of the productions tailor-made for the website phenomena YouTube, Facebook, MySpace, and Webkinz qualify as folk practices, and if so, well, so what? What are the various cultural texts, and contexts, of e-mails, text messages, listservs, blogs, vlogs, and homepages and how do they diverge from the face-to-face, in situ experience of field-recorded material? Is disembodied storytelling on the Internet really folkloric, after all? Is it real, even if it is in real-time? Or in computer lingo, what happens when in addition to digitizing folklore, for example, sending or posting jokes they heard orally, people virtualize it? How do new media technologies featuring the Internet—such as netbooks, video game units, media players, iPods, smartphones, and iPhones—relate to cyberculture?

These are key questions because folklore—a fundamental, timeless form of communication—is inextricably tangled up in the Web. Folklore as an expression of tradition has to be present on the Internet because increasingly e-mail and listservs, often incorporated into the Web, have become the primary way that people *message, connect,* and *link,* if not talk, to one another, and hence incorporate the symbolic and projective functions that folklore distinctively provides. When people e-mail or post to a board, they often invoke, and evoke, folklore as a cultural frame of reference for creatively relating experience, particularly in narration and imagery that respond to ambiguity and anxiety. If saying that folklore is on the Web or is produced about it are relatively safe cultural calls, the signal claim that the Internet acts folkloricly may give pause (see Dundes 1980, 17–19; Dundes 2005, 406; Ellis 2006). Yet upon reflection, the Internet as an expanding folkloric thoroughfare may help explain aspects that have confounded those technopundits who were sure that the vampire in the machine sucked users dry of their culture and creativity. As an icon of mass media, the Internet was certain, they said, to alienate us all and obliterate the last semblances of community and art we have (Ronnell 2001; Ross 2001; see also Benjamin [1936] 2007). How, then, has it been a tool of social connection, and consequently, of new expressive lore engendering digital, or virtual, culture?

To begin answering these questions, I move from the manifest appeal of the Internet as a social networking tool to the less discussed, but critical area, of its folk logic, which is steeped in the psychologically created frame of an open medium. In addition to suggesting concepts to guide the interpretation of folk web practice and sources for the social construction of the folk web, I provide a case study involving cultural responses to tragedy in 1987 and 2007 that allows me to compare folklore as oral and Internet traditions.

Social Factors and Folklorization

The basis of the claim for the Internet taking on folkloric qualities is the medium's interactive, instrumental quality; that differentiates it from television and radio, which divides people between broadcasters and listeners or viewers. Internet users are captivated by its capability to simultaneously send and receive, produce and consume, write and read (Tabbi 1997; Zukin 2004, 227-52). Precedent can be found in vernacular uses of photography, photocopying, and faxing. They invited manipulation of images and text to create a play frame in which humor, pathos, and memory were shared among members of a social network. The playful manipulation often came from an anonymous source that signified commentaries we might call *metafolklore* on values and attitudes about the very technology and institutional contexts that made the images and text possible (Dundes [1966] 2007b; Dundes and Pagter 1975; Fineman 2004; Mechling 2004, 2005; Preston 1994; Roemer 1994). Many of these broadside-type sheets, surreptitiously produced in and circulated from photocopy rooms, found their way to bulletin boards and office walls, creating a foundation for the humorous postings one sees on the Internet today.

In my experience, folklore was present at the beginnings of computing, even before Internet and e-mail burst on the scene. When in its Neolithic stage of the 1960s I began computing, as one of the select high school math-team members who formed a geek clique, the gargantuan machine we thought was wondrous in its power was barely capable of a few mathematical calculations. But it still seemed light years ahead of the slide rules we were carrying around, and the idea of wiring into a machine what we did in our heads made us giddy. The machine was *the brain*, and we marvelled at its symbolization of things automatic, how it seemed self-acting, with apparently a life of its own. It suggested autonomy; unlike the automobile, it could run itself, evident in the digital installation of *autorun*. It could speak, through programmed message responses to user actions. I recall philosophical discussion of automorphism, the reproduction of forms, as a representative system. I wrote a program to generate automorphic numbers, maybe as a precursor to folkloristic fascination with repetition and variation of forms. These numbers are those that when multiplied result in the number appearing in the total (e.g., 5 x 5=25; see Kobayashi, Schmid, and Yang 2008). Binary language, the programming fundament of 1s and 0s that spawned a new science, also gave rise to inside jokes written into notebooks, such as "There are only 10 types of people in the world—those who understand binary, and those who don't."

Reflecting back on it, I see the humor laid the groundwork for understanding the significance, as folklore, of multiple meanings in digital thinking. For the uninitiated, 10 refers to the number ten, but in binary, it means the number two, and in keeping with the praxis of writing programs, the joke makes sense only when written. It also has its variations, often given serially like a discussion thread, such as "There are only 10 types of people in the world—those who understand binary, and those who get laid"; "There are three kinds of people in the world: those who can count, and those who can't"; "I must have heard that joke 1100100 times"; and "1010011010, the number of the Beast"—666 in binary (Beatty 1976; Binary Jokes 2008). In response to the spate of lightbulb jokes all the rage at the time, computer geeks could imagine an automated light bulb that changed light bulbs: "How many lightbulbs does it take to change a lightbulb? One, if it knows its own Gödel number" (see Dundes and Renteln 2005, 187). Much of the discussion was about speed that like acting out a heroic John Henry test, could be shown to outpace human effort. The buzz was about the advent of a new Pax Automatica age ushered in beside the cultural revolution by youthful rebellion. It would be one in which society depended on information and information gave youth power, or so we surmised from memorization of Marshall McLuhan's work, which pronounced the revolutionary implication of instantaneous, automatically provided information, mediated through technology (McLuhan [1964] 1994; see also Virilio 2001).[2]

The room the machine occupied was papered with photocopied, scatological folk wisdom, such as "Garbage In, Garbage Out" made to look on a flat sheet like a homespun motto; a flow chart beginning with the question "Does the Damn Thing Work?" and showing the arrow for *no* leading to a command box plainly advising "Shitcanit"; and an instructional graphic captioned "Understanding the Technology" that showed a toilet with arrows pointing to the input and output areas and a backup system of a chamber pot (compare Dundes and Pagter 1991b, 161–62; Dundes and Pagter 1996, 120–21). Perhaps inspired by this risque gallery that other rooms lacked, giving us a special status and some weird looks for our geekness, our first deviations from the instructional text included cartoon characters made from computer-generated lines and circles. In an animated way, it showed we had a life and could humanize science. That material representing playing with the machine generated more excitement than long invariable printouts of calculations and data, truth be told. I do not recall talk of sneaky viruses at that time, but frequent reference was made to the ghost or devil in the machine and the belief that the thing had a mind of its own, which is still echoed today (Jennings 1991, 143–58). We did not call this material folklore, but it was significant to our folk logic regarding the control we exercised over the technology and the world we wrought, as we struggled to make the huge technological dragon do our bidding (see Dundes and Pagter 1996, 6–7, 58–61). Others made this folkloric connection about the artificial being that humans then seek to rein in, judging from the naming of an early supercomputer developed in the 1950s as Golem after the Jewish legend of a creature made from clay.

Alan Dundes was among the first folklorists during the 1970s to spot the computer's leavening of folklore: "So technology isn't stamping out folklore; rather it is becoming a vital factor in the transmission of folklore and it is providing an exciting source of inspiration for the generation of new folklore" (1980, 17). The folklore he reported, as early as 1958, was about computing as a suspect occupational pursuit on the periphery, probably because of the potential for human displacement. Thus he documented esoteric lore of computer programmers and an exoteric tradition in the general society about the computer and those who were authorities on it. He explained the rise of this jokelore about computers and computer programmers as a function of a need by suspicious folk to project symbolically, and externalize, anxiety about the change wreaked by technology, anxiety that appeared to be part of the modern condition. In advance of security fears and rumors about the Internet leading to scam and identity theft, Dundes noted that "there is widespread genuine anxiety that the use of the computer to gather personal data may bring us to the point where dossiers contain more information about a person than the person himself knows" (1980, 18).

Such fears, including that machines would replace humans in controlling daily life, have been enduring concerns as computer technology has advanced. They have forced reflection on issues of control and power, culturally perceived as a conflict between the promise to individual users that they can hold the "power of the Internet" in their hands and the realization that self-interested multinational corporations exact tolls on the information superhighway. Although Dundes did not predict the Internet would be the dominant interactive medium and household appliance it became, he, in thematizing folklore about the computer, offered a hypothesis about human control through vernacular means that in its comprehension of the impelling urge by users to create folklore-type materials in and about digital technology, anticipates the Web. As he put it, "it is folklore itself—including the joketelling process—that ultimately separates man from machine, or does it?" The example he gave was this: "A super computer is built and all the world's knowledge is programmed into it. A gathering of top scientists punch in the question: 'Will the computer ever replace man?' Clickity, click, whir, whir, and the computer lights flash on and off. Finally a small printout emerges saying, 'That reminds me of a story'" (Dundes 1980, 18–19).

Thing is, what constitutes a story in the new media is related differently than elsewhere, on humor sites where viewers rate the story's funniness and respond with variations or in blogs and chat rooms where they editorialize. Even more than transmitting items classifiable as stories that are comparable to analogues in pre-digital form, people on YouTube, Facebook, and MySpace employ emergent interactive practices—represented by that "clickity, click, whirr, whir, and the computer lights flash on and off"—that users in the Internet age identify with digital custom. These demand our critical cultural attention.

During the 1990s, when the graphical interface of the World Wide Web became widely available, the Internet took on more of the characteristics of a visual culture than an electronic post office or business tool. The development of Web 2.0, referring to the quantum leap of the Internet from step one's display to a multiuser *platform*, resulted in an explosion of expressive material moving online, which widened computing from techno-headed, self-isolating geeks to nonspecialists, ordinary users, engaging in daily activities online. Arguably, it made the Internet more of a folkloric thoroughfare and mediator than it was when it was still conceived as an intelligence, military, or academic tool or as a desktop publication. It could now be used easily to create public activity in the form of social networking sites, wikis, and blogs; it allowed audiovisual uploading as well as downloading, collaboration as well as individual tinkering. If in my technologically Neolithic stage, folklore was outside of our awareness even when we engaged in it, by the time Web 2.0 burst on the scene, with the beginning of the new millennium, reference by developers, not folklorists, to the folk character of the Internet was explicit. *Folksonomy*, a portmanteau (one of many in digital culture, indicating fusion and hybridization as technological evolution) of folk and taxonomy, entered Internet lingo to stand for the emic, or user-generated, practice of collaboratively creating and managing tags to annotate content (Howard 2008a; Mika 2007). Folksonomies are ubiquitous in popular social bookmarking and photography sites such as Flickr, Librarything, Esnips, and Del.icio.us, where users are aware of who created tags and can see other, assigned tags. The vernacular implication is that this kind of taxonomy can provide an alternative to the corporate-controlled search engine with its monopolistic, industrial image. Another significant connotation is recognition, in the growing, user-generated fondness for folksonomy, that patterns of emic categorizing and organizing in the openness of cyberspace are key cultural practices defining boundaries and shared ways of thinking about information and, hence, are markers of identity.

A key characteristic of the Internet that distinguishes it from face-to-face talking is how visual it is. Users look at a screen, allowing images and texts to be combined. Adherents to verbal communication might argue that this visibility takes away from the use of imagination to picture what is heard. Yet visualization on a screen adds a level of suspicion about whether what one is looking at is "real." That is why, I contend, people think of Internet information as simulated, or *virtual*, which is probably derived from the term *virtual image* in optics. Unlike the sense of touch, which can be used to verify physical evidence, sight merely identifies and is known to be manipulable. Suspicion can be created that one is "just seeing things," witnessing an optical illusion, or viewing an altered image. If one of those claims are true, you are liable to be accused of being "out of touch with reality." Touch, though it also can be manipulated, especially if not supported by sight, is considered in vernacular logic more reliable. Sure facts are tangible, gripping, clinching, and hard. Visual information, as the proverb "Seeing is believing" attests, involves belief rather than certainty. The proverb used to continue with "but feeling's the truth." The special experience is one that "touches us deeply." To be sure, photographs are posted on the Internet as visual proof, but arguments, and narratives, can arise about the activities outside the frame or the accuracy of the image inside the frame. Especially when images are broadcast from peer to peer in a play frame, the Internet becomes folklorized through the discourse of belief involved. The perceptions that every picture tells a story and that it attracts unseen viewers only add to the Internet's folkloric dimension.

The Internet's visual character gives the impression that it broadens experience. One can see off into the distance, but touch is at hand. Locality—where one lives and interacts with others—is described in terms of touch as well as tradition—the earth beneath your feet, the feel of familiar furniture, the handshake on the street. Sight looks out on the horizon rather than feeling at home; ringing in one's head might be the expansive sense of the visual conveyed by *see the world* or *look to the future*. The Internet carries this sensory implication further by reference to the World Wide Web and with the visual connotation of Google, the largest search engine. A Google Doodle (a variant of the company's logo) featured eyeglasses on the logo. The founders actually took the company name from *googol*, which refers to the large number 10^{100}, but many users perceive a connection to googly eyes. (Following this idea of visual broadening, the first search engine was called the *Wanderer.*) The rhetoric of the *information superhighway* and *cyberspace* expresses working the Internet to accelerate away from the here-and-now and the potential to take in everywhere and everything. As exhilarating as that sounds, it does not come without some anxiety about freedom and the information overload involved. Questions of identity and security arise, for if someone can be everywhere, then to where and to whom does one belong? Where is the safe haven of home? A formidable folk construction to temper the radically individualized world of the digital screen is the creation of groups linked by sites identified as such or as lists and networks. Folklore also arises among users to caution about unfamiliar sites and attachments as one wanders afield from the homepage or gets too curious or lascivious about what is out there. They include stories of attack sites ("CNN News Alert," "Pictures of My Party"), virus-infested attachments ("Shakira's pictures," "Snow White and the Seven Dwarfs"), and worms ("An Internet Flower for You," "A Card for You") released by virtual tokens from abroad ("Virus Hoaxes & Realities" 2008).

The visual practice of web posting differs from the vernacular use of photography, photocopying, and faxing because it is more widely available and can be more thoroughly personalized. In Dundes's joke, the machine runs by itself; on the Web, people imagine that they personalize the machine in their own image and often approach it like a workshop in which the screen constitutes a virtual canvas or desktop. Users can arrange and symbolize material on the Web as virtual reality to create a persona that was literally screened through postings and sought-out kindred spirits. The wonder of the Web is the graphic material open to view—graphic in a visual sense and also in its uncensored quality, suggesting the freedom of expression of a folk, or informal, commons in which participants regulate action through tradition rather than through arbitrarily imposed rules. Cognitively, a binary has been constructed between analog print as the regulated, institutional world of potential censorship and the digital Web as the open, uncensored folk domain.

Theoretically a wide open field, the Internet's cultural hangout has proved especially attractive to youth, who, the public imagines, better their elders with the informational capital of new media and often use it as a secret language beyond parental and professorial monitoring (Bronner 1995, 232–46; Sullivan 2005). In an individualistic society placing faith in technological progress, the energy of youth is channeled into innovation that will displace the establishment culture of older stuffed shirts; fashion, fads, and trends of the young dictate the popular culture, media and retail outlets remind consumers. Children embrace the communication potential of the folk Internet and shape it into their own image and culture supposedly because they are preoccupied with social and pubertal concerns rather than business applications.

Youth has also influenced the growing compactness of the Internet, which can be utilized on the run and in private, away from home and the watchful eye of authority.[3] Youth are thought to engage the Internet particularly because they have more to say, fantasize, or worry about, and they derive gratification from widening their circles of contacts into definable networked cliques. It enables their transition out of the home, giving them the physical mobility and social connections often associated with cultural passage into adulthood. The openness of youthful endeavor is indicated by the number of electronic means to tell others what one is doing. Facebook has a prominent feature of posting what one is doing presently and Twitter is a service to stay connected through the exchange of quick, frequent answers to one simple question: what are you doing? This linkage of action to age is yet another way that the Internet mediates and alters tradition.

Also conspicuous on the Web are efforts to virtualize rituals of change, joy, and grief, such as virtual wedding chapels, church services, and cemeteries (Goethals 2003; Hutchings 2007). The folk web has not in reality replaced rites of passage, but it often elaborates upon them in virtual photo sites, which arguably have transformed album keeping and photocopying of humor into digital culture. As the folk web is embraced by all ages, beginning even before children can read, it becomes part of ritual routine, through creation of electronic family albums, virtual cafes, and support groups composed by parents; niche sites for ethnic-religious networking; matchmaking and chat rooms assuaging loneliness for singles; and memory-making by older adults in scrapbook and memorial sites. So don't get me wrong; I am sure that graybeards can pute with the best of the young whippersnappers, but my point is that cultural expectations have been created for who is wired and doing the wiring of society. The old pastoral model of folklore that evoked wisdom of yore being *handed down* by a golden ager may lead us to think that digital culture displaces tradition, but we might instead conceive of digital culture fostering a *handing up* of vernacular knowledge by young, wired wizards with mythic imagination and social ebullience.

A dramatic tension is apparent in the metafolklore about the Internet hosting an unseen power who can spy one's codes and inscriptions. Theoretically, power is assigned to the user to select who sees them—all or some—but fear of unwanted viewers—lurkers, authorities, and hackers—generates a folklore of its own. If the Internet is performative by virtue of the self-conscious act of *going to a site* for viewing or listening, it is surely different by virtualizing a context of security and secrecy that does not depend on a time and place of assembly (Laurel 1991; Simmel 1906). People presume that communication in this medium ripples like a wave outward and can be caught by any number of strangers; an important function of folklorization of the Internet is the interpersonal controls that people impose to secure the channels or conduits of interaction. The Internet's saturating, expansive features to facilitate *logging on anywhere* and being *always on* raise images of defying nature and sleep in a 24/7 format and are frequently mentioned as defining characteristics of the medium. People on the Internet do not ask whether it is too late to call with a story, and posters of images appreciate that they *go up* instantaneously and are always retrievable. More than miming the actions of natural reality by giving flowers or posting a note to project feelings onto objects or language, while working in a structural form confined to three dimensions, the representation on the screen evokes in our minds the possibility of innovation in expanded, stringed dimensions and of reconstitution of traditions in new, unforeseen or hidden perspectives that only the computer can reveal (Randall 2002; Waldrop 1985; Weingard 1988).

Besides freedom of expression, the Internet putatively liberates artistic communication from materiality, but hardly immaterial, the folklore of the Internet is consequential stuff that invites human participation. In this way, it is conceivable to envision the difference in method and theory between natural and virtual reality that Kirshenblatt-Gimblett invited folklorists to contemplate by thinking about the betwixt and between characteristic of Internet communication. Additionally virtual traditions deviate from the definition of folklore as artistic communication in small groups, which Dan Ben-Amos inventively suggested as a modern definition of folklore in context; in a digital age they appear as layered (and often non-linear) symbolizations or processes in multivariable, interactive networks (Ben-Amos 1972; Labbo 1996; Laske 1990; Sommerer and Mignonneau 1999). Although naturalistic tradition is often associated with precedent from way back when, the Internet's flattening, or disregard, of time invokes the view that something being on the Internet is sufficient to show this pre-existent characteristic of tradition. The implication is that this something has its own independent existence that involves an artificial fusion of new and old, text and image, and creativity and tradition. Folklorists and other cultural scholars may be concerned that in this kind of tradition the electronic tools of forwarding and copying and pasting standardize and stabilize texts, taking away the variability that marks cultural identities in natural contexts, but the serial reproductive process of homepages and forums appears to foster commentary and communal alteration, often with an instrumentality that signifies cultural space (Baker and Bronner 2005, 346).

A process of bricolage, that is, combining different images to create new forms, appears in the new media transmission and is characteristic of a consumer society, and there is evidence of alterations and selections that represent national and regional identities, such as the cultural divides in the global Internet phenomenon of 9/11 humor (Ellis 2003). These variable photo pastiches and riddle jokes divided between an American leitmotif of masculinist unity under stress facing an exoticized, feminized enemy and European satire deflating American leadership and arrogance. American jokes often expressed a militarist desire for revenge, such as the common joke, "What is Osama bin Laden going to be on Halloween? Dead!" British jokes, by contrast, blurred the tragic events with images drawn from the media, as in "Bin Laden is going to be on [a cooking show] next week. He'll show how to make a big apple crumble" (Ellis 2006, 630; compare Dundes and Pagter 1991a). After following the quick folkloric response on the Internet, folklorist Bill Ellis pointed out that "American jokes and British jokes were available to both cultures online, sometimes posted together on the same message boards. However, it seems clear that regionally generated social rules about humor continue to play an important part in determining which jokes spread and where they go" (Ellis 2006, 630). This symbolization is a reminder of the function, indeed the imperative, of folklore as a culturally variable frame in which to express or resolve feelings, ambiguities, and conflicts under conditions of stress. It also suggests not quickly dismissing nationalistic and regional affiliations in the embrace of the Internet as a global village in cyberspace that subverts nation-states on land (Stratton 1997). The Internet incorporates folklore by offering spontaneous transmission bounded by a number of social, localized configurations, and one might argue that it expands the folkloric frame because it extends the creative, reproductive, and often transgressive capability of oral communication with visual imagery and instantaneous response. Indeed, to spotlight the interactive quality of the Internet, many sites encourage agonistic, rather than harmonious, relationships. On these pages, a button is frequently labeled with the folkloric idiom *talk back*, inviting an impudent reply that will start a heated exchange, virtualizing and ritualizing *getting in your face* (Millard 1997).

Symbolically, the Internet may be cast by Hollywood as a displacement machine reminiscent of industrial giants obliterating cottage-housed artisans, but it is also a tool for maintenance of diverse subcultures because it allows multi-layered social interaction that is difficult to maintain in a dispersed society. In this regard, it is deep as well as open; users often talk about subtexts and an archeology of sites, with hidden links or tags that reveal meanings not apparent on the surface (Wilbur 1997). Although the openness of cyberspace is hailed, dangers are narrated in a folklore about fringe or nefarious groups latching on to the Internet and masking their predatory intentions with slick homepages. Supposedly a tool of massification, the Internet has also spawned a belief that it expands social diversity by allowing communication of people on all sorts of interests or fetishes (Poster 2001). To account for multifarious networks fostering idiocultures (cultures created through shared group interactions rather than through their place on the land) on the Internet, we can apply the multiconduit hypothesis from folkloristic theory. It holds that "folklore texts do not pass through an orderly, regulated trail from person to person but generate their own, specific linkages that carry messages through society" (Dégh 1997, 142; see also Dégh 1993; Dégh and Vázsonyi 1975). Thus textual and visual reproduction on the Internet does not necessarily homogenize cultural expression. Instead, the Internet's potential for free, spontaneous transmission fosters renewal and innovation by participants working within a traditional frame of reference. Indeed the posting of sources in website counters, e-mails, and listservs suggests a quantification of the multiple conduits of transmission that is onerous to attain in the naturalistic field and when observed often presumes degeneration (see Ellis 2003; Fine 1979, 1980, 1983; Oring 1978). The belief is pervasive in cyberculture that expressive payloads users launch into cyberspace are always new, "to boldly go where no man has gone before," to quote from an often folklorized line from the television show *Star Trek*. Fear and folkloric belief in conspiratorial, imperial deception reigns among open-source advocates who worry that cyberspace will not always be open or deep—rhetorical representations of virtual folklorization—as the state or corporation seeks to regulate it and bring it under its wing rather than letting the masses constitute it (Stelter 2008; Truscello 2003). Thus the metafolklore of the Internet also refers to the possibility that the folk web will be shut down or forced underground. Its practice can therefore change, and that leads to examination of the characteristics that now allow it to function for social and cultural purposes.

Digital and Analog, Analytical and Relational, Visual and Virtual

An Internet means of transmission raises questions about what kind of cultural practice on digital equipment constitutes folkloric enactment. The association of generations and periods of time with technology, such as the computer age and the iPod generation, implies that lives are structured by what we own and do. Such generational labels refer to tools that users harness for individualistic purposes; users are in a sense digital selectors who can create multiple personas suited for different web events. People materialize digital power in everyday life by hanging equipment on belts, which is reminiscent of emboldening gun holsters from the Wild West; opening laptop lids as if lifting a treasure lid or secret spy code unit; and flipping open phones with a sound effect like an attention-grabbing switchblade. Whereas going to the mailbox by your house is an occasional, pastoral behavior, or what computer geeks derisively call *snail mail*, the cyberculture instantaneous experience of checking and receiving mail is constant and intrusive, especially when engaging in instant messaging, a rhetoric that suggests instant gratification. Although inexpensive webcams, often built into computers, make it possible to look our conversation mates in the eye, communicative practice on the Internet surprisingly has resisted going live.[4] Or maybe it is not so surprising if one considers the folkloric qualities that people want to embed into their interaction. Being disembodied allows for role playing, speech play, visual representation, bricolage, and sometimes anonymity, each of which supports elaboration of the self—and connection to a group—through expressive material. The frame requires some boundaries to manage risks in communication. Some limitations are policed and legislated, and a tradition of folk regulation has arisen governing such transgressions as those represented by the vernacular terms *flaming*, *snarking*, *lurking*, *spamming*, *phishing*, *socking*, and *thread bumping* (Millard 1997; Stivale 1997). In other words, the Internet opens up investigation not just of the texts it produces but the behaviors it spawns, which draw attention to themselves as repeatable *practices* related to logging on and thereby rhetorically become ingrained into culture as *praxis*—representations for generalizable actions such as interfacing and downloading (Bernstein 1971; Bronner 1988a; Johnson 1999; Lavazzi 2001).

Talk of an all-encompassing digital age and digital culture constructs a binary with analog culture that merits closer scrutiny. This binary, which privileges the advancement of digitization, implies a number of structural oppositions: large/small, new/old, artificial/natural, formal/informal, electronic/manual, and discontinuous/continuous. The implication of this rhetoric is that thinking has shifted as the technology and culture have changed. Emblematic of the digital/analog difference is the clock. The analog version is understood by positions of hands on a dial that make reference to the natural occurrence of lines and shadows formed by the sun, which can be read by relative positions. *O'clock* thus signifies the position of an observer in the center, where 12 o'clock considered straight ahead. The digital clock takes out representation and the observer. Time is instead represented in exact numbers or language that can be received anywhere and in any form. Display is continuous and does not represent position so much as express a code. Analog is considered more interpersonal and tactile because it can be equated with the direct perception of sensation (Gregory 1970, 162–66; Stewart and

Bennett 1991, 24–29). Digital is conceived as artificial and solely visual as it depicts time in alphanumeric symbols or icons framed in mechanistic rectangles instead of analog's naturalistic circles and hands.

Digital comes from the Latin *digitus* for finger, suggesting discrete counting, converting real-world information into binary numeric form. Analog contains reference to the Greek *logos* positing meaning that comes from its related senses of "word" (or "say") and "reason"; folklorists use *analogue* in its sense of an item in relative position to another. Further, the strategy of holding up group and context as vital to the definition of folklore is analogic because it is relational, emphasizing the immediate characteristics and fragmentation of the event, or performance. Whereas, *repetition* and *variation* and *practice*, which are more commonly applied to folklore in new technology, including the Internet, have a digital connotation that underscores linear continuity and aggregate data (see Bronner 1988a, 2000; Dégh 1994; Drout 2006; Dundes and Pagter 1975; Köstlin and Shrake 1997; Koven 2000). Analog culture, often attributed to the touch-oriented world of tradition, especially in pre-modern society, derives meaning from sensory aspects of perception (Stewart and Bennett 1991, 28–32; Bronner [1986] 2004). Cultural practices are more often circumscribed than delineated. People derive significance from face-to-face encounters because the appearance of people, what they do, and how they do it convey an encircled, functional reality (Stewat and Bennett 1991, 29). Thus storytelling in analog culture is an event defined not just by a text but by a physical setting and the perceptions between tellers and audience (Georges 1969; Oring 2008).

Digital culture emphasizes representations of reality and outcomes of *messages*. Thus it may seem to connect more people, but it judges meaning less from social relationships and appearances than from textual similarities. Arguably, in an analog context, meaning is attached immediately to events as they are perceived within a small group; it is more sensitive to the natural, immediate social context. It privileges the ground of turf while digital values the action of surf. Both analog and digital culture are capable of producing and expressing tradition, but they may perceive it differently. Analog culture might be said to be relational and localized, with a high degree of sensitivity to experience, context, emotions, relationships, and status—within a place. Digital culture relies on analytical, inductive thinking that takes observable events to form informational pieces linked in causal chains and categorized into universal criteria (Stewart and Bennett 1991, 41-42; Cohen 1969, 841–42; M. O. Jones 1971). Much of this linkage, analytical thinker Alan Dundes pointed out, tends to be linear and is reflected in folklore, particularly folk speech, that is oriented toward vision rather than touch, the individual rather than the group, an outcome rather than a process, the future rather than the past, and progress rather than stability (Bronner [1986] 2004; Bronner 2007; Dundes 2004; Lee [1950] 1968). We can understand the misplaced perception that the Internet is devoid of folklore as a relational, evolutionary outlook: anything digital is equatable with machinery that replaces the human capacity to emote and embody. But viewed operationally or analytically, digital culture as represented by the Internet is replete with *construction* and *assemblage* of multi-layered messages into virtual, rather than natural reality. One of those constructions is the presumption that digital is preferable because it is more efficient, more essentially human, leading to a certain illusion that the digital world is culture free. One can arrange a continuum of thinking set, as it often is, in scenarios appropriate, for example, to decision making. It is indeed possible to analyze the folklorization of the Internet as the cumulative acts of organizing and tagging an ever-expanding array of messages. These acts are focused less on the immediacy of the event than on its spread, creativity, traditional character, simultaneity, and heterogeneity of transmission (see Bronner 1986, 122–29; Lowe 1982; McCallum 2001).

As daily practice rather than special performance, the Internet structures perceptions outside of users' awareness. One can talk about how folk beliefs about Internet usage involve its global reach, classlessness, democratization, and gender neutrality (see Poster 2001; Wallace 1999), but expressed beliefs about the Internet do not always characterize it consistently. In the rhetoric of transmission, the Internet is frequently noted for both its mass globalization and acquisitive individualism as well as its freedom and collectivity, even by its most avid, or addicted, fans. One can discern cultural expectations when logging on that affect the kind of traditions created online. Cognitive associations are frequently made between geekdom and being emasculated, yet holding cultural, if not social capital. Country singer Brad Paisley in 2008 had a chart-topping hit with "Online" that was replete with these beliefs. He sang over and over again, "I'm so much cooler online" and explained, "When you get my kind of stats, It's hard to get a date, Let alone a real girlfriend, But I grow another foot and I lose a bunch of weight, Every time I login." As these lyrics indicate, the Internet lends itself to hyperbole, which often translates into rumors, legends, and humor of tall-tale proportions.

In his compilation organized around American regions, *The Greenwood Library of American Folktales*, Thomas A. Green listed over eighty discrete texts he contextualized as folklore in cyberspace. Many are oral legends and chain letters adapted to the distributive medium of the Internet with the instruction to "forward asap," but others use a digital medium to comment on electronic communication's distinctive qualities. An example is the rumor that the federal government will charge a 5-cent surcharge on every e-mail delivered to offset losses by the U.S. Postal Service (Green 2006, 4: 262–64). A variant accuses newspapers and the popular press of repressing the story. It invites users to harness the power of the Internet to "E-mail to EVERYONE on your list." It speaks to the democratizing, freedom ideal of the Internet and at the same time to the belief that superstructures representing the power elite inevitably flex control. As one variant states directly, "The whole point of the Internet is democracy and noninterference" (Green 2006, 4: 264). This idealization of the Internet as an untethered, unbureaucratized *commons* suggests that although it is certainly viewed as postmodern in its transcendence of space and time, it is popularly constructed in the model of the premodern village, which raises comparisons to a global village governed by tradition rather than nationalistic rule of law. Its interactive empowerment and constructiveness are among its culturally expected, addictive features. We can connect this belief to the multiconduit model of folklore. Folklorist Linda Dégh, writing about the conduits of face-to-face communication, asserted that "transmission of traditional messages in natural contexts is essentially free; arbitrary limitation of this freedom encroaches upon the normal functioning of the conduit" (Dégh 1997, 143).

References to the democratization of the Internet in popular discourse raise the question of its American-ness or Western-ness, especially considering the big developer names of Microsoft, Apple, and Google are American-based (Stewart and Bennett 1991, 17–44; Cohen 1969; Lee [1950] 1968).[5] What is implied by the American preoccupation with the constructiveness of culture, counter to the European emphasis on the rootedness and givenness of folk culture in the natural landscape and the Asian perception of groupness constituted by social homogeneity and historical antiquity (see Bronner 1998; Dundes 1982)? American conceptions have often been distinguished by presenting culture as an outcome of social interaction, even if temporary and overlapping actions. Instead of comprising received traditions to be unselfconsciously followed, culture—and websites—can be constructed, created anew, to meet needs of the moment or person (Mechling 2006). In a constructivist concept of culture, individuals choose with whom they affiliate and the customs in which they participate; they may hybridize different traditions to create a distinctive cultural persona. Alan Dundes characterized his definition of folk group, for instance, as a "modern" and "American concept" due to the idea of social linkage rather than birthright: *"any group of people whatsoever* who share at least one common factor. It does not matter what the linking factor is—it could be a common occupation, language, or religion—but what is important is that a group formed for whatever reason will have some traditions which it calls its own" (Dundes 1965b, 2).

Dundes's reference to "two or more persons" as the social minimum of the group rhetorically implied that these persons produce culture working in interaction with one another. This constructivist outlook, which does not assert a baseline for the extent, location, economic status, literacy, or antiquity of the group, lends itself to the centrality of the network as the social basis of folkloric communication on the Internet. Using *network* as a term before the advent of the Internet, folklorists Beth Blumenreich and Bari Lynn Polonsky understood that "folklore is individually determined and based, not 'group' determined and based. Moreover, the individual's folklore is determined by the nature of his interactions and experiences. This suggests that folklore can be most profitably studied in terms of interactional communicative and experiential networks—ICEN's, as we shall call them" (1974, 15; see also Augusto 1970; Fine 1983). Blumenreich and Polonsky conceptualized networks to be face-to-face connections of choice in which obligations are decentered from family and community and recentered in the heterogeneous organizations that the individual chooses. Unlike communities in which one resides and consequently interacts with others, networks are broadly expandable and transcend time and space. Virtual networks, according to a dictionary of *New Keywords* for the information age, are central to the development of choices, and "imagined to be a means of establishing electronic communities (networks of people sharing beliefs and/or interests at a distance) at a time when long-term communities are said to be disappearing" (Webster 2005). Networks are integrally tied to technological change that facilitates increasing, simultaneous flows of information through cumulative, expandable social conduits. Although the buzzword *information* makes the communication sound like bundles of sterile minutiae, folklore is one of the strategies commonly employed to give a sense of tradition and hence identity to participants in the network, and to enliven the information with a cultural frame of reference.

Transmitting Tradition in Analog and Digital Eras: Lessons from the Budd Dwyer Saga

One way to test the production of tradition through interactive or mediated networks is to compare the production and use of lore in analog and digital eras. I had a chance to do that by being in the middle of an oral joke cycle that emerged in 1987 in Pennsylvania, and in the twenti-eth-first century took new forms on the Internet, for a global audience. The subject of the humor was Pennsylvania State Treasurer R. Budd Dwyer who committed suicide at a televised news conference in the capitol building in Harrisburg. For months, regional media had been devoting coverage to Dwyer's conviction for accepting a $300,000 bribe in exchange for a no-bid computer contract. Corruption trials were noth-ing new to the state capital, but what was unusual was Dwyer's promi-nent executive position. Prosecutors had brought a parade of underlings in for graft, but Dwyer was the highest official in the Dick Thornburgh administration to come to trial. If he made headlines as a big fish, he also drew notice for hanging around local watering holes. Asking to be called by his chummy middle name of Budd rather than his first name Robert, Dwyer was known for his neighborly familiarity around town, and he had a cherubic face and congenial style. He came from the unassum-ing-sounding town of Meadville and, after starting out as a high school civics teacher, worked his way up in the Republican Party from state senator to state treasurer. He was a regular sight on Harrisburg side-walks, and he had the reputation for being approachable and affable. Some whispered that he got ahead by being the party's water carrier, that he was just a bumpkin, but regardless, he was recognized as one of the state's political honchos.

January 22, 1987, looked like an ugly day to commuters descending on Pennsylvania's state capitol as cheerless dark clouds hung over the city. Cleanup had finished of inauguration celebrations two days ear-lier for the new Democratic administration of Robert P. Casey, and state workers settled back into their routines. The statewide magnet of the Pennsylvania State Farm Show in Harrisburg, an indoor agricultural fair attracting half a million visitors, had cleared out a few days before, as the winter holidays became a distant memory. The day started with one of those January frosts that brought a frown to the thousands who made their way to work for the area's largest employer—state government. To top things off, a heavy snowfall that began that morning snarled traf-fic and kept children from school. As the snow depths increased, state workers were sent home, and most schoolchildren who never ventured out were taking seats in front of their televisions. Budd Dwyer decided to go ahead with his scheduled press conference anyway. The next day he faced sentencing, and he was looking at the likelihood of a long prison sentence for the federal crime. Most commentators expected Dwyer to use the occasion to reiterate his innocence and announce his resignation. Reporters, photographers, and television camera operators gathered in

his office at 10:30 a.m. Several noticed that the furniture had been rear-
ranged to create a barrier between where Dwyer was about to speak
and the reporters, but they made no protestation of the set-up. When
Dwyer entered the room, he insisted that the door to the adjacent room
be closed, restricting the room to 30 or so reporters and a handful of
aides. These were unusual actions on the state government beat, but the
reporters figured these were unusual times for Dwyer, the state's highest
fiscal officer, now facing disgrace.

Dwyer read a long rambling statement declaring his innocence. He
opened by saying, "This has been like a nightmare, like a life in the twi-
light zone. It wouldn't surprise me to wake up this minute to find out I
was home in my bed and had just had a terrible nightmare. That's how
unbelievable this has been. I mean, I've never done anything wrong and
yet all this horrible nightmare has occurred to me." Dwyer blamed former Governor Dick Thornburgh for starting the probe because of a feud
between them, and he criticized the press, FBI, judge, and jury for their
handling of the case. But he saved his harshest words for the aggressive,
ambitious state prosecuting attorney with the flashy name of James West.
He then called for a review of the judicial system, a system that he felt
had failed him. Occasionally he seemed to force back tears as he hurried
through his speech. He skipped past pages of the text and told reporters
they could read it later. Some of the reporters from television stations pre-
pared to leave, but Dwyer called them back, saying, "I think you ought to
stay, because we're not finished yet" (Cusick, Meyers, and Roche 1987).

After about 25 minutes, Dwyer came to the last page of his speech.
He did not read it. Instead he handed three sealed envelopes to his
aides.[6] He reached into his briefcase on the desk, took out a manila envelope, and pulled out a .357 Magnum revolver. He held it up and with his
other hand reached out like a football back fending off tacklers. Several
reporters began to yell at him, "No, no, don't do this." Over the shouts,
he announced, "Please leave the room as this will, as this will hurt
someone." He looked like he was about to say something else, but as the
shouts of the reporters grew, he put the gun in his mouth and holding
the gun with both hands pulled the trigger. Forty-seven-year-old Budd
Dwyer died instantly. His body fell back against the wall and slouched
down in full view of whirring cameras. Blood splashed behind his head
and dripped down from his nose. Dwyer's press secretary closed out the
event by stepping out in front of the body and saying, "All right, show
some decorum."

Shortly after 11 a.m., the largest of the midstate's television stations
interrupted programming and reported the news of Dwyer's suicide.

With no warning of graphic content, the station ran the video without editing. A flood of calls came into the station protesting showing the tape when so many children were home watching. Drawing comparisons to coverage of the Kennedy assassination and the Challenger shuttle disaster, the station answered on the air that it was reporting the news as it happened, even if it was disturbing, and showed the tape again, though warning viewers this time about the graphic contents. Other stations also showed video but edited out Dwyer pulling the trigger. They offered phone numbers of crisis intervention centers to help those who had watched the video and felt anguish as a result.

The unread portion of Dwyer's statement revealed that the suicide for the cameras was planned. It stated, "I am going to die in office in an effort to see if the shameful facts, spread out in all their shame, will not burn through our civic shamelessness and set fire to American pride. Please tell my story on every radio and television station and in every newspaper and magazine in the U.S. Please leave immediately if you have a weak stomach or mind, since I don't want to cause physical or mental distress." But distress he did cause, among many viewers, who phoned stations to request shelving the video.

The story went national quickly. Cable News Network (CNN) showed a slightly edited version of the video, while the major networks carried the news without showing the tape. The Associated Press sent out photos showing the entire sequence of Dwyer's suicide, but included the warning: "They are very graphic photos of Dwyer with the gun in his mouth and pulling the trigger. We call to your attention that they may be offensive to some readers." Newspapers across the country included stories on the event, but Pennsylvania's offered the most graphic depictions, most notably the *Philadelphia Inquirer*, which to the chagrin of many readers splashed photos on its pages of Dwyer putting the revolver in his mouth and falling to the floor (Cusick, Meyers, and Roche 1987, 16A). Ironically, in many circles the media's handling of the event became the story rather than Dwyer's message. *Time* magazine, for example, commented that "while most newspapers and TV stations carried only edited footage of the incident, two Pennsylvania stations aired the full sequence of the suicide—prompting hundreds of viewers to phone in protests" ("Milestones" 1987). A few days later reports of a televised suicide by a public official in Australia, apparently in imitation of Dwyer's event, came on the air and kept the controversy stirred. Looking for precedents to mark the events as a pattern, a search of news archives came up with the televised suicide in July 1975 of Christine Chubbuck, a host of a local variety show in Sarasota, Florida, but it had not had the worldwide attention grabbed by the act of political figure Dwyer. The Dwyer story resurfaced on 19 June 1987, in one of those "ripped from the headlines" fictional adaptations on the popular television series *Hard Copy* broadcast by CBS. Perhaps replacing Dwyer with a female lead was a nod to Chubbuck, but the plot clearly echoed the details of Dwyer's case. In the show, a public official is hounded by reporters for her alleged participation in a kickback-for-contract scheme. She calls a televised press conference, declares her innocence, pulls a gun out of her purse, and in words reminiscent of Dwyer's, says, "Leave this room if you can't stand the sight of blood" before she commits suicide. The drama implied that media coverage drove her to ruin, and she got back at the press by committing the suicide in front of the reporters and cameras.

The show did not revive Dwyer's story. In reality, the national networks had given time on one night to the story. Stations in Pennsylvania continued their coverage for weeks with reports of reactions from various officials, speeches at the funeral, and subsequent investigations. By most accounts, Dwyer's suicide hit Pennsylvanians, especially Central Pennsylvanians, hard. The counseling center at Penn State Harrisburg put out a statement five days after the suicide reading, "We are aware that the events surrounding the recent public suicide of State Treasurer, R. 'Budd' Dwyer have generated considerable discussion and reaction in our community. We also know that a public and traumatic event of this kind may impact on individuals in different and sometimes unexpected ways." The center invited individuals to air their feelings with them. Also venting their feelings were reporters on the capitol beat who had been part of the news rather than spectators to it. They were now being interviewed instead of doing the interviewing. The questions were difficult: Could they have stopped it? Could they have known? Did they contribute to it? (Smith 1987; Parsons and Smith 1988).

During the weeks that followed Dwyer's suicide, reporters regularly queried psychiatrists for advice. Most commented on the feeling of hopelessness that Dwyer must have felt at a time when he thought he had achieved the pinnacle of success in public life. Dr. John Fryer, deputy medical director of the Philadelphia Psychiatric Center, was quoted as saying, "To do it in this way is to really get back at everybody and make sure nobody will escape. The rage must have been overwhelming. The time-honored theory about suicide is aggression turned inward. But it was Dwyer's public expression of rage that separates him from most suicide victims." Dr. Steven Schwartz, chief of adult psychiatric services at Thomas Jefferson University Hospital, added: "It's a nice extra bonus to make others suffer like they tried to make him suffer. The act was directed at newspeople and the populace who hounded him giving them something to remember. If you're going to do such a grand act of autonomy and power, why not do it on the biggest stage you can? It's screaming to the world, 'You didn't do anything to me, *I* did to me!'" In addition to speaking on talk shows and news programs, psychiatrists went out to the schools and spoke to schoolchildren who witnessed the event (Herskowitz 1987; Lewis 1987).

Nowhere in the coverage was the rise of jokes about the event mentioned. Nor was humor circulated through youth networks mentioned anywhere as a way to adjust to the trauma of the event. But the lore was hard to miss. The jokes began spreading the day after the event. Among the first I heard were "What was the last thing Budd Dwyer's wife said to him?" (answer: don't go shooting your mouth off) and "What was the last thing to go through Budd Dwyer's mind?" (answer: his teeth). The jokes were brought to my attention by students in class at Penn State Harrisburg, the school where Budd Dwyer's son was enrolled. A reporter who had been interviewing me about folk beliefs of Central Pennsylvania asked me whether I had heard the jokes. When I asked him whether he was questioning me for an article, he replied that no, he did not think his paper would run such a story because it might be construed as in bad taste. Instead, he was asking me for personal reasons. He had gone to a journalism convention in South Carolina, and when the Pennsylvania reporters got together, he said, "all they did was tell these jokes." "No one else knew them," he added, "just the Pennsylvania people." Yet the jokes had the characteristics of other joke cycles based on televised tragedies, such as the Challenger space shuttle disaster of 28 January 1986, jokes which coincidentally were getting around again after replays of the event on its one-year anniversary (Bronner 1988b, 129–30; Oring 1987; Simons 1986; Smyth 1986). Jokes in the Challenger cycle, many referring to schoolteacher-astronaut Christa McAuliffe, had precedents in oral tradition. A joking question making the rounds after the tragedy such as "What was the last thing to go through Christa McAuliffe's mind?" (Answer: ass, teeth, sheet metal, fuselage, tile) resembled jokes about Grace Kelly's fatal auto accident of 1982 such as "What was the last thing to go through Grace Kelly's mind?" (ass, windshield, teeth). Probably older is the bawdy joking question often collected from youth, "What's the last thing to go through a bug's mind when he hits the windshield?" Answer: "his asshole" (Barrick 1987; see also Barrick 1982). The central characters in these jokes were celebrities who all had connections to the technology that did them in (McAuliffe

to spacecraft, Kelly to a luxury automobile, and in Dwyer's case to con-
tracted computers). Humor about all three also played on the unnatural
deformity of their bodies as a result of unexpected tragic events that
were intensely photographed or filmed.

Mac E. Barrick, a folklorist at Shippensburg University, also in
Central Pennsylvania, heard the Dwyer jokes too. We polled our classes
immediately to trace the cycle of lore as it took its course, and compared our findings. When Barrick interviewed his students on February
4, all twenty-six had heard the jokes. I also had twenty-six students,
and on January 28, twenty-two of twenty-six had heard the jokes. Of
those twenty-two, nineteen had seen the unedited version of the video
(eighteen in Barrick's class), and sixteen thought he was guilty (fifteen
thought so in Barrick's class). Fifteen of the students knew at least two
jokes, five knew three, and two knew one. From whom did they hear
them? They said other college students. Making other inquiries, I found
that the jokes were not restricted to college-age youth. I heard them from
children as young as the sixth grade and from adults in their thirties,
but I concluded that they were most popular in the age of adolescence
through the early twenties.

A total of 23 percent of respondents told me they heard a Budd
Dwyer joke the day after the suicide, but over 86 percent heard their
jokes three to five days after the suicide. Both men and women heard the
jokes, but men appeared to prefer telling them. In Barrick's class, equally
composed of men and women, 36 percent heard the jokes from both men
and women, whereas 64 percent heard them solely from men.

The joke cycle had two waves. During the first wave in the first five
days after the event, the most popular jokes were joking questions playing on the answer "don't go shooting your mouth off." The questions
varied from "What did Budd Dwyer's wife (mother, press secretary) say
before his press conference?" to "How did you know Budd Dwyer was a
politician?" Second in popularity were joking questions playing on beer
commercials or beer characteristics. One might hear "What did Budd
Dwyer's press secretary say to the coroner?" The answer: "This Bud's
for you." Or there's "What do Dwyer and flat beer have in common? No
head." Or "What kind of beer has no head? Budd-Dwyser." And "What
happens when you shake up a Bud? It blows its cap." Third in popularity were joking questions offering another misplaced phrase or pun.
"What were Dwyer's last words to his wife?" one asked, and then sup-
plied the answer of "I need this job like I need a hole in the head." Then
there's "What's worse (or better) than a pistol in your washer?" Answer:
"A bullet in your Dwyer." Other jokes were in the form of remarks, such

as "Budd Dwyer got so fed up at work the other day he shot his brains out, but now he has half a mind to go back to work." This could also be rephrased as a joking question such as "Did you hear that Budd Dwyer shot himself? Now he has half a mind to go back to work." These jokes apparently have cognates in humor about the head injury to James Brady during the assassination attempt on Ronald Reagan in 1981. The "hole in the head" answer in the Dwyer jokes has precedent in "What did James Brady say to Reagan that day? I need this job like I need a hole in the head." And there was the follow-up: "What did James Brady say later at the hospital? I have half a mind to go back to work."

During the second wave of orally circulated jokes, students composed new jokes or recycled Challenger disaster jokes by applying Dwyer to them. Typically offered at bar or dorm get-togethers, the jokes in this cycle rarely went beyond the group. Some of the composed jokes were: "What did Budd Dwyer say to his secretary at the end of his press conference? The envelope please." "What did the guy say when he went into a bar? Gimme a Bud and blow the head off of it." "What's Budd Dwyer's favorite beer? Colt 45." "What's Budd Dwyer's favorite toothpaste? Aim." "Why did Budd Dwyer put money behind his head? He wanted to see his face on a dollar bill." "What's the Budd Dwyer memorial coin? A washer." A large share of the composed or adapted jokes were sexual in nature: "What does Budd Dwyer have in common with a good Catholic girl? No head." "What do Tom Selleck's girlfriend and Budd Dwyer have in common? They both had Magnums go off in their mouths." "What did Budd Dwyer and Liberace have in common? They both put things in their mouths they shouldn't have." "What's the difference between Budd Dwyer and Rock Hudson? Budd Dwyer put a bullet in his head and Rock Hudson put a head in his butt." The common recycled Challenger disaster jokes were: "What color were Budd Dwyer's (Christa McAuliffe's) eyes? Blue—one blew here, one blew there" and the one about the last thing to go through his (previously her) mind. "What's the new Capital Cocktail," another joke went, and the answer was "Straight shot and a Bud" (the Space Shuttle Cocktail was "7Up and a splash of Teacher's"). The second wave in the Budd Dwyer joke cycle subsided by the end of February, and in March when I asked about the jokes, no new ones had been heard.

The Budd Dwyer joke cycle took on the swift-timing and mass-society characteristics of other celebrity tragedy jokes, but the Dwyer jokes were restricted almost exclusively to Central Pennsylvania. Although the entire nation had heard of Dwyer after the event, it was in Central Pennsylvania that adjustment was called for; it was in Central

Pennsylvania that the suicide was graphically displayed; and it was in
Central Pennsylvania that Budd Dwyer's name and, particularly, his
image were familiar sights. He was a person who you could run into
having a beer in a local tavern or conversing on the street. The jokes thus
created an incongruity between the unassuming figure and his celebrity
status. There were overtones of the bumpkin overwhelmed by the city,
but mainly, especially to those living around Harrisburg, the jokes were
understood in the context of political corruption so familiar to state government (Keisling and Kearns 1988). In addition to covering Dwyer's
case, Harrisburg's media reported at the same time news of graft in con-
tracts for the building of the capitol addition and the indictment of several state judges for accepting bribes. Along with Dwyer, the Republican
Party chairman was convicted and several other state officials were
implicated. As Frank Lynch, a reporter for Harrisburg's *Patriot-News*
at Dwyer's trial, told me, "Everyone did it, but Budd Dwyer just got
caught, that's all. Budd became the symbol of Pennsylvania politics"
(Bronner 1988b, 86).

But it was the way Dwyer went out of politics that attracted humorous comment. It was the airing of the analog tape of Dwyer taking his
own life and seeing the bloody result that forced young viewers to come
to terms with the harshness of death. Perhaps especially wrenching for
vulnerable adolescents was this public figure's ultimate statement of failure and hopelessness, an avowal that was repeated a few days after the
suicide by a teenager in York, Pennsylvania, who took his own life by
shooting a gun into his mouth. In the first wave of jokes, related in face-
to-face encounters within the local setting, could be heard the outlets, on
the one hand, of laughter at a community tragedy. On the other hand,
to many young men, telling the jokes was a sign of their toughness, an
aggressive demonstration of their ability to be unshaken by the horror
of the graphic suicide. Still, most of the students I interviewed acknowledged that laughing at the event in the days following the suicide eased
the tension in the air. Many of the students interviewed also considered
the jokes irreverent and derived adolescent satisfaction from the rebel-
liousness of telling them, at least to one another. The event was a disaster
to Pennsylvanians not only because of the taking of a life but because
the corruption that they knew ran rampant and was taken lightly had a
tragic end. It was a disaster because it brought death close to home, close
to children American society tries hard to shelter (see Dundes 1979, 3-14).

The first wave of Budd Dwyer jokes had raised talk about the televised broadcast of his suicide, his guilt or innocence, and the context of
political corruption around the city in general. The second wave focused

on the act of joking itself. It played with the joking form, rather than providing humorous comment on the historical and political context. In the second wave of jokes, a shift is apparent from Dwyer's predicament to creating humor through the extension of word play and the realization of incongruity. The jokes emphasized the sexual and violent content that marks other joke-telling sessions during the college years. Dwyer became a temporary vehicle for varying the expression of these themes. But these jokes were not successful; they did not spread and they often received a grudging reception when they were originally told.

Budd Dwyer jokes spread orally had a limited time and place, but on the Internet Dwyer lore has taken a different visual form and has gone global. Twenty years after Budd Dwyer's death, a Google search of his name produced 37,600 sites. Among the sites were several tributary memorial sites, MySpace and Facebook pages using his name (including a few rock bands), http://www.budd-dwyer.com.remember.to, and lots of wikis on his biography, including gorewiki.org on which a clip of the shooting looped repeatedly. The jokes resurfaced, either on sites dealing with sick jokes generally or on humor sites (often under the subject category of *suicide*) that prefaced the jokes with explanations of Dwyer's conviction and press conference. Although some of the sites referred to the jokes as texts of particular meaning to Pennsylvanians, most networks categorized them more generally. For example, the Comedy and Jokes Community included Dwyer's death among a "list of crazy, weird and even funny deaths of prominent people in the last 100 years" (posted 29 August 2008). The most common joke listed among different sites was word play connecting Budd Dwyer with commercial icon Budweiser beer: "What's the difference between Budd Dwyer and Bud Lite? Bud Lite has a head." In fact, many sites misspelled Budd's name as Bud, assuming that it was a nickname that fit his constructed persona of victimized everyman.

More likely than repeating jokes, Internet chatters discussing Dwyer were fond of spouting a joking proverbial comparison, "Like Budd Dwyer, I'm going out with a bang" (Domi 2008). Discussing a rumor that the Dwyer saga would be made into a movie, one discussion group started a thread of humorous comments: "He sure went out with a bang. Hahahahaha; Hey man, nice shot! Muhahaha; Now that's what I call a sack lunch" (Mencia 2008). A MySpace page repeated the "out with a bang" line but used it to express gothic subculture by respecting Dwyer's "style" for going "out with a bang and make sure those who did you wrong remember it forever" (Laurelei 2008). Dwyer's name along with the "bang" line came up often when a suicide made the news. When a

Pennsylvania district attorney went missing in 2005, a poster in a discussion thread commented "I guess he didn't want to go out with a bang like Bud Dwyer" (Will 2005). Different anonymous posters contributed to a parody of the typically just-the-facts Wikipedia entry for Dwyer in the Uncyclopedia. The "out with a bang" line was there expressed as "Dwyer's career had hit a rough spot, but he still managed to go out with a bang" and a spinoff at the end, "He then proceeded to give the audience a piece of his mind; those closest to him received that and more" ("Budd Dwyer" 2008). Whether functioning as "gross humor" to shock readers by its insensitivity and therefore question societal norms, or to temper disturbing thoughts of death, the repetition and variation of the "out with a bang" remark resonated with viewers because of Dwyer's public event and subsequent celebrity status. If Dwyer jokes had previously been symbolic of cultural communication that one would not read in the newspapers, Dwyer images in the digital age signified the openness of the Internet and the ability—in some cases, the obsession—with making a public mark in cyberspace. Among the many suicides discussed, Dwyer's stood out because it was public, as the Internet was, and vivid footage challenging social norms was available.

Dwyer was known to many viewers only on the Internet, where he achieved cult status for engineering his own death on tape. Dwyer's parting sentence, "Stay back, this could hurt someone," is frequently cast in a play frame through a list of comical, "famous last words throughout history" that is posted on many sites. Dwyer's name also rates listing along with celebrities Rosie O'Donnell, Michael Jackson, and Maury Povich as an example, in chat jargon of IDIFTL (I did it for the lulz), referring to an internet drama one causes ("I Did It for the Lulz" 2008). Reporting Dwyer's notoriety on the Web under the headline, "Dwyer Suicide Lives On," the print version of the *Philadelphia Daily News* informed readers that "The former Pennsylvania state treasurer is an *Internet cult figure*, his final moments posted on Web pages as a curiosity or a *sick joke*" (Russell 1998; emphasis added). The reporter thought the main audience for the "gruesome suicide" was youth because the subtitle of the piece was "Sex Isn't All That Parents Should Monitor on the Web" (Russell 1998). In keeping with the untethered reputation of the Internet, many bloggers narrated the footage as evidence of governmental conspiracy, suppression, or vendetta. Posts, expressed like urban legends, stated that independent investigations proved that Dwyer was framed and hounded to his death. Unlike television, which hid reality for the benefit of corporate suits or governmental higher-ups, the Internet opened access and invited commentary much as oral tradition might. In culture critic's Christie Davies's words, "Television is hegemonic, the Internet libertarian" (2003, 30). She theorizes that "Television, far from creating a global village, destroyed local communities and institutions, leaving behind a mass of atomized and alienated individuals, but the Internet is now enabling them to recreate virtual substitutes for the world they have lost . . . [the Internet] is a free, decentralized electronic medium in an otherwise controlled and restricted age" (Davies 2003, 34). Dwyer jokes in 1987 responded largely to television and commented on its moral authority to suppress a public suicide as well as the adjustment to the images that leaked through. By the Internet age, the Dwyer tape was widely available and prompted more belief and narrative response than textual production. It brought out the line between the folk and official web.

Another common reaction to Dwyer's footage on the Web that raises comparison to folk communication systems is that it haunts. It is narrated in terms reminiscent of ghost stories or spectral sightings and the figure of Dwyer can appear to be a dubious image rather than a real person. When jokes circulated at the time of Dwyer's suicide, the connection to everyday life was clearer than years later when the footage was posted on the Internet. "Videotape instantly helps negate the 'real-ness' of any situation," journalist Daniel Kraus wrote of the Dwyer Internet tape thirteen years after the public suicide occurred. He observed that the Dwyer tape has a "friend-of-a-friend" validation because someone tells someone else to view it and "conjure up very similar scenarios time and time again" (Krauss 2000). As it showed up on various sites, the footage lost clarity each time it was copied and redubbed; the blurry man on the tape looked ghostly, several posters commented. As with ghost hunters and legend trippers who go out in search of an encounter with the dead, viewing the tape involves both a morbid urge to view death and a repulsion from it. Seeing the footage invites narrative speculation about Dwyer's motivation or the forces that worked upon him that might also work on the viewer. Discussing the tape on MetaTalk, Phaedon wrote, for example, "I couldn't believe what I saw at first was real," to which Vacapinta responded, "It's a video of a desperate man blowing his brains out in public. It's haunted me since" ("Suicide Video Link" 2007). Daniel on MySpace independently wrote on his page, "This one haunted me . . . as desensitized as I thought I was, this one's been beating up my noggin for a couple of days" (Daniel 2008). He narrated that "You basically see him make the decision to end his life in his eyes, and you hear the gunshot, and the next thing you see is his lifeless body" (Daniel 2008). Along with the feeling of being haunted by the Dwyer footage the reactions mentioned include disbelief in the action viewed and the strong lingering character of it. Although a supernatural element is not apparent in most posts, the footage elicits responses that it is "unbelievable" and "incredible," which leads to comments addressing the unnaturalness of the death. It suggests a common folk strategy of ghost stories and beliefs to elicit responses about unnatural death and the vulnerability of mortals (see Thomas 2007a).

Whether framed as sick, apparently insensitive humor or tormented, sensitive narrative, Dwyer's story apparently carried a different message on the Internet in the twenty-first century than it did in dorm talk sessions in the twentieth. Whereas in its oral communicative context of Central Pennsylvania, it often was accompanied by comments on the problem of local corruption and the desperation of a popular public figure, Internet discourse turned his name into a metaphor for a stupid or outrageous media act. As a result of Internet posting of his death tape, Dwyer according to blogger David Eisenthal, "became something of a . . . joke" by two decades after his death (Eisenthal 2007). As blogs invite feedback, Eisenthal received several responses, many of which noted how easy it is to view the video of his death on the Internet, as it should be, which stood in contrast to how much controversy was raised when it was on television. The implication in the digital age is that the prosumer Internet, unlike consumer media, is an open public commons in which anyone can express opinions and all information is appropriate; this process comes to the fore in the posting of shocking images. In web discourse Dwyer became more a character in a narrative than a person with a biography. And that discourse takes on the character of conversation in a dorm or back room, which is instantaneous, even simultaneous, with content that emphasizes the colloquial, often defiantly incorporating, in the frame of the discussion thread, what elsewhere would be considered taboo or indecent.

In 2008 the wiki and chat site Urban Dictionary listed six different definitions of *Budd Dwyer*, arranged into a linear thread. The site has the participatory feature of allowing viewers to rate each definition, which reveals the cultural production of celebrities through perceptions. The first posted definition was "to commit suicide on television," and it gave the example of "they feared he could pull a Budd Dwyer." One topical reply worried that resigning New York governor Eliot Spitzer would "have a Budd Dwyer moment." Another definition referred to the difference between understanding the event on television and on the Internet with the comment "this was pre-internet, mind you, so they weren't used to seeing stuff." It received the most votes of approval, perhaps because it reminded viewers of the openness of the folk web and assured contemporary users that they were wiser and more aware than the days when the airwaves were censored. One poster complained that Dwyer as a term was not sympathetic; "he was an attention whore drama queen," Tien Duong baldly wrote, but his comment received more thumbs-down than thumbs-up symbols. Clearly not feeling pressure from any censors, Reservoir Dog got approvals for reporting the term used during fellatio. The poster explained "When getting a blow-job from a hot girl, you cum so hard that it shoots out her nose simulating Budd Dwyer's public suicide" ("Budd Dwyer" 2008). Usage was not due to Dwyer being a household name, which he was not, but to the easy availability of the suicide video on the Web, which gave him notoriety for a new generation.

The visual material was grist for thread mills that impelled posters to express beliefs—and express metafolklore about modern mass media. Internet images of Dwyer's suicide invite evaluations of the immediacy, and even exhibitionism, involved in making a mark in post-modern digital culture.[7] On the blog Modern Television, filmmaker Phillip Patiris posted a photo of Dwyer but resisted showing the "cheap thrill" of the video clip. He explained that despite his "unassailable belief that the wide-open web as a culmination and synthesis of all previously existing media is a place where anything and everything should (must) be presented . . . it's about time that people were forced to develop for themselves that lost, civilized art of responsibility and *discerning* by giving them access to every temptation available" (Patiris 1999). He argued that the Internet was unbridled and uncensored in the spirit of oral communication, but restraints, in the form of netiquette traditions, were developing to guide use of the Web. On the folk web, accusations, using folk terms, that posters are *flaming* (being intentionally provocative or insulting) or *snarking* (portmanteau of snide and remark) are akin to children's folk jeers, which keep group members in line by shaming them into conforming to standards of behavior (Knapp and Knapp 1976, 58–75). The disadvantage on the Web is that a jeerer cannot get in a culprit's face, but group pressure is applied through the discussion thread, often using the power of the Internet's instantaneity. The spread of Dwyer as a character or metaphor led Patiris to comment, for example, "It's all so instant here in cyberspace . . . witness e-mail and newsgroup flaming and the rise of incivility as people give in to their immediate and emotional impulses, immediately transmitted to the whole world, a form of exhibitionism" (quoted in Lynch 1998).

The video of Dwyer's suicide appears in several versions, short and extended, on YouTube, among other sites. The conversation in dorm rooms and offices in 1987 has been replaced by a running thread debating whether the video is camp or creepy. The first post to the extended version was "I just pissed and shit my pants," one of several referring to losing bodily functions while watching it. Whether or not that was a positive or negative statement, it was followed with the applauding line "That was a good screamer! Good job!" and the not so laudatory "D*it that scared me!" Often posted as a link with an invitation to view it, the video also provoked some irate posters to complain about the posters who had "shit on them" or "fucked with their heads." Viewing a visual image without historical context, some posters questioned the veracity of the footage and filled in a plausible narrative. RJAHaven, for instance, commented "Does he really shoot himself in here or is this a spoof?" to which michaeldog responded that it was real and "he committed suicide so his family could reap off the benefits" (HurricanEAJW2 2008). As if to underscore the openness of the Internet, a frequent comment on the cultural impact of Dwyer's event was to refer to a sketch for a television pilot by comedian Norm MacDonald in 2005 mimicking Dwyer's comments before committing suicide at a press conference. Although that never made it to television, as the story goes, on the Internet one can freely view and respond to videos about suicide, intermeshing both the comedic and the serious.[8]

The understanding of the Internet as open and visual was apparent, for example, in the case of "90 Day Jane," who announced her intention on a blog to commit suicide on the Web in ninety days. She in fact referred to Dwyer and Chubbuck's televised public suicides as models for her act but insisted that she was not depressed or seeking attention. She did intend to comment on the alienation of her young generation whose "biggest obstacle is beating Halo 3" ("'90 Day Jane' A Hoax, Takes Down Site" 2008). Responses ranged from sympathetic notes to vulgar accusations. She blogged each day leading up to her announced doomsday and received hundreds of comments on each of her posts. Word got around the Web and apparently college lounges, judging from the poster who wrote "It was all my college spoke about in the last week" ("'90 Day Jane' A Hoax, Takes Down Site" 2008). One curious fellow blogger, wrote, "Like any site you hear about from a friend, there are thousands of other 'friends' out there telling their friends, and *your* friend is surely not the *first* friend to tell their friends" ("'90 Day Jane' A Hoax, Takes Down Site" 2008). Alarmed by the reaction, she shut down the site and explained that her blog "was meant for me and (what I ignorantly thought would be) a small number of people who might find it on BlogSpot. It is the result of me tapping into the darkest part of myself and seeing where it led" (Douglas 2008). She imagined the site in a play frame, wherein the context would be understood by participants as if they were located in a social space, but as a viewed image, it spread quickly and was used to comment on the function of the Internet as a cultural location. She recognized that on the Internet people intensified their honesty and emotion. What began as a commentary on the "true human connection on the internet" ended up showing the extent of folkloric construction as the Internet distributed the material and image of a disturbing topic.

Classic theories to explain suicide concern who is likely to take their lives and the motivations for doing so. Emile Durkheim (1951) in particular argued that each society has a collective inclination toward suicide, and he posited social causes for its regularity. Dwyer's case combines elements of each of Durkheim's three categories of suicide—egoistic, altruistic, and anomic—and this encapsulation of social motives in a public declaration is partly responsible for its notoriety. In the egoistic category, the underintegration of the individual into society is brought into light; altruism is at work in advancing a religious or political cause, reflecting a heightened sense of integration; anomie results from problems coping with new opportunities or developments, especially when the person has been previously representative of societal beliefs and practices (Simpson 1951, 14-15). Coupled with this social perspective is the psychoanalytic view that suicidal individuals seek to internalize aggression they hold toward others. In any case, suicide draws attention to itself because it is considered unnatural, particularly with modernization and its premise of progress and increased ease of life due to technological innovation. Suicide is intrusive and transgressive, therefore, because it uncovers the remaining deep crisis in modern society (Simpson 1951, 17).

The Internet records folk commentary on suicide and makes it part of the process of questioning modernization. Arguably, the Internet brings suicide out into the open; made public through Dwyer footage and 90 Day Jane blogs, it becomes more vivid and accessible. That presentation raises conflicts that drive narrative and belief about the *collective conscience*, to use Durkheim's terms, at work in a cyberculture. The circumstances of Dwyer's suicide became on the Internet secondary to the perceptions of it by postmodern viewers. Memories of the act, especially in relation to historic corruption, were not solicited as much as ethical considerations of it as disrupting public, bureaucratic life. The Dwyer tape came to symbolize the Internet itself and forced reactions as a metamessage about the cultural implications of a technology that allows viewing of a suicide tape. Whether treated as comical or haunting, Dwyer's footage is among notable images on the Internet that compel folk responses as a way to deal with postmodern anxieties and ambiguities. Posters put themselves in Dwyer's shoes and created narratives that conveyed or subverted values for the present day. One telling response, which was uttered frequently, was that the video made posters think about what it meant when frustration led them to say they wanted to "blow their brains out" or shoot themselves. They thus used the Internet as an imaginative platform to question the boundaries between fantasy and fact, virtuality and reality, life and death.

Logic and Psychology of Internet Praxis

The Internet's distributive traits separate it as an electronic medium from the one-on-one communication of telephone calls and fax machines. The Internet layers an assortment of captioned material, graphic and textual, brought together through the marvel of electronic cut and paste on a *page* or *site* (often *under construction* in computer lingo) in a process comparable to the bricoleur's overlay technique in scrapbooking and album keeping. The scrapbook is a personal document, and yet is made attractive and recognizable to others because at some point it is shared in a selected network of family and friends. Sites such as Facebook and MySpace, especially, virtualize and folklorize the scrapbook and album by programming that encourages users to make comments and effect designs for *friends* to view and respond to with their own remarks. *Blogs* (a portmanteau of web and log) can have handles or tags rather than real names and often thematize the cultural frame of reference around special interests or identities (Lieber 2009). Although bloggers have been compared to diarists and e-mail to postal writing, the distinctive features of visualizing discussion *threads* and leaving comments and responses as *posts* merits a different kind of comparison to the anonymous or tagged messages in latrinalia that have been documented as folklore (Dundes [1966] 2007a). Defecation inspires writers to inscribe traditional verse on stalls, such as "To the shithouse poet/In honor of his wit/May they build far and wide/ Great monuments of shit" and "Those who write on shithouse walls/Roll their shit in little balls/Those who read these words of wit/Eat the little balls of shit" (Dundes [1966] 2007a, 372–73). Inscriptions are often arranged in a vertical chain with an initial message followed by responses by different writers below it. Linguist Allen Walker Read hypothesizes a motivation for these anonymous writers that can be extended to Internet posting: "the well-known yearning to leave a record of one's presence or one's existence" (1935, 17). That writing in this individualized context is often associated with defecation led Alan Dundes to relate this impulse to an infantile desire to play with feces that was displaced by *making one's mark* on the wall (Dundes [1966] 2007a, 373).

An analogue is apparent to this scatological function in the posting of photocopied humor on bulletin boards and cubicle walls, which often subverts the corporate, machine-like setting with visual references to bathroom behavior, where nature calls and people are naturally themselves. Internet users may also associate the bathroom with modern ritual beliefs, from calling out in childhood revenants such as Bloody Mary in the mirror to narrating deaths and assaults occurring there during adulthood. My interpretive purpose is not to reduce all Internet usage to the expressive process apparent in latrinalia (you might call that *bullshit*, but isn't that more evidence of the cultural trope?). It is to extend the Dundesian interpretation of grafitti as a projection of infantile repression of scatological taboos to the psychology of folk empowerment in the technology-driven information age by comparing the latter to the naturalistic context of toilets. Folklorist Jeannie Thomas noticed in 2007, for example, the preponderance of bathroom ghosts in modern folklore and theorized that the bathroom has a liminal location in the home or institution: "it is simultaneously the unclean room and the room where we clean our bodies. As such, it is a place we feel ambivalent about, and it is associated with significant cultural issues: body functions that are seen as unclean, disease, sexuality, dirt, health, and intimacy" (2007a, 38). Of special significance to the computer metaphor is the notion of restrooms as public places where people rely on technology to do private things and therefore feel vulnerable. Many of the prime images offered on the open medium of the Internet—health, death, sex, and social connection—extend the issues Thomas mentions that are raised by the sequestered bathroom. The computer's space is often envisioned as an artificial-sounding cubicle or station that is necessary to daily function but also may cause discomfort because of a person's inadequacy with the technology or fear of being overwhelmed. Defecation can produce both relief and shame, and its product, known euphemistically as *presents* in childhood, is equated in folklore to official *paperwork* on a desk or screen. In corporate lore distributed by photocopiers, fax machines, and computer, for instance, the image of an outhouse or a child on a potty appears, with the caption, "The job is never finished until the paperwork is done!" (Dundes and Pagter 1975, 160–62). The action of the toilet is further symbolized as a model for information technology in humorous signs such as "We Welcome Advice and Criticism and always *rush* Them through the Proper Channels (One flush usually does it!)" (Dundes and Pagter 1991b, 102).

Before you roll your analog eyes, consider this: regardless of whether the Internet is hailed or reviled for enabling the rapid distribution of material, much of that material is labeled as rumor that is said to *smear* and slander (from the root for scandal or shameful conduct). As I noted in responses to the Dwyer suicide tape, many posters linked the presentation or viewing of the material to defecation ("I shit in my pants watching," "intense shit," "holy shit," "some kind of shit."). Of folkloristic significance is that Internet practice is widely viewed as yeast for *spreading* stories that call for an evaluation of their truthfulness (see Mikkelson and Mikkelson 2008; Oring 2008). Indeed, a website launched in 2008 with the domain name Fightthesmears.com was predicated on the presumption that the Internet fosters the *zooming* of hearsay, according to a report in *Time* (Tumulty 2008). Particularly sensitive to "the blogosphere's superheated rumor mill," according to *Time*, presidential candidate Barack Obama referred to "dirt and lies that are circulated in e-mails" being "pumped out" (Tumulty 2008, 40). Prime examples of popular Internet sites promoting verbal smearing are the-shit.net, JuicyCampus.com (replaced by collegeacb.com), and hecklerspray.com, replete with scatological references in their titles and aimed at youth. Another, spokeo.com, which is advertised as a social-network-based deep search engine, shows on its home page a string of teenage girls whispering, with hands over their mouths, in one another's ears above the text "Want to see something juicy?" As of 2008, YouTube featured 4,160 videos posted with titles that included "talking shit" and Facebook listed over 500 groups for "talking shit." Many of these posts relate their sharing of *inside* or *juicy* information as providing *the straight poop*.

What is the connection to latrinalia? A play frame is established in the stall in which a person is released from the restraint of workaday society, and the wall becomes an open, uncensored discussion board and canvas on which creative messages and drawings can be sequenced, similar to the heralded form and function of many blogs (Longenecker 1977). An individual in the stall, itself located within official space, connects to other people anonymously while engaging in a natural act. Many listserv postings, too, are framed as informal rather than business and relay rumors with the invitation to give feedback. Accusations of *playing on the Internet* often imply that the user is engaging in idle *chatting* or rumor-mongering with others. The privatized context of defecation in a public, institutional setting compels us to consider the psychoanalytic interpretation of graffiti and threading as using an infantile smearing impulse to signal human freedom, especially in the symbolic equation of playful writing and anality, whicht bears application to the pose of sitting in front of a screen (Dundes [1966] 2007a).

Is there symbolic significance in the fact that Facebook's primary form of communication is privatized *writing on the wall*? Another clue to the folk logic of the Internet is MySpace's two standard *blurbs*, in computer lingo: "About Me" and "Who I'd Like to Meet." The use of blurb is an Americanism referring to a short, overblown endorsement of a book; it has a connection in sound and meaning to the colloquial use of *blurt* (usually accompanied with *out*) for anal wind. In computer talk, it is common to refer to having a flood of messages fill up a user's drive, which is periodically emptied, and the user anally feels impelled to organize accumulated material into boxes that can be emptied. Notably, odious messages labeled *junk*, or *spam* (from stigmatized canned luncheon meat), suggest repulsion against being befouled or smeared (expressed in the satire of the traditional proverb "To err is human, to really foul things up takes a computer."). Excretory references to digital work are also apparent in the common computer-age adages "Garbage In, Garbage Out" and "A clean house is the sign of a broken computer." Early in computing, UNIX users assigned scatalogical names to punctuation marks such as *splat* for an asterisk and programmers' lore referred to the *bit bucket*, a magical trash can in which computer gremlins stash or excrete gobbled data (Beatty 1976; Jennings 1991, 105). Later *bladder* or *bladderball* became terms for an obnoxious string of emails sent to a large list, rather than being contained. Self-referential responses to rumors about the Internet, such as the one that Congress will vote on whether or not phone companies can charge long-distance rates for accessing the Internet, repeat variations of "When will people realize that they are spreading any shit they believe into," "these people are full of crap," and under the heading of "Polluting Internet," the "videos [on the rumor] are all a bunch of crap load of shit" ("2012: The Year the Internet Ends" 2008; see also Green 2006: 4 262–64).

Anxiety that the folk character of the Internet will be lost comes through in a narrative directly relating defecation with computer use. In 2003, a story circulated that Microsoft was developing an Internet-capable toilet. In some reports, it was called an iLoo (from the British term *loo* for toilet). According to the narrative, the stall would be equipped with a wireless keyboard and an extensible, height-adjustable plasma screen located directly in front of the seated user. The story appeared to confirm that no place was immune from the Internet's reach, but a detail also equated human control with wiping and smearing: the toilet would come with special paper imprinted with URLs that users may not have tried. Snopes.com, a reputable urban legend reference site, declared iLoo a hoax but quoted a newspaper interview with a Microsoft official who said, "People used to reach for a book or mag when they were on the loo, but now they'll be logging on! It's exciting to think that the smallest room can now be the gateway to the massive virtual world" ("iLoo" 2007). The excitement the official cited presumably extends to being seated at the screen within a cubicle, where privatized *logging on* enacts the titillating, smearing praxis of building "far and wide, great monuments of shit."

Although it is often noted that folk initialisms are common in electronic communication, rarely interpreted is the preponderance of scatological references in online chat lingo:

> AS = Ape Shit
> BAG = Big Ass Grin
> BS = Bull Shit, Brain Strain, Big Smile
> BTSOOM = Beats the Shit Out of Me
> CYA = Cover Your Ass
> DILLIGAS = Do I Look Like I Give a Shit
> EE = Electronic Emission
> ESAD = Eat Shit and Die
> FOS = Full of Shit
> LMAO = Laughing My Ass Off
> PITA = Pain in the Ass
> SEG = Shit Eating Grin
> SOGOP = Shit or Get Off the Pot
> SOL = Shit Out of Luck
> SOS = Same Old Shit
> SSDD = Same Shit Different Day
> TS = Tough Shit, Totally Stinks
> TSFY = Tough Shit For You
> UY = Up Yours
> WTSDS = Where the Sun Don't Shine
> WTSHTF = When the Shit Hits the Fan
> YGBSM = You Got to be Shitting Me
> YS = You Stinker
> ("List of Chat Acronyms & Text Message
>   Shorthand" 2008)

Maybe some of this impulse comes from the ejective or retentive praxis of users in a seated position. Much visual humor associates toilets and electronic technology involving inputs and outputs. The position of the user may invite commentary because it brings into question boundaries of private and public, play and work, natural and technological, and freedom and restraint that are of concern on the Internet. The common folkloric forms of initialism are more than linguistic devices to save space; they also signal subversion of the institutional use of initialisms and acronyms in bureaucratized modern life (Jennings 1991, 91–108). Visualizing the computer as a toilet (such as in the examples I previously mentioned from my math team experience) reflects the need to humanize technology and institutions, lest they replace or control humans, but it also is congruent with the social negotiation between the pleasure derived from ejection and the social restraint on its appearance (Jones [1912] 1961, 413–37). Moving beyond one-on-one communication, the Internet frequently makes use of an informal, scatological frame of reference to distribute playful material widely, which is tantamount to the smearing of feces, such as in references to the ease of *slinging mud, dishing dirt*, and *spreading shit* online. In this way, it signifies exhilaration, maybe compulsion, and a certain amount of aggressive rebellion. In the writing-defecation equation, one leaves a potentially embarrassing or satisfying remark and maintains a presence in a globalizing medium that blurs the divisions between private and public. This is not to say by any stretch that on the Internet users are imitating defecation. The point is that rhetorically, scatological initialisms and symbolic references to smearing signal, indeed demarcate, the folk web.

To be sure, users locate the folk web by referring to other transgressive practices. The fact that information is most often viewed without direct contact with its creator fosters the emergence of a metalanguage for expressing the gesture, emotion, veracity, and humor that typically accompanies face-to-face interaction. For example, online chat noticeably employs initialized sexual expressions that are transmitted by both men and women as *natural* symbols of aggression, particularly by teenage users: WTF for What the Fuck, FFS meaning For Fuck's Sake, FOAD for Fuck Off and Die, GFY for Go Fuck Yourself, GTFO for Get the Fuck Out, and STFU for Shut the Fuck Up. Users with whom I discussed this penchant suggested to me that less stigma is attached to disembodied swearing online and it marks messages as conversation, especially youthful talk associated with being brash and high-spirited. As with scatological references, this swearing also helps to demarcate a folk or play frame characteristic of the folk web. Referring to the presumption that in an analog world typing is considered formal or is institutionally supervised, a representative comment was that tapping out or texting

WTF provided a high, or felt transgressive in a way that speaking the words, if one was inclined to do so, did not. This rhetorical strategy raises questions about the symbolization of phallic or pubertal power in technology (essentialized, for instance, in light bulb jokes in which there is a double entendre for screwing in a light bulb as sex and technology), and for many cultural critics, about the gendered or patriarchal posturing of the Internet (Dundes 1981; Miller 2001). In relation to the previous argument that scatological impulses are projected onto the *Net* (slang for Internet that draws attention to its function as a catchall receptacle as well as a linguistic clipping of *network*), one can note the fear of being smeared extended to being feminized sexually. This is evident in the motifemic slot filled by *fucked* or *fouled*: SNAFU (Situation Normal All Fouled/Fucked Up), FUM (Fucked/Fouled Up Mess), and FUBAR (Fouled/Fucked Up Beyond All Repair) (Jennings 1991, 107). The adoption of these terms from military lore may not be coincidental, because an analogy can be made between soldiers entering a vernacular cultural register with this speech and computer users as indoctrinated, masculinized trainees using the computer as a phallicized weapon (Fleece 1946). In addition, the Internet historically has roots in military intelligence and is often associated with other institutionalized groups such as universities, hospitals, and corporations. Moreover, the Web can be construed in digital folk belief systems as representative of a formal, routinized organization that users need to humanize or even subvert (often signified by creative variation and parody) and about which they need to vent aggression.

Folklore about the Web often creates, as its other, a money-grubbing bullying elite aligned with corporate, scientific, and government interests that seek to control, censor, and bureaucratize the Internet. The folk web in this construction represents the tradition of a democratic, participatory commons and the value of openness and inclusiveness. The cyberculture wars are imagined as a David-Goliath battle of ordinary, disempowered people affiliating with tradition against scientists and bureaucrats who carry the brand of technology and modernity and would deracinate the Internet commons. Yet despite the cautionary tales and rumors of the end of the open Internet, the mass of user-generated data on the Web suggests the expansion of a folk system, at the dawn of the twenty-first century, that is characterized by peer-to-peer sharing of handed-down wisdom and by the priority of practice over scientism. A notable declaration of user independence for the Internet, in the touchstone technology publication *Wired* magazine, carried the headline "The End of Theory," printed as "The End of Science" on the magazine's cover (Anderson 2008). The basis of the shift in authority, according to the magazine's editor Chris Anderson, is the "massive corpus" of reachable information that is a sign of a new revolutionary epoch dubbed the "Petabyte Age." In previous iterations of data, organizational analogies were used: folders, files, and libraries. "Petabytes," Anderson wrote, "are stored in the clouds" (2008, 108). By this cosmological analogy information is visualized, in almost supernatural terms, as being beyond human reach and comprehension.

Technically, a *petabyte* is equal to one quadrillion bytes (1000^5 or 10^{15}) and symbolizes an extraordinary amount because of the significance of *quad* (from the root for *four*), a unit representing abundance as *three* in Western thought stands for completeness (Dundes 1980). It also refers to automorphism because of the fifth power (five being an automorphic number) to which the official measure of 1000 is put. In Internet usage, the vast amount of data can be expressed in petabytes: Google processes about 20 petabytes of data a day. "This is a world," Anderson philosophizes, "where massive amounts of data and applied mathematics replace every other tool that might be brought to bear . . . Who knows why people do what they do? The point is they do it, and we can track and measure it with unprecedented fidelity" (Anderson 2008, 108). Web phenomena are therefore described as patterns rather than models, rationalized in analytical terms as correlations rather than outlined relationally as causation. It may appear, as Anderson claims, to be "a whole new way of understanding the world" (2008, 109), but it also may be a virtualization of a mythic world in which one's experience is connected to everyone else's. The essence of the mythic, as stated by anthropologist Eric Dardel is placing oneself "in the current of the whole world's life" ([1954] 1984, 229). He contrasts the modern world, "dominated by logical and historical concerns, with our explanations ruled by the principle of causality," with the mythic, "which shows itself in convictions or in beliefs, in 'verities' which we declare to be true" ([1954] 1984, 230). The mythic as seen on the Internet is *present*, not in the past or future, and it is not set in place but in repetitive patterns with sources in precedents that we may call tradition. This comes out in the awe for the mass of data in its fantastical universe. Not envisioned as comprising things such as those in a file, cabinet, or library, it is ethereal, an *ethernet*, and references the lights, whirrs, and clicks that manifest cosmic forces. There people engage mythic meanings, especially through the Internet's responsive quality, which produces relational narratives by users in the play frames, commons, or *rooms* of the Web and raises discourse about the logic of virtuality.

Although an argument can be presented that Internet communication in on-line cafés or chat rooms simulates the mythic, it does not necessarily result in the production of expressive lore. To be sure, many networks revel in their group's thematized communication with its initialisms, narratives, and beliefs that distinguish the group and represent the Internet as a cultural space. Carrying over the idea from community life of creating lore so as to give identity to the group, communication on the Internet is culturally marked by self-referential genres. An example is the neologism *meme* for a digital file or hyperlink propagated quickly from peer to peer on the Net. Many memes are in fact folkloric because they often take the form of catchphrases, rumors, schemes, and legendary material, and arguably this praxis has a folkloric reference because it is taken from the Greek root of *mime* for imitation or repetition, but has been altered to sound more like *gene* as the unit of cultural transmission on the Net (Jeffreys 2000). The invented term draws attention to the Net's state of matter as data, reproducible and variable, and its difference from the social forces in life. Such constructions force folklorists— and other scholars of culture—to think long and hard about standing on the shoulders of giants who restricted their concept of folklore to oral or naturalistic tradition.

How folklore is enabled for its users by virtualization and how it is differentiated from the face-to-face world referred to as analog culture demands rethinking assumptions and questions about the workings of tradition, once thought to be a product or relic of the past, arising out of the land and group or belonging to *others* who are at a remove due to their lack of technological advancement or cosmopolitanism (see Bronner 1998). The issue with virtual tradition is not so much to ask whether geeks, gamers, and bloggers constitute a folk group the way a previous generation of folklorists, confronted with the assembly line, phonograph, and telephone, asked "Is There a Folk in the City?" and "Is There a Folk in the Factory?" (Dorson 1970; Nickerson 1974). To be sure, that can be answered with lists of computer slang, emoticons, and initialisms that mark cultural knowledge and, consequently, identity for a group (Jennings 1991; Jordan 1997; Preston 1996). The significance of understanding the Internet rhetorically as a folk system is its suggestion of ways that technology allows everyone to enact, and alter, in some form tradition, whether thought of digitally or analytically. This is especially compelling as the Internet becomes more portable and pervasive, becoming the primary mediator of cultural connection. Boundary maintenance occurs not so much by the corporeal traits of ethnicity, region, gender, and occupation, although they may enter into the communicative equation. One affiliates with any number of over-lapping, often temporary global and local networks, lists, and interests, often corresponding to age and organizational divisions. And most per-plexing to communicative scholars like folklorists, these affiliations are often imagined through multiple avatars, roles, profiles, personalities, and addresses. So who is doing the talking—or connecting?

The answer to this question returns us to the original point about the significance of conceptually putting the Internet and tradition together. As a fundamental human capacity and need, the production of folklore to represent tradition is a continuous vital force, and it is imperative to view how it is enacted with, and problematized by, media, old and new. Indeed, we may comprehend the way, in a new wired age, folklore is digitized and virtualized, or we may folklorize the age, perhaps outside our awareness. Or to quote the motto I see now on the wall of the com-puter lab, put up now by a new-generation geek, "Oh, what a tangled Web we weave when first we practice."[9]

Notes

1. In my background this assemblage is familiar rather than sui generis, as many web aficionados would claim. Talmudic study involves navigating pages that have a central textual core surrounded by commentaries, often at odd angles, in different domains on the page. See Rosen 2000.
2. I have argued in *American Folklore Studies: An Intellectual History* (1986) that the incorporation of the rhetoric of technology into the intellectualism of the 1960s, which represented in part a shift in cultural applications of the history of science from natural history to physics, influenced the rise of interaction, network, and dynamics as keywords in folkloristics. See Bronner 1986: 106-29. Indeed, discourse on harnessing computers as an analytical tool goes back to this period (see Dundes 1965a; Holbek 1969; Maranda 1967; Petöfi and Szöllösy 1969; Sebeok 1965).
3. Miniaturization in Internet-equipped devices may also be a function of the influence of Japan's technological designers who operate in what has been dubbed a *compact culture*. Major Japanese computer manufacturers such as Sony, Toshiba, and Hitachi catered to the demands of consuming Japanese youth, who do not have privacy in small dwelling spaces and use the devices in mass transit and public areas. The pattern of compactness was prevalent in Japan before it became widespread in the Americas and Europe (see Lee 1992; Yoshida, Ikko, and Tsune 1982).
4. Precedent can be cited for this cultural response in the history of technology. At the 1964 New York World's Fair, Bell Telephone hailed the "pictureph-one" as the next mass cultural appliance. Video technology allowed speak-ers on either end of the telephone to see each other, but despite a formidable marketing campaign, consumers did not buy into the vision. Historians of

technology generally agree that consumers wanted to preserve the informal-
ity of appearance that not seeing callers permits (see Lipartito 2003).

5. Stewart and Bennett (1991) culturally exemplify the difference between
    analog (relational) and digital (analytical) thinking as a contrast between
    Buddhist and Western approaches to perception. They offer different inter-
    pretations of a folk proverb to make their point: "The American proverb,
    'still waters run deep,' (as a way of describing a quiet, thoughtful person)
    would be rendered differently by the Chinese. In Mandarin, a profound
    thinker would be described as 'great' or 'valuable' rather than deep. Also, in
    Japanese, horizontal allusions to size, rank, or multiplicity more often ren-
    der the quality of thought than vertical allusions to depth. Both for the Chi-
    nese and Japanese, the thinking process is seen as much less deep than it is
    by Americans and other Westerners. External social roles and relationships,
    for instance, receive much more emphasis than the nature of one's thought
    processes. Put differently, the Chinese and Japanese tend to have a highly
    developed sociological sense but make relatively little use of psychological
    analysis" (24–25). Another difference is in ordering knowledge. As Stewart
    and Bennett (1991) explain, Buddhists' "perceptual theory minimized the
    distinction between direct sensory information and knowledge obtained
    through fantasy or inference, inducing them to treat perceptual objects and
    mental products similarly. Concrete objects and abstract concepts were situ-
    ated side by side on a single dimension, and abstract ideas could be repre-
    sented as concrete objects. The objective world was exhaustively described
    but without the rank ordering which Westerners impose on reality by clas-
    sifying objects and events according to their importance" (24). For other
    comparisons of Asian and American thinking processes related to tradition,
    see Bronner 1998, 475–82; Nakamura 1964, 130–33; White 1994. Lee (1992)
    particularly adapts this contrast to technological differences.

6. Later it was revealed that one envelope contained instructions for Dwyer's
    funeral; another held his organ donor card; and the third contained a letter
    to Governor Robert Casey asking him to appoint Dwyer's wife, Joanne, to
    succeed him as state treasurer (see Cusick, Meyers, and Roche 1987, 1).

7. As an example, see the digital folk art of a fictional *Nintendo* "shooting"
    game featuring Budd Dwyer (with an exploding, pixelated face) as the main
    character: http://bluntobject.files.wordpress.com/2009/06/429px-budd_
    dwyer_nes.jpg (accessed 30 June 2009).

8. Although the image and audio track of the suicide footage did not get re-
    aired on television in the digital age, they were featured on a number of
    commercial films and CDs. Probably best known is its use in the movie
    Bowling for Columbine (2002) and the singles "Hey Man, Nice Shot" (1995)
    by alternative rock band Filter and "Get Your Gunn" (1994) by Marilyn
    Manson.

9. The phrase is a takeoff on the poetry of Sir Walter Scott, renowned for his
    folkloristic collections as well as creative writing, in *Marmion* (1808), Canto
    Sixth, stanza XVII. His poetic lines were "Oh what a tangled web we weave,
    When first we practise to deceive!" Sometimes a variation of the computer
    satire is "Oh what a tangled website we weave."

Chapter 2

Guardians of the Living: Characterization of Missing Women on the Internet

Elizabeth Tucker

As Richard A. Lanham suggests in *The Electronic Word*, the World Wide Web facilitates information-sharing that is both fluid and democratic (1993, 106). One important kind of information-sharing occurs on websites devoted to women who have disappeared, probably because of violent death. Since the Internet became popular in the early 1990s, it has served as a locus for predation and consolation, as well as expressions of confusion and resolution. The Internet theorist Sherry Turkle explains that all of us who spend time on the World Wide Web become "dwellers on the threshold between the real and the virtual, unsure of our footing, inventing ourselves as we go along" (1995, 10). So it is not surprising that websites about missing women have developed folkloric patterns. Rumors about sightings of the missing woman comprise one form of folklore. Another pattern is the "missing woman" or "missing child" hoax. A website about the disappearance of the nonexistent girl Penny Brown, for example, is still available on the World Wide Web ("Missing Child"). Articles about University of Wisconsin student Audrey Seiler, who faked her own abduction in the spring of 2004, contribute to the impression that one should not necessarily believe what one reads online.

Other folkloric patterns have emerged as well. The subject of this chapter is the relationship between websites' renditions of missing women's stories and legends about the ghosts of murdered women that describe violent death followed by benevolent haunting of the place where the woman died. One section of my book *Haunted Halls* (2007) analyzes "wailing women" ghosts, who warn living women to steer clear of the dangers that led to their own demise. These dangers include men's predatory behavior, isolation from others who can help, and over-indulgence in alcohol. Stories about places haunted by wailing women teach both women and men to be careful, while also offering them a good scare, especially around Halloween.

I could tell many legends about female college students who died in troubling circumstances, but the two that have the closest connection to the subject of this chapter are the stories about Shelley Sperling at Marist College in Poughkeepsie, New York, and Elizabeth at the State University of New York at Cortland. Shelley Sperling died after her boy-friend assaulted her in Marist College's dining hall in 1975. More than twenty years after her death, students in her residence hall complained that Shelley's spirit was turning their lights and TVs on and off. I inter-viewed a former resident assistant for the hall, Christina Hope, who cre-ated a website in memory of Shelley because she felt it was very impor-tant for other students to know how Shelley died. While working on the website, Christina Hope saw an apparition of Shelley in her residence-hall room. Once the website was finished, signs of Shelley's presence diminished. In contrast to this complex of narratives, stories about the ghost of Elizabeth at SUNY Cortland show no evidence of being founded on a historical death. Students in Cheney Hall say that Elizabeth, who died after being pushed downstairs by her boyfriend, haunts Cheney's staircase to protect other women's safety. Her own tragic death makes her a guardian of current students; Elizabeth has, according to recent narratives, saved women who have drunk too much alcohol from falling downstairs (Tucker 2007, 134–52).

Many websites for missing women include stories about how indi-vidual women disappeared and how they lived before their disappear-ances. There may even be several postings by people familiar with the circumstances that preceded the disappearance. Often these writers consider how morally and safely the woman conducted her life before-hand. Did she work hard? Did her recreations involve risk-taking? Once a woman has disappeared, even small daily decisions may seem signifi-cant. Gathering details of this kind is part of the interactive storytelling that happens in cyberspace.

This storytelling follows patterns established by *legend*, a conver-sation-based genre with a close connection to the stresses and strains of everyday life. Ghost stories comprise one subcategory of the legend genre. Elliott Oring defines legends as "narratives which focus on a single episode, an episode which is presented as miraculous, uncanny, bizarre, or sometimes embarrassing" (1986, 125). Jan H. Brunvand explains that legends get readers' or listeners' attention through "a strong basic story-appeal, a foundation in actual belief, and a meaningful message or moral" (1981, 10). One legend that scares adolescents is "The Boy Friend's Death," which luridly describes the murder of a young man who hikes down the highway to get gas after leaving his girlfriend in his locked car. According to Brunvand, this legend warns young people to avoid danger but also "reveals society's broader fears of people, especially women and the young, being alone and among strangers in the darkened world outside the security of their home or car" (1981, 11). Such widespread fears often come to the surface in people's interactions on websites for missing women. Through characterization of women who have disappeared, storytellers share their concerns with fellow users of the World Wide Web.

Some listeners accept ghost stories and other legends as true stories, while others question their veracity. The liveliness of legend circulation depends upon believers, skeptics, and other people who take a stance in between those two extremes (Dégh and Vázsonyi 1973). By questioning the truth of a narrative, people enhance its potential significance. Elliott Oring explains that whether such narratives are true or false is not important; what matters is the process by which "the art of legendry engages the listener's sense of the possible" (1986, 125). Even if we feel reluctant to accept a story at face value, we may enjoy pondering its potential significance.

Linda Dégh and Andrew Vázsonyi (1975) have explored how people with common interests transmit folklore through social conduits: one interested individual shares a story with another; as transmission continues, the story grows and changes. Gary Alan Fine (1979) applies the hypothesis of multiconduit transmission to boys' storytelling in Minnesota. In my own research on ghost stories, I have found that a shared interest in supernatural events stimulates storytelling in small or larger groups. The Internet offers exciting potential for story transmission. Those of us who study supernatural narratives are just beginning to understand how people share legends and develop legend characters through the Internet.

Ghost stories feature certain kinds of characters. Jeannie Banks Thomas delineates typical male and female legend characters: the "Extreme Guy" and the "Deviant Femme." Violent, angry, and wild, the Extreme Guy wreaks havoc on innocent people. The Deviant Femme chooses to live by her own eccentric rules rather than accepting society's restrictions on women's behavior (2007b, 91–102). Her daring rejection of "safe" rules for women makes her a fascinating person. Some Deviant Femmes become eccentric and violent because of the Extreme Guy's influence; an example of this kind of character is Mary of the "Mary's Grave" legends on Long Island in New York. After Mary is raped and beaten by her father, she kills her baby and slaughters farm animals in a satanic ritual. Finally, she kills herself and then lingers at the place where she died to shock and frighten adolescent visitors (Tucker 2007, 201–02).

After visiting numerous websites dedicated to missing women, I have come to the conclusion that the characterization of some women who have disappeared fits Thomas's Deviant Femme concept to a certain extent. Website visitors' stories about missing women tend to highlight any daring, deviant behavior of theirs before their tragic disappearance. In some cases this behavior pattern seems relatively low-key, while in others it becomes sensational, with strong moral overtones. While legends provide the main pattern, folktales—narratives about events in a fictive realm that offer some guidance for real life—also offer a framework for portrayals of missing women.

In addition to highlighting daring or deviant behavior, the characterization of missing women in newspapers, on television, and on the Internet has focused on women of privileged backgrounds. *Washington Post* reporter Eugene Robinson suggested that the media "[choose] only young, white, middle-class women for the full damsel treatment" (2005). "Full damsel" refers to the well-known image of the damsel in distress: a lovely, imperiled woman who desperately needs to be rescued. This term brings to mind suffering princesses and other female characters in traditional folktales, as well as P. G. Wodehouse's novel *A Damsel in Distress* (1919). On a CNN program in 2006, Sheri Parks, a professor of American Studies at the University of Maryland in College Park, invoked the phrase "Missing White Woman Syndrome" ("Diagnosing 'Missing White Woman Syndrome'"). This term has become so well accepted that it has its own acronym, MWWS, and its own article in Wikipedia ("Missing White Woman"). That article mentions a corollary term, "Missing Pretty Girl Syndrome," commonly known by its acronym MPGS.

Keeping in mind that legends focus on worries about women who take risks and push the envelope of acceptable behavior, I suggest that some Internet sites for missing women tend to emphasize a previously unnamed subcategory of MPGS: "Missing Party Girl Syndrome." As perceived by journalists and website participants, the "Party Girl" has too much fun and does not take enough precautions. Stories about her behavior before her disappearance tend to emphasize her failure to do certain things that might have given her sad story a different conclusion.

Among the many available websites about missing women, I have chosen several that characterize missing young women as "Party Girls" who have taken too many chances. These websites follow the MWWS pattern. In contrast, I have also examined a website about a number of young and older women of different ethnic backgrounds who tragically disappeared and were, in some cases, found to have become victims of a mass murderer. All of these websites invite visitors to express opinions and tell stories of their own in response to information and photographs. By examining postings on a number of sites, it is possible to trace elements that show the influence of traditional legends and folktales.

Disappearance in Aruba

Some of the most frequently visited websites are the ones dedicated to eighteen-year-old Natalee Holloway, who disappeared in Aruba in the spring of 2005. Many of these websites welcome comments from anyone. "Blogs for Natalee," for example, has an open chat room and postings from registered visitors; it also offers a "Shout Box" and a "Virtual Hope Quilt for Natalee Holloway." About.com, which covers a wide variety of topics, has encouraged interactive conversation about Natalee Holloway's disappearance ("News and Current Events"); so has TripAdvisor.com (2005), which lets travelers exchange positive comments and warnings.

One of the most interesting interactive sites, Scared Monkeys, has a section that posts information on a long list of women who have disappeared ("Scared Monkeys Missing Persons Site"). The portion of this site devoted to Holloway includes numerous articles by journalists, interview transcripts, photos, videos, and other material. Each missing woman has her own forum, on which active members, known as *Monkeys*, can post material and discuss Holloway's case; non-Monkeys can also participate in the discussion. Many Monkeys identify themselves as women who are eager to help solve Holloway's case. On this website and others, women tell stories, chat, and commiserate with each other. Men also participate, but not as frequently.

During the two-and-a-half years since Holloway's disappearance, reports on television and on the Internet have provoked countless comments. Early media coverage focused on the last time Holloway's friends saw her; the fact that she was drinking at the bar Carlos and Charlie's and then left with three young men became the basis of her sad story. Private detective Charles Montaldo summarized what happened: "Witnesses said Natalee was last seen leaving a nightclub in a car with three males"

(2008). This brief description identifies the missing young woman as a "Party Girl" who wants to have fun but does not take precautions. A focus on the young woman's unwise separation from her friends mirrors the legend's didactic emphasis on terrible consequences suffered by women who go out into the world without proper safeguards.

Two frightening consequences of isolation in an unsafe social environment can be overindulgence in alcohol and exposure to dangerous drugs. Visitors to interactive websites such as "Blogs for Natalee" have discussed these subjects in detail. On 23 July 2007, for example, a male "Blogs for Natalee" participant with the screenname "MIP6" commented that "[Natalee] was drinking 151 shots on her own long before doing shots at C and C" and was "so hammered she had to be helped back to her room the night before." This posting's harsh tone provoked a rapid retort from "Granny Toad," who wrote, "Shame on you . . . So, MIP6, your position is that the victim drank and drugged herself to death then disappeared herself." Her response's sarcasm put MIP6 in his place, reminding him that Holloway was a victim who had tragically and mysteriously disappeared.

Date-rape drugs and nonconsensual sex are other disturbing subjects. Andrea Greenberg authored the earliest study of legends that combine drugs and sex (1973), while Fine and Johnson's essay on the "Promiscuous Cheerleader" focuses on adolescent males' legend telling (1980). Jan Brunvand analyzes "Spanish Fly" narratives (1984, 133–34), and I have collected a number of legends about "roofies" (rohypnol) given by men to young women in clubs (2005, 98–99). Fear of men preying on women through date-rape drugs has encouraged the spread of legends on this subject, as well as warnings passed from one woman to another.

Website visitors' comments on Holloway's tragic disappearance have included expressions of sadness, anger, and support for members of her family, as well as accounts of personal experiences. While these stories vary, their common theme is worry about Holloway and other missing women. A married woman's posting to TripAdvisor's "Aruba Forum: Alert" in June 2005 describes an encounter in the bar where Natalee was last seen: "When we saw her leave she left by herself. No one was with her, but we did notice some local guys talking with her while she was in there." Notice that the phrases "by herself" and "no one was with her" highlight her aloneness as a figure in a legendlike scenario that is mysterious, uncertain, and dangerous.

A posting on an About.com message board five months later suggests a more hopeful but unconvincing outcome for Holloway's story: "On November 5th 2005 a friend and I went to a night club in Manhattan

Kansas where I do believe I seen Natalee Holloway. She was not 21 yet around 5'9 or 5'10 about 130 to 140 lbs (maybe). She might of met this guy on her trip and come back to Kansas with him" ("News and Current Events"). Still other reports place her in Mexico, where kidnappers have taken her. These and additional rumors have fed the dialectics of Holloway narratives. Some narrators believe in their sightings, while others do not; what ties them all together is their hope for a positive or at least a clear conclusion. Both "true" and "false" Holloway figures contribute to this process.

Psychics' investigations of Natalee Holloway's disappearance have also added intriguing material to websites. Accounts of their work have some similarity to ghost stories about haunted places, including college buildings, but these accounts focus more on the psychic's efforts to contact a spirit than the spirit's own attempts to be recognized. Marie Saint Claire (2005), a psychic with an Internet following, posted her investigation on the website Underworld Tales. Saint Claire had three psychic experiences while seeking to contact Natalee Holloway's spirit. The first was a "vision that nearly grew into a full remote connection" in which the girl, wearing a swimsuit, "looked beautiful under the water, her long blonde hair flowing around her like an angel's." The second communication involved rough male voices, "Over here" and "Turn around," interpreted as vocalizations by Holloway's killers, and the third included a view of Holloway running on the beach followed by a glimpse of her killer's face.

Saint Claire's discussion of her contact with Holloway's spirit includes messages from readers who want to help solve the case. One message from a citizen of Aruba suggests three interpretations of the word "Mont," which came to Saint Claire as a clue. Another message mentions the reader's own visions of Holloway, which include "pink flags," "a dab of purple," and "a strong odor of seafood." This reader, who concludes that Holloway died on a beach and was transported on a boat, added: "I hope I'm wrong. I hope she's just sitting on an island somewhere having a good time before she goes to college." This wistful statement shows how important it can be for a website visitor to envision the folktale's "happily ever after," although available evidence discourages that conclusion.

On Court TV's "Missing in Paradise," which aired on 29 June 2007, psychic profiler Carla Baron and medium John Oliver visited Holloway's high school and a beach in Aruba, communing with her spirit and deciding that she might have been drugged, raped, and left to die on the beach. Although none of these suggestions added new material to public media speculation, the dramatic enactment of Holloway's death made her spirit's presence seem real; viewers' comments show that a significant number of TV watchers took the show seriously. "Truthsoflife," for example, wrote: "Carla, I swear I saw Natalee morph in your eyes for a brief moment in the back of the car. You were reading about the drug she was given. I have the chills" ("Talkback").

Websites dedicated to Natalee have frequently mentioned her mother, Beth Holloway. Shortly after hearing about her daughter's disappearance, Beth Holloway (also known as Beth Holloway Twitty) gathered photographs from home that could be used in a search. Realizing that media reports of the disappearance might not portray her daughter fairly, she requested a copy of her daughter's high school transcript (2007, 11). In her book, Holloway's description of Natalee as a successful student, dance team member, and scholarship recipient has provided a counterweight to the persona of the "Party Girl" who separated herself from American friends. This negative characterization, presented both in media reports and in legends, has had an educational impact, but Beth Holloway has found another way to encourage young people to stay safe. She has given many lectures at schools, churches, and other organizations on how to travel safely and her International Safe Travels Foundation website (2007) offers valuable help to young website visitors and their families.

Dancer with No Shoes

In contrast to Natalee Holloway, whose disappearance started a tidal wave of publicity, another woman who disappeared in 2005 got a relatively small amount of attention from the mass media. Lynn Moran, a Massachusetts childcare administrator and former dancer, vanished in the harbor area of Portland, Maine, on Columbus Day after leaving her shoes, cell phone, and purse in a male acquaintance's apartment. Local news reporters covered this event, and Moran's family offered a $10,000 reward.

Like Natalee Holloway, Lynn Moran disappeared in the midst of festive socializing. Both women were drinking, and both were in the company of men. There, however, the resemblance ended. Natalee Holloway was eighteen years old, while Lynn Moran was a twenty-four-year-old professional woman who had worked with children. Holloway vanished in Aruba, where the judicial system was unfamiliar to most Americans, while Moran disappeared in the comfortably familiar harbor district of Portland, Maine.

Comments on "Scared Monkeys" shortly after Moran's disappearance show the impact of journalists' emphasis on her clothing at the time when others last saw her. The article "Lynn Moran, 24: Missing in Portland, Maine" (2005) notes that a "witness told police Moran was alone and wandering around the Old Port shopping district barefoot and wearing a men's long-sleeved shirt"; she "had left her purse and cell phone at her friend's apartment." This focus on aloneness, transgender clothing that suggests a man's presence, and lack of a cell phone for protection rapidly generated dialog among women who were reading "Scared Monkeys" postings.

On 26 October, "Jillian in Boston" posed a brief but important question: "Why the hell are we losing so many girls?" The next day an answer came from "icey": "I guess we have always lost so many girls, but our focus before Natalee was not as intense as it is now." In a second paragraph, she surmised: "I hope and pray Ms. Moran is OK, but the witness sighting is very troubling. It almost sounds like she could have been drugged and perhaps ran away from where she was at (men's shirt and no shoes)." Her third paragraph offered a lesson for young women: "We have to be more proactive in life. If the 'passerby' mearly [sic] approached the girl and asked if she needed help, perhaps there would be no disappearance to report!" This three-paragraph statement goes from answer to interpretation and ends in a moral. As in many horror legends, instructive content predominates.

Lisa, another participant in the "Scared Monkeys" blog on Lynn Moran's disappearance, posted the following answer to Jillian's question on 27 October: "It does seem to [be] a lot more missing women reported and in low crime areas; Portland, ME, Thunder Valley Casino, etc." After this brief but reflective reply, Lisa offered some firm words of advice: "Hate to say this, but in some of these cases, the women were promicious [sic] and took chances with men they barely knew. With the advent of date rape drugs, women should really be on guard and travel with some 'real friends,' not the ones who would leave you for a guy." This sequence—an answer followed by a lesson to be learned from a tragic situation—mirrors the order of icey's earlier posting.

As on websites about the disappearance of Natalee Holloway, women's discussions about Lynn Moran on "Scared Monkeys" show the influence of horror legends about women in unsafe social situations. While no available information suggests that date-rape drugs caused Lynn Moran's disappearance, reports of her unusual behavior suggest this possibility. Mysterious circumstances generate conversations in which legends influence people's reflections and concerns.

While some comments on Moran's behavior show the influence of folk legends, others indicate that the folktale has some impact as well. Media reports and website conversations emphasize Moran's kindness and interest in children, her talent as a dancer, and her mysterious, inexplicable choice to go outside on a rainy night without cell phone, purse, or shoes. Like Cinderella, deserted by magic after midnight, Moran seems lonely, unprotected, and unconnected to conventional sources of help. She is a "damsel in distress," with no fairy godmother to keep her safe.

The discovery of Moran's body in Portland Harbor on Halloween 2005 resulted in a verdict of accidental drowning after excessive drinking. Although some perplexed conversation continued on websites, there was little further reporting and no psychic investigation that could generate ghost stories. Her quickly resolved disappearance did not have the wide media appeal of Natalee Holloway's case, but in both situations the description of an attractive, not sufficiently careful young woman who went out alone has had didactic value.

Vancouver's Missing Women

Unlike websites dedicated to young women who disappeared after going to parties or bars, "Vancouver Eastside Missing Women" sadly commemorates the lives of sixty-two women whose involvement in dangerous lifestyles resulted in premature death. These women disappeared from the east side of Vancouver during the late 1990s and early 2000s. Alcohol, drug use, and prostitution had put the women at risk. The size of this group makes the extent of these dangers clear. The group is multicultural, including Black, Native American, and white women. They do not fit the pattern of "Missing White Woman Syndrome" or "Missing Pretty Girl / Party Girl Syndrome," but they have received a large amount of coverage in the media.

One of the reasons why this website has received so much attention is its focus on the tragic details of a mass murder. In 2002, pig-farm owner Robert Pickton was charged with the deaths of twenty-six Vancouver women; he was convicted of six counts of second-degree murder in 2007. DNA analysis gradually revealed which women had become Pickton's victims, but the case remained mysterious. Drug use and prostitution seemed to be part of the matrix that had led to the women's deaths, but details were hazy. A few women whose names and pictures had appeared on the website were found to be alive, and other missing women were added to the list ("Vancouver Eastside Missing Women").

Grieving relatives and friends posted comments on this website's guestbook for the whole group of women ("Vancouver Missing, Guestbook"). Many guestbook visitors expressed sadness, outrage, and an insistence on the improvement of living conditions for women in Eastside Vancouver. A guestbook on a second website gave concerned visitors another opportunity to express their feelings. A recent posting to that site from Vancouver resident "Marianna" includes both personal storytelling and a call to action:

> I am very sad to see Michelle Gurney. She is my niece, my son's cousin. I met her when she was a little girl; she lived with her mom and brothers near Commercial Drive. I think she was about five; the cutest little girl. It is unbelievable that in Canada, in Vancouver, there are no homes for these street women to be safe, to find help, to live and get the counseling and support they need. What is wrong with our society that we just treat young women as worthless, just because they have become involved in the drug and prostitution lifestyle, usually because they need some help?? We still don't have any centres for First Nations young people who are on the street! Why don't we have resource centres to serve people's needs? I grieve for Michelle. (E-GuestBooks.com 2008)

Marianna's compelling statement makes the need for better support for women very clear. She identifies the source of the problem as society's neglect of women who have broken rules for proper moral behavior through involvement in "the drug and prostitution lifestyle." These women have, to some extent, followed the Deviant Femme pattern identified by Jeannie Banks Thomas (2007b); they have pushed aside society's rules for proper conduct. Marianna observes, however, that this rejection of those rules probably occurred because the women "need[ed] some help." Marianna's sad story, followed by her insistence on change, follows conversational legend patterns in that it links personal experience and interpretation with a lesson for others. The story does not, however, invoke the negative characterization that became an issue on websites for Natalee Holloway. The gravity of mass murder seems to have decreased that kind of characterization, making kinder interpretations more frequent.

"Vancouver Eastside Missing Women" deliberately portrays the softer side of the women who disappeared and died. Steve Mertyl's (2006) essay about Brenda Wolfe, a woman who disappeared from Alberta in 1999, identifies her as a "Downtown Eastside guardian angel" who was "not afraid to roust rowdy drunks—male or female." A friend of hers, Maggy Gisle, remembers Wolfe "in the midst of three men, whaling on all three of them at once" and protecting prostitutes from people who tried to make them pay for using street corners. Gisle explains that she "got scared straight" after hearing stories about the disappearance of her street friends.

Like the ghosts of murdered women that allegedly haunt some institutions of higher learning, Wolfe is depicted as a strong person who tried to protect others before becoming a victim of violence herself. Since she used drugs and worked as a street enforcer in a rough neighborhood, her story on the website reminds women to take care and stay clean. Although she is not precisely a ghost, Brenda, as a character in others' narratives, becomes a representation of risks that women should avoid. Her power as a protector of prostitutes and a beater of three men makes her a hero similar to "John the Bear" (Thompson 1968, 3–8) in European folktales. A "guardian angel" while alive, Brenda expresses concern for other women after her death by her role in stories told about her.

None of the other women depicted on the "Vancouver Eastside Missing Women" website seem quite as formidable as Brenda Wolfe, but descriptions of many of them by friends, relatives, and reporters emphasize positive characteristics. Mandy Blakemore, for example, was "a fun girl who always smiled; she never had a bad word to say about anyone." Marilynne Neill, "a good person with a big heart who truly cared about people," was "trying to get out of [drug using] and change her life when she went missing." This sad sequence of attempted change followed by disappearance also emerges on other websites about missing women, including Jessie Davis, who disappeared and was found murdered in the spring of 2007 (Montaldo 2009). The lesson here seems to be that trying to change is not enough; only immediate transformation of a risky lifestyle will keep a woman safe.

What, then, is the relationship between ghost stories and narratives that characterize missing women on websites? Although most missing women are not portrayed as ghosts, their stories bear a haunting resemblance to legends about women who die violently and return as ghosts to protect others. In the renditions I discuss here, ghosts are not the guardians of the living; the real guardians are the women who share rumors and legends, including, in some high-profile cases, rumors and legends about ghosts of women who have vanished. Women's storytelling about risks that result in death relies on legend patterns, with some inclusion of folktale characteristics. Many descriptions of women's lives before their tragic disappearances emphasize their angelic qualities, including kindness and concern. By hearing such narratives, women learn how important it is to go out in groups of friends, to avoid dangerous areas, and to watch how much alcohol they drink. Although some material posted on the Internet seems dubious and untrustworthy, these narratives for women's education have the ring of truth. Websites keep such cautionary narratives circulating, reminding people of the strength and power of caring women.

At the beginning of this chapter, I cited Sherry Turkle's assertion that all of us are "dwellers on the threshold between the real and the virtual, unsure of our footing, inventing ourselves as we go along" (1995, 10). Examination of websites dedicated to missing women makes it clear that visitors to these websites not only invent themselves as teachers of important lessons, but also participate in creating characters that have meaning for large groups of people. Future studies of such websites can yield insights into Internet identity formation and community-building, as well as efforts to facilitate social change. Doing their best to save young women from harm, future users of the Internet will tell stories that merit close attention.

Chapter 3

The End of the Internet: A Folk Response to the Provision of Infinite Choice

Lynne S. McNeill

Digital Folk Culture

I was working in the kitchen with my husband one night, preparing a dish of deviled eggs to bring to a dinner party, when I was first struck by just how much influence digital culture has over our daily lives. As a household we are, of course, as wired-in as many people are these days—we communicate via e-mail and text message on a daily basis, and we use the Internet to plan our trips, buy gifts, and arrange our schedules—but this was something more, something deeper. My husband was carrying a plate of boiled eggs from one counter to another when he lost his balance. He saved himself from a fall, but the eggs weren't so lucky; as I watched, they slid to the edge of the plate, teetered on the lip, and finally fell, bouncing away across the kitchen floor. In his moment of frustration, grabbing hopelessly at the falling eggs, my husband exclaimed, "Control Z!" I looked at him in surprise. Still holding the plate, he bemusedly explained, "Undo—it's the undo command. I wanted to undo it." He said he could picture himself instinctively reaching for the keyboard—ring finger on the CTRL button, middle finger on the Z—the minute he realized the eggs were falling. It was his first, immediate reaction to a mistake. CTRL-Z! Undo.

My husband and I were born on the cusp of what Marc Prensky has dubbed the *digital native* generation, people born close to 1980 who are all "'native speakers' of the digital language of computers, video games and the Internet" (2001a, 1). My husband and I were born in 1976 and 1977, respectively, but as the first online bulletin board systems were up and running in the late 1970s, we technically get in under the wire. Birth dates aside, my husband's digital reaction to a real-world mistake clinched it for me; in a way my parents never will be, my husband and I are fully ensconced in a digital culture that shapes how we perceive the world around us.

Prensky's idea of digital natives has become a key concept in the field of education, where scholars are trying to figure out exactly how (and how much) to alter their pedagogy for a generation of students whose perceptions of the world (if not the very structures of their brains) are likely fundamentally different from those of previous generations (see Bennett , Maton, and Kervin 2008). The trouble, of course, is that the majority of the people who are behind current pedagogical decisions are digital *immigrants* who, while adapting to their environment—as do all immigrants to varying extents—still retain their accent, which can be seen in "such things as turning to the Internet for information second rather than first, or in reading the manual for a program rather than assuming that the program itself will teach us how to use it" (Prensky 2001a, 2). According to Prensky, other nondigital accent markers are:

> printing out your email (or having your secretary print it out for you—an even 'thicker' accent); needing to print out a document written on the computer in order to edit it (rather than just editing on the screen); and bringing people physically into your office to see an interesting web site (rather than just sending them the URL). (2001a, 2)

These behaviors alienate natives, who perceive in them a distinctly foreign, and somewhat incomprehensible, worldview.

While the implications for education are fascinating, what I am interested in here is the basic idea that the digital world is a *culture*, one that a person can be native or nonnative *to*. Folklorists have recently been challenged by a host of apparent "traditions" that emerge at lightning speed from the Internet and its attendant technologies, and the question of whether or not folklore can be found in this environment remains somewhat up in the air. I feel that the idea of a digital culture is not simply a metaphor that can be expanded into further metaphorical concepts such as nativity, but that it is also an accurate, literal description of a component of digital society. Ward Goodenough's definition of culture, first penned in 1957, long before the Internet was an everyday reality, posits that a society's culture is made up of "whatever it is one has to know or believe in order to operate in a manner acceptable to its members" (1964,

36). Any newcomer to an Internet chatroom, or a Facebook page, or even a back-and-forth mobile phone texting scenario, will know that there exists a certain shared body of knowledge about how to behave in such settings. Folklorist John McDowell similarly suggests that folklore "is the study of traditional modes of expression and thought as they surface and evolve in the course of social interaction in human communities" (Williams 2001). Both these definitions target the fact that culture, and more specifically folk culture, deals with knowledge gleaned from social interactions. As Bruce Mason notes, the Internet "is a 'virtual' home to many millions who have gone ahead and made the Net a space in which to create a lived culture" (1996, 4). Monica Foote agrees: "Those who frequent chat rooms and use instant messenger programs have developed their own folkspeech, [and] online communities function according to their own sets of customary behavior" (2007, 27). As with any process of acculturation, newcomers to these digital situations aren't handed a manual about how to express themselves most effectively to the locals; they learn as they go, informally picking up on how best to blend in through observation and participation. Hence, a digital culture.

Digital natives, those people whose entire lives have been spent immersed in digital culture, live in a world defined by constant connectivity—"being in touch with friends and family at any time from any place" (Frand 2000, 14) is both important to them and easily achieved through communications technologies. This interactivity is at the core of the distinction between a generation whose main observed technology was television and one whose main observed technology is the Internet, and it is this possibility for interaction that allows folklore to flourish and a distinct culture to develop in a digital setting. Browsing the Internet is not a passive experience—users are contributing, communicating, learning, and teaching by example within a community whose ability to erase geographical limitations is astounding. This, of course, defies the original purposes of the Internet; no longer simply a tool for particular realms of activity such as business or government, the Web, just like any public gathering place, has become a setting for normal, informal, daily social interaction. And just as with any other location where such interaction occurs, folklore emerges. As Georges and Jones, in their excellent introductory text *Folkloristics* explain:

> The word "folklore" denotes expressive forms, processes, and behaviors (1) that we customarily learn, teach, and utilize or display during face-to-face interaction, and (2) that we judge to be traditional (a) because they are based on known precedents or models, and (b) because they serve as evidence of continuities and consistencies

through time and space in human knowledge, thought, belief, and feeling. (1995, 1)

It will become evident that communications technologies, especially the Internet, provide the setting for such folkloric emergence and transmission.

The main difference between the Internet as a setting for social interaction and a more concrete location in the "real world" is the speed at which information can be located and socially exchanged. Even the telephone, once the peak of communications technology, pales in comparison: while one can call a friend who lives in another country and immediately be able to communicate freely, one cannot pick up a phone and ask to be connected with someone—anyone, anywhere—who shares his or her interest in, say, mushroom identification, or hostelling, or furniture making (see Rheingold 2000). The Internet, on the other hand, allows like-minded people who would never otherwise meet (whether due to physical, geographical, or situational obstacles) to find each other almost immediately. It is the *pace* and *scope* of these social processes that have increased so exponentially.

Despite the common judgments of nonnatives, the social connections that digital natives forge over the Internet are genuine and very real. Setting aside the question of social connections initiated and sustained entirely over the Internet, digital natives conduct much of the business of their everyday family and friend relationships through digital mediation as well. Jason Frand notes that digital natives do not perceive communications technologies as "technology" anymore, and compares the situation to the telephone, which many digital immigrants see as a fairly unmediated form of personal communication:

Alan Kay, a member of the 1970s Xerox PARC team who went on to help create the Apple Macintosh, has described technology as 'anything that isn't around when you're born.' Stated another way, if you can remember using your first one ever, it's technology. For most of us with an industrial-age mindset [as opposed to an information-age mindset, which Frand associates with the digital natives]—those of us who are in our mature years (say, over thirty)—telephones, automobiles, and television aren't technology, but computers, the Internet, the Web, and the expanding world of cellular telecommunications are all technologies. Technology, then, to the information-age generation, is everything that surrounds computers and is made possible by computers, but only incidentally the computers themselves. (2000, 16)

I have found this to be true among my college-age students (and among many of my peers as well). For example, in the study of folklore great emphasis has been put on orality and the face-to-face context in which folklore is learned and performed. This idea has, of course, already been complicated by the learning and dissemination patterns of such folk forms as graffiti, autograph-book verses, and chain letters (both paper and e-mail forms), and I often find myself explaining the concept to students as person-to-person rather than face-to-face, as the former is a phrase that still emphasizes the individual, personal communicative qualities of folk culture that distinguish it from the mass broadcasts of most popular culture, yet one that also allows for mediated interaction. Interestingly, however, Frand's observation that digital natives no longer see their communicative tools as mediating technology is accurate. I would argue that my students increasingly consider online chatting, social networking, and mobile-phone texting to be a form of unmediated face-to-face contact. Their Facebook pages and MySpace profiles are as much a daily presentation of self as their demeanor and speech are in real-life social settings. Distinguishing these virtual spaces from "real life" is actually inaccurate—they *are* real life to the people who use them. The digital natives identify so strongly with their phones and online accounts that they do not recognize any meaningful difference between casual interaction through technology and casual interaction in person—texting and chatting *are* "face-to-face" communication.[1]

Considering this, it is completely natural that folklore would emerge in these social contexts—folklore emerges *anywhere* where informal, everyday, face-to-face social interaction takes place. As Dell Hymes explained in his presidential address at the 1974 AFS meeting, "folklorists believe that the capacity for aesthetic experience, for [the] shaping of deeply felt values into meaningful, apposite form, is present in all communities, and will find some means of expression among all" (1975, 346). There is no reason why a digital community should be treated differently than any other community that Hymes may have been describing. It may take on new forms and shapes, and may be transmitted in new ways, but folklore is definitely alive and well in the digital world.

The emergence of traditional expressive forms on the Internet, and the observation and re-creation of them by other people in new contexts, has not gone unnoticed by the Internet community itself, which has adopted the concept of *memes* to identify what folklorists would call folklore.[2] According to memetic theory, memes are small, self-replicating cultural units (Dennett 1990, 128), "ideas or fragments of ideas which are capable of being replicated as they pass from brain to brain and thus are subject to evolution in the form of random mutation and selection" (Foote 2007, 31). While the content may not always fall into what a folklorist would identify as "traditional," Richard Dawkins (who coined the term as the cultural analogue to genes) offers a definition of memes that comes close to folkloric ideas:

> Examples of memes are tunes, ideas, catchphrases, clothes fashions, ways of making pots or of building arches. Just as genes propagate themselves in the gene pool by leaping from body to body via sperm or eggs, so memes propagate themselves in the meme pool by leaping from brain to brain via a process which, in the broad sense, can be called imitation. If a scientist hears, or reads about, a good idea, he passes it on to his colleagues and students. He mentions it in his articles and his lectures. If the idea catches on, it can be said to propagate itself, spreading from brain to brain. (1976, 206)

This description could very easily apply to the transmission of folklore; while not focused on a particular group within which a meme (or a tradition) is transmitted, the basic idea of a piece of lore surviving through a combination of successful transmission and cultural relevance (a process of natural selection, Dawkins would say) is not far off base. The adoption of this term by Internet users to describe aspects of Internet experience (images, videos, phrases, exchanges, etc.) that are propagated via the tools of the Web (e-mail, blogs, forums, etc.) should be of interest to folklorists. Monica Foote, in an article on avatar images in online communities, encourages the use of memetics in folklore study, but she does caution that the two areas are not interchangeable:

> The scope of study of memetics is much wider than that of folklore, as anything whatsoever created by imitation falls within the purview of it, rather than just that material which fits the narrower definitions of traditionality and belonging to the folk. That is to say, all folklore is made up of memes, but not all memes are folklore. (2007, 31)

Realizing these limitations, it is still useful to consider the Internet content self-consciously labeled by users as memes, as this designation will often point the way to genuine digital folk traditions.

There have been a wide range of Internet memes that have waxed and waned in popularity over time, and as digital culture has shifted and evolved, the memes associated with it have evolved as well. Taking the digital-native metaphor to its extreme, we actually a have more complex situation than the simple dichotomy between immigrants and natives. We have digital *settlers* as well, nonnative adults who pioneered new frontiers of digital technology and who are responsible, as are all pioneers, for shaping the cultural foundations upon which future generations would build their native lives. These digital settlers perhaps know the roots of digital culture better than many of the natives (who may easily be unaware of how their own culture came to be while still functioning perfectly within it), and these settlers' needs, desires, and efforts are distinct from the culture that is now emerging within a fully formed setting. Web 2.0, an Internet defined by interactivity and collaboration, is the result of the digital natives' growing influence over their own domain as they age. If we look back to the inception of the Internet as a general-use communication medium, we can see that memes, the folklore that emerged from early social interaction on the Web, reveal much about the acculturation of a digital pioneer settlement.

The Last Page

In the mid- to late 1990s, the Internet was coming into more general use and was just beginning to reveal its applicability to consumption, information retrieval, and virtual communication. ARPANET, the military body that initially governed the Internet, was decommissioned in 1992 and the U.S. government relinquished control over the majority of its infrastructure, leaving behind a web of interconnected private service providers that would become the Internet as we understand it today. According to one timeline, the 100,000 web servers in use in January 1996 exploded ten-fold in just over a year to 1,000,000 web servers in April 1997 (Information Today 2007).[3] This exponential growth in servers is also reflected in individual users. In 1996, approximately 45 million people were using the Internet; when NASA broadcast pictures from the Mars Pathfinder online in 1997, NASA's website had 46 million hits in one day. By 1999, the Internet browsing population had tripled to 150 million users ("Internet Timeline" 2000, 68). Jon Guice of NASA's Ames Research Center feels that it is the assessment of the Internet's history in terms of *users* rather than *technology* that reveals the surge. He enumerates networks, computers, users, and locations:

> In 1994 the global Internet, defined as access to e-mail, comprised over 15,000 networks, 2.5 million permanently connected computers, and 25 million people in 125 countries, by one estimate. By the close of the next year, the number of networks, computers, and people had roughly doubled. Statistics such as these are controversial in their details, but no one disputes the upward curve. Even the most conservative definitions yield results showing what any experienced Internet user can attest to: rapid growth. (1998, 203)

This explosion of generalized use of the Internet for social, commercial, and business purposes in the late 1990s sets the stage for the arrival of a fascinating Internet meme. A number of websites cropped up at this time, each claiming to be the "end" of the Internet. Despite the sensationalistic possibilities, these sites are not an "end" in the sense of the demise of the concept as a whole, but the "end" in the sense of the end of a book, the "last page," as some sites call it. This Internet meme comes in a variety of forms, but the message is consistent: that the user has reached the end of the Internet and must now stop browsing or turn back. Many versions of this website go beyond simply announcing the end and offer suggestions as to what the user should do now that he or she has reached the end. The following are a selection of such texts:

> Attention, please.
> You have reached the very last page of the Internet.
> We hope you have enjoyed your browsing.
> Enjoy the rest of your life.

> Congratulations, you have reached the End of the Internet. To get back to the Other End of the Internet please click on the back button on your browser 3,307,998,701 times.
> Many thanks.
> The Internet Team

> The End
> Turn back you have reached the
> Last page on the Internet.
> (Note: for safely reasons will the last surfer please switch off all the servers before leaving.)

> WARNING
> You have reached the end of the Internet.
> There is nothing more to see.
> Please go back now.

> You have reached the end of the Internet.
> If you think you have reached this page in error you have not. It is simply because you have been online too long and had nothing better to do.
> This Is The Very Last Page On The Internet.
> Please turn off your computer!!!
> Go outside and play!!!
> The End.

You Have Reached The End Of The Internet
There is nothing more to see or do here.
Turn off your computer.
Take a break.
Go for a walk.
Read a book.
Have a cup of tea.
Sit and stare at the natural world.
You get the idea . . .
Remember to wiggle your toes and get out of your head.
Thank you and have a nice day!

Attention:
You have reached the very last page of the Internet.
We hope you have enjoyed your browsing.
Now turn off your computer and go outside.

You have reached the end of the Internet.
We hope you have enjoyed your experience.
Now go outside and play.

The Page at the end of the Internet.
Well Done! This is the last page.
You have now reached the end of the Internet. This is it. There are
no more links and no more pages to visit.
This means that you can now turn off your computer, make yourself a nice cup of tea, and contemplate what you are gong to do with
the rest of your life now that you've finished viewing the Internet.

This is just a small sampling of numerous iterations of the End of the
Internet (EOTI) meme. The traditional elements that are preserved
across all the versions are plain to see: an announcement of the end and
a recommendation of what to do next. The dynamic elements typically
come in the specific recommendations of what the user should do, but
even here we have some consistencies; suggestions that target a natural,
peaceful life—making tea, reading a book, going outside—are predominant. The visual makeup of the sites is also a dynamic element, but the
majority of the variations are in the details, such as font size and color.
Almost all of these websites are very simplistic in design.

Most use only text and basic (if any) graphics. This perhaps indicates
their creation by nonprofessional users, but the lack of interactive and
collaborative qualities also reveals the sites' *terminus ante quem*; these
sites are strictly a Web 1.0 phenomenon.

As far as being a form of folklore, these websites are closely related to the fax and copier lore that Dundes and Pagter collected in their four *Paperwork Empire* volumes ([1978] 1992, 1987, 1991b, 1996). For all that these websites make use of their digital nature, they might as well be printouts. They also share the burden of newfangledness that Dundes and Pagter had to wrestle with when identifying their Xeroxlore as legitimate folklore:

> One thing this volume clearly demonstrates is the existence of folklore in the modern urban technological world. The idea that folklore reflects only the past is incorrect. Yes, some folklore reflects the past, but there is also folklore, ongoing, current, which reflects the present, the culture of today. As more and more individuals move from rural to urban settings, a trend which is observable in many parts of the world, the folklore of offices and of bureaucracy is bound to continue. The office copier greatly facilitates the transmission of this folklore. For this reason, we think it is incumbent upon folklorists to document this tradition, and to document it as it happens. Were folklorists to wait fifty or one hundred years to investigate the traditions contained in this book, they might be unable to do so. (1991, 20)

If copier technology facilitated the rapid transmission of folklore, the Internet has multiplied that speed exponentially. It is similarly incumbent upon folklorists to document the early instances of emergent folklore on the Internet, before it disappears or its irrelevance to current culture becomes too great.

Xeroxlore is actually an excellent precedent for the acknowledgement of static web pages as items of folklore; Dundes and Pagter were fighting against understandings of folklore that relied heavily upon chronology, communal (re)creation, and orality. Thus they had to turn to more pragmatic indicators of folkloric nature when identifying photocopy and fax materials as folklore:

> It is possible or likely that there are individual creators for every item. Our point is that an item, however or whenever created, becomes authentic folklore once it has undergone repetition and variation. We have multiple versions—with variation—of almost all the items. (1987, 14)

Similarly, the EOTI sites—although each is created by an individual—come in multiple versions; every one has its own levels and types of variation from the others. And like all folklore, all versions are equally legitimate; there is no one "correct" or "authentic" version. In the true spirit of folklore, we can even find parodies of these websites, and, as Grant C. Loomis points out, parody "implies a familiarity with the original creation" (1958, 45). In parodies, we see a powerful generic sensitivity to the original form, with enough conservative elements remaining amid the humorous changes for the original to be a reference point. Thus, we find:

> Beginning of the Internet.
> This page is the beginning of the Internet.

and

> Welcome to
> The Middle Page of The Internet
> This page is dynamically adjusted to remain at the exact middle
> of the Internet. If you have browser problems, or if pages take a long
> time to load, please visit this page to reorient your browser.

If the parody proves the rule, then we get a clear confirmation of the generic conventions of this folk form.

As a folklorist, my curiosity has been piqued by the question of *why* this Internet meme was so popular in the mid-to-late 1990s. Most of the sites were created during this period, and most have not been updated since. My attempts to contact the originators of the sites met with poor results. It may be that the contact links for the sites are out of date, or perhaps my queries were diverted to junk-mail folders, but I only heard back from a few creators. Of the responses I did receive, none was very satisfactory. One was quite straightforward: "When did you make this?" "1994." Why? "Lack of motivation to make anything worthwhile." "What were your inspirations?" "Beer." Another response was a bit more thoughtful: the creator wanted to inspire people to "get back to the basics" and live unplugged for a while.

I imagine that the many other iterations of the EOTI meme can also be explained as falling somewhere between these two divergent motivations. The similarities in wording (and occasionally in form) clearly indicate monogenesis—most of these pages are created by people who have seen one already. The message resonates enough for people to want to re-create it themselves rather than simply refer friends and family back to the same page they discovered. What motivates the replication of this folk form? Why was the idea that the Internet has a "last page" so resonant with the early online community?

If the Internet were a book, actually able to have a last page, its hyperlinked nature—where within a given page there are one or more links to other pages containing related information—makes the Internet read less like a novel and more like a Choose Your Own Adventure book.[4] Anyone who has ever temporarily marked their place in one of these books to jump ahead and read both possible plot options—and perhaps even the choices those options would each eventually lead to—can relate to how stressful it can be navigating the Internet at times. One can never be sure if one is getting the complete picture or missing out on some key point of information. I believe that it is this quality of the Internet, the overabundance of options, which made the idea of the "end" of the Internet such an appealing one to early users.

The Psychology of Choice

In the fields of personality and social psychology, research into the issue of *choice*—paralleling the Internet boom and beginning in the late 1990s— is applicable to this subject. The basic idea is that when it comes to making decisions, the more options one has to choose from, the better. As psychologist Barry Schwartz notes, when it comes to choice, "the presumption is, self-determination is a good thing and choice is essential to self-determination" (DeAngelis 2004, 56). This idea is often thought to be "common wisdom" or "intuitively appealing," phrases used in many studies of choice, but Alexander Chernev, a professor of marketing, has a more scientific view:

> This assumption is consistent with the prediction by classic economic theories that larger assortments should always be beneficial for consumers because they provide for a potentially better match between consumers' own preferences and the product offering. (2003, 170)

The scope of this idea is impressive, and, as explained by psychologists Sheena Iyengar and Mark Lepper, it is not limited to simple purchasing situations (which is where many marketing studies apply it):

> It is the common supposition in modern society that the more choices, the better—that the human ability to manage, and the human desire for, choice is infinite. From classic economic theories of free enterprise, to mundane marketing practices that provide customers with entire aisles devoted to potato chips or soft drinks, to important life decisions in which people contemplate alternative career options or multiple investment opportunities, this belief pervades our institutions, norms, and customs. Ice cream parlors compete to offer the most flavors; major fast food chains urge us to "have it *our* way" (2000, 995; emphasis in original).

Early psychological studies agreed with this, too; for example, people were found to be happier when given the opportunity to choose between several different activities to perform than when assigned one by a moderator (see Zuckerman et al. 1978). This and other research appeared to show that the provision of choice increases motivation and enhances performance on a variety of tasks.

But numerous later studies indicate that empirical evidence runs contrary to this idea; there is a limit to the level of choice that is desirable. As a recent article in the *Monitor of Psychology* asks,

> Do you like your orange juice organic or regular, with or without calcium, or with minimal or maximal pulp? How about your toothpaste? Is it the herbal variety with added fluoride, the cavity-busting option with baking soda or the original formula with flavor crystals? Or *maybe*, the thought of having to select any of those options is keeping you out of the grocery store entirely—you'd rather scrape by on what's still in the house. Although an explosion of consumer choices may mean we sometimes get exactly what we want, too many choices can also overwhelm us to the point where we choose nothing at all. (DeAngelis 2004, 56; emphasis in original)

Anyone who has ever gone to a grocery store to buy shampoo can probably relate to this; a quick trip to my local Albertson's revealed that there are 127 different brands of shampoo for sale there. It is perhaps easy to imagine the frustration of living in a small isolated community and having only two brands of shampoo to choose between, but for as much as 127 initially seems like a better spread, it's not difficult either to imagine (or perhaps to recall) the stress of choosing just one from all of those options.

Most of the research that has been conducted on this topic deals with consumerism. A 2000 study in the *Journal of Personality and Social Psychology* used jam selection at an upscale grocery store as the field experiment. After the preliminary surveys had been completed—surveys designed to ensure that neither group of proffered jams (all of them from Wilkin & Sons, purveyors to her Majesty the Queen) included the most preferred or the most disliked jam options—the psychologists spent two consecutive Saturdays ("neither of which fell on a long holidays weekend" they assure us) at a tasting booth in the grocery store. One day they offered a limited selection of jams—only six kinds. The second day, they offered an extensive choice—twenty-four types of jam. The results were striking. While the extensive-selection booth showed more initial attractiveness to customers, drawing in bigger crowds of interested shoppers, the percentage of visitors who actually made purchases was almost entirely from the limited-selection table (Iyengar and Lepper 2000).

This same result has been seen in numerous other studies involving a wide range of products and other choices. While some work has been done to identify the mediating factors in this debate—to discover why sometimes the traditional expectation that greater choice is better does pan out[5]—the implications remain the same. The closer the number of options in any decision-making situation gets to infinity, the less inclined people become to actually take any of them.

This idea has rapidly gained widespread attention with regard to increasing choices within the realm of popular media. A recent *Los Angeles Times* article urged readers to "step back from the media buffet":

> As a nation, we spend on average two months of every year watching TV. Perhaps it's *not* crazy given that, according to the 2006 International Television and Video Almanac, we have 392 cable channels to choose from and 40,000 DVD titles. And let's not forget the 175,000 books published annually, or the hundreds of movies released each year and the billions of Internet pages. [And] still we want more. (Abramowitz 2007; emphasis in original)

Film producer Michael London attributes much of today's media-binging to the new opportunities for entertainment and quasi-entertainment presented by the communications industry:

> I've always been a media junkie. I've always been vulnerable to disappearing down the rabbit hole. When the rabbit hole has gotten bigger and deeper through the Internet, for people like me who multitask, it's created a real danger. It creates a perfect meltdown scenario to people who are vulnerable to trying to do too much at once. You can sit in your office, and you can be having a phone conversation while reading *Variety* online, and answering your e-mail, and having an IM chat with somebody. It sounds crazy, but it's not an exaggeration. (Abramowitz 2007)

Interestingly, the whole promotion of choice in the media—the idea that "new technologies would make possible greater individual choice of what to see and hear, and of when to see and hear it" (Berger and Burke 2005, 217)—paints readers, listeners, and users entirely as consumers, emphasizing the idea than even when the goal isn't explicitly consumer driven, the concepts from the marketplace will still be applicable.

Jeffrey Cole, director of the Annenberg School for Communication's Center for the Digital Future, has been conducting a long-term study on this very issue. After surveying 2,000 households over the past six years, he and his researchers discovered that some of the most advanced users of technology were saying that they were starting to feel like they *had* to check their e-mail before going to sleep. As Cole notes, "it's really a function of being overwhelmed by the amount of things technology makes available" (Abramowitz 2007). If 127 kinds of shampoo at the store is overwhelming, consider the tens of thousands of results for "shampoo" on the popular shopping website Amazon.com. Whether the goal is shopping for products or interacting with friends, the Internet provides boundless opportunity.

The increasing pressure to take advantage of all of this at once is a serious issue; as Michael London noted, it's easy to experience a "meltdown" when trying to take it all in. When it comes to digital natives, however, multitasking is recognized as one of their unique skills:

> Digital natives are used to receiving information really fast. They like to parallel process and multitask. They prefer their graphics *before* their text rather than the opposite. They prefer random access (like hypertext). They function best when networked. They thrive on instant gratification and frequent rewards. (Prensky 2001a, 2; emphasis in original)

Digital natives are born into a world that bombards them with information from every angle—their coping mechanisms are built into their worldview. But what of the digital settlers and immigrants, those who have to undertake the (sometimes painful) process of acculturation to digital society, those who haven't been learning since birth how to navigate the endless possibilities that technology affords?

The ability of the Internet to exponentially multiply options in just about any decision-making situation—what to buy, where to invest, what treatment to seek, what information to utilize, how to fill spare time—makes it the ultimate arena for oppressive levels of indecision. As a research tool, the Internet has been compared to the ultimate library, but as the Online Computer Library Center (OCLC) notes,

> the library has long been a metaphor for order and rationality . . . Contrast this world with the anarchy of the Web. The Web is free-associating, unrestricted and disorderly. Searching is secondary to finding and the process by which things are found is unimportant. "Collections" are temporary and subjective, where a blog entry may be as valuable to the individual as an "unpublished" paper as are six pages of a book made available by Amazon.com. The individual searches alone and without expert help and, not knowing what is undiscovered, is satisfied. (OCLC 2003)

While this seems to imply that ignorance is bliss—that Internet users don't know what they're missing when they find a limited amount of information on the Internet—I would argue that in many cases, especially for those who were adults when the Internet became available to the general public (and who recall the diligent, comprehensive research processes demanded by physical information collections), the opposite is true. While Internet searchers may indeed only be able to actually inspect and process a very limited amount of the information on the Web, these individuals are presented at every turn with an endless pool to choose from. In some cases, this is touted as a benefit of the Internet; access to information is no longer limited to what any particular institution is willing to reveal:

> The common theme is that the Internet is a popular, liberal, democratic, or even anarchistic medium. While having origins in the U.S. Department of Defense—a perennial irony for these stories— the Internet has grown to be a nonhierarchical arena for the free exchange of ideas and information. (Guice 1998, 202)

But for someone who is attempting to be comprehensive in a search for information, the lack of boundaries is a burden; when presented with unlimited information, searchers are very aware of the avenues they're *not* able to pursue. The process of deciding which of the vast array of information options to choose as one's smaller selection of usable data puts the searcher into the same position as the hesitant-to-buy, extensive-choice, jam-selecting group, but to an exponentially greater degree.

We can see Internet companies such as Yahoo, MSN, and Google attempting to address this with specialized search engines that filter the infinite information for us, that pick the best for us, that do the work for us. But the problem still remains, especially now that those filtering sites themselves are rapidly multiplying. Will I find the best deal through Amazon.com or through Yahoo!.Shopping? Will there be a specialized website I'll miss out on if I stick with the major search engines? How do I know when I've looked at enough? If twenty-four types of jam are sufficient to cause buyers to leave empty-handed, then the information available on the Internet is certainly enough to stunt any decision-making process. And yet, decisions must be made.

Conclusions

As an Internet meme—a form of folklore created by and relevant to digital settlers and immigrants—End of the Internet websites provide form and expression for the growing cultural tension that emerged in the mid-to late 1990s as the Internet's exponential growth began to reveal the roles it would play in daily life. These websites, created at a time when non-native users dominated the creation of Internet content, dramatize the anxiety that the seemingly infinite nature of the Internet caused, despite the surface-level assumption that the increase in options provided by the Web could only be a good thing. Instructions to turn off the computer and join the "real world" imply that to these users, the Internet is not the real world, an idea that digital natives would find dubious. Another common suggestion, to "go outside and play," implies that surfing the Internet is work rather than entertainment, highlighting the often-stressful nature of web browsing for those who do not see it as a regular setting for casual interaction. For digital immigrants, the basic idea that the Internet *has an end* was resonant and meaningful, simply because it allows for the reassuring notion that options are anything but infinite. For digital natives, the infinite nature of the web is simply a given, a construct that levies no increased burden of effort simply because there never was a time in their lives when the options were fewer. In the emergence of Web 2.0 and its expansive opportunities for collaboration and interactivity, we can see the maturation of the digital natives as they begin to take the reins in the formation of their own cultural landscape. Soon, the message of the EOTI sites, which even now are rarely updated, will be completely irrelevant to users as the population of digital immigrants gives way to a complete culture of natives. So, while it's still meaningful: This is the end. Log off, shut down, and go outside and play.

Notes

1. Interestingly, my students now make a distinction between texting or chatting and e-mail, which is seen as a much more indirect form of communication, probably due to the time-delayed nature of the interaction. While texting and chatting are conducted in real time, as an in-person conversation would be, e-mails are non-immediate, and thus are relegated to "business stuff," as one of my students put it. According to this student, e-mailing is for intermittent communication with parents and professors; texting and chatting are for socializing with friends.
2. A Wikipedia search for "Internet Phenomenon," a common phrase used to identify an image, video, phrase, or idea that moves through the digital community gaining variations and parodies, automatically redirects to "Internet Memes."
3. By 2002, it had multiplied by ten again.
4. This is a series of children's books published by Bantam from the late 1970s to the late 1990s. They were written from a second-person perspective and

featured multiple possible endings, based upon what line of action the reader chose at various points within the narrative.

5.   Often this occurs when there is a pre-articulated combination of ideal attributes. In other words, when a consumer enters into a purchasing situation with a set of desired qualities that they want their final purchase to have, then a larger selection is helpful, as there is a greater likelihood of the specific qualities being shared by one product, and the (otherwise stressful) process of elimination is expedited by the predetermined criteria.

Chapter 4

The *Forward* as Folklore: Studying E-Mailed Humor

RUSSELL FRANK

Folklore in the Age of Electronic Reproduction: Text and Context

On Sunday afternoon, 12 February 2006, I checked the *New York Times* website, as has been my custom since 9/11, to see if anything horrendous had happened since the morning papers arrived on my doorstep. The breaking news was that Vice President Dick Cheney had accidentally shot a quail-hunting buddy in Texas (Kornblut 2006).

The timing of the story was remarkable for me personally. The day before the shooting I had asked a friend to help me collect topical folklore, which I refer to as *newslore* (Frank 2004), by asking *his* friends to send me any e-mailed items they received. That Sunday morning, I had made the same request of readers of my column in the local newspaper (Frank 2006). By the end of that week I had hauled in forty-six jokes: thirteen Bush jokes, nine Cheney jokes, six Enron jokes, three Bill and/ or Hillary Clinton jokes, and fifteen miscellaneous jokes, half of which I would consider newslore (see the appendix at the end of this chapter for a sampling).

The volume of material I received suggests that e-mail has become a robust medium for the transmission of jokes, especially topical jokes. As I will attempt to show in this chapter, these forwarded e-mail messages, or *forwards*, challenge canonical folkloristic ideas about the importance of performance and context and the roles of individual creativity and audience response in textual variation. At any given moment they may also be a reliable guide to those news events, public figures, and joke types that have captured the public imagination. The jokes in my collection consist of verbal, visual, and verbal/visual jokes, but most of the examples I will include here will be visual and verbal/visual ones, since they represent a more significant departure from traditional joke cycles than the verbal jokes.

The advent of netlore came at an awkward time in the history of folklore studies. Beginning in the 1960s and culminating in 1972 in a special issue of the *Journal of American Folklore* that was subsequently published as a book (Paredes and Bauman 1972), the dominant paradigm for folklore research shifted from collecting and comparing folkloric texts to observing and describing when, how, and why those texts emerged in specific social situations. Text was inextricable from context; to study folklore was to watch it being performed.

The shift in research methods was wholly consistent with long-standing conceptualizations of "the folk" as members of small communities whose interactions with each other are mostly face-to-face. But while the research paradigm was shifting, more and more people were gaining access to electronic media that allowed them to communicate in ways that did not require them to be in each other's presence. And some of that communication, inevitably, was folkloric in nature. If these mediated folkloric communications differed from face-to-face communications only in lacking the full-bodied presence of the participants, folklorists could perhaps have safely ignored them and continued studying folklore in more contextually saturated situations. But, of course, each new medium changes to some degree the *way* people communicate.

In his collections of "folklore from the paperwork empire," Alan Dundes made a convincing argument for considering hand-drawn cartoons and parodies of memos, government documents, news releases, and the like as folklore despite the lack of oral performance (Dundes and Pagter [1978] 1992, 1987, 1991b, 1996). By collecting and presenting the texts with little regard to their contexts, Dundes reminded us, first, of the intrinsic value of the texts themselves, and second, of the essential role of the analyst in making sense of those texts. "No piece of folklore continues to be transmitted unless it means something," he wrote, "even if neither the speaker nor the audience can articulate what that meaning might be" (Dundes 1987, vii).

With the advent of computer-mediated communication, however, other folklorists offered evidence that those who interact electronically constitute, as John Dorst put it, "communities that, though dispersed, display attributes of the direct, unconstrained, unofficial exchanges folklorists typically concern themselves with." At the same time, Dorst conceded that these exchanges "are not readily susceptible to the conventional methods of performance analysis and ethnography of speaking" (1990, 180). Similarly, Bill Ellis wrote that the existence of virtual communities "challenges our assumption that folklore is the property of small, localized groups," while acknowledging "the difficulty of gathering contextual information" (2002, 1).[1]

Yet Ellis (2002), Baym (1993), and Fernback (2003) have gone a long way toward showing the possibilities of "virtual ethnography" (Mason 1996) by focusing on online discussion groups. Whether they are fans of daytime television soap operas, as are Baym's informants, or contributors to an assortment of message boards, as are Ellis's and Fernback's sources, these people are doing more than exchanging items of folklore; they are conversing, and their conversations include their reactions to the folklore.

Still, even if virtual relationships offer some of the satisfactions of the face-to-face variety, virtual ethnography cannot possibly have the texture of an account of actors, scene, and setting, especially if most of one's material comes, as mine does, via e-mail rather than participant-observation in a virtual community. Here, the element of performance is almost wholly absent. As Brad Templeton, founder of the Rec.Humor. Funny site, puts it: "You don't get the advantage of delivery, surprise or a funny face. You don't get a drunk audience [usually] or a chance to use your great German accent. You must prepare a joke that stands on its own" ("Submission Guidelines").

By "prepare," Templeton seems to mean "invent." Most of us, though, simply read or pass on jokes invented by unknown others. In what we might call (updating Walter Benjamin) the age of electronic reproduction, we pass these texts along in a form that is identical to the form in which we received them. Forwarding an e-mailed joke does not even entail retyping it: one hits the forward button, and the joke from the incoming e-mail is automatically reproduced in the outgoing e-mail. In other words, variation, long an identifying feature of oral tradition, has become the exception rather than the rule.[2]

The other half of the folklore-as-performance equation, of course, is the audience. We can, as Ellis has done, ask receivers and forwarders what they thought of this or that joke, but we cannot reconstruct their facial expressions, body language, and verbal responses, if any, at the moment they opened the e-mail. In a face-to-face joke-telling situation, the audience might signal appreciation for the joke by laughing, smiling, nodding, or commenting. Members might feign appreciation either to spare both parties the awkwardness of a "lead balloon" moment or to conceal the fact that they didn't get it. Or they might express disapproval or indifference, verbally or otherwise. Those reactions may then influence the telling (or withholding) of additional jokes.

These kinds of interchanges can be approximated by newsgroup or forum members who participate in threaded discussions, or by instant-message partners who may, in addition to commenting verbally, deploy such Internet slang as LOL (laugh out loud) or even ROTFL (rolling on the floor laughing), or emoticons like the ubiquitous :-) or ☺.

The audience for an e-mailed joke will typically, though not invariably, receive the joke in private and may elect to spike it without opening it, spike it after opening but not reading it, spike it after reading it, forward it with or without comment, or respond to the sender. Feedback, then, is less observable, less immediate, and by no means assured. (In a face-to-face encounter, even a non-reaction is a reaction.) At best there may be short attestations to the quality of the item in question, either in the subject line or in the body of the e-mail. These may be appended by the friend who forwards it to you or by some earlier link in the chain of forwarders. A few examples from my own inbox:

- Subject: Laugh for the day
- Subject: Fw: You'll love this one! Give it a minute to load.
- Subject: Fw: Fwd: a little laugh??
- Hi, this attachment is hysterical; I hope you can unattach it and laugh along with it.
- Here's a good one.
- Hi Russell. Just got these today . . . Have a chuckle.
- No matter your political persuasion, these may make you chuckle—unless you are a personal friend or relative of Mr. Whittington [Vice President Cheney's victim].
- Would be funnier if it wasn't so tragic.
- This is one from my son in Issaquah, Wa. You will laugh!
- You might really like this one!
- This is definitely worth the look!!!
- Hope this works—it's a hoot!!

Meager as they are, these little blurbs offer insight into an aspect of joke transmission that rarely occurs in face-to-face contexts: the pivot from hearing a joke to telling it. If someone tells me a joke, I'm not likely to immediately re-tell that same joke unless I know a variation or think the first teller butchered it. But if I receive a good joke by e-mail, I am quite likely to forward it. My comment, if I add one, may be read as both my reaction to the joke as an audience member/recipient and as my introduction to the joke as a performer/sender.

Also implicit in subject lines and appended comments is the awareness that the tingle of anticipation we once felt in response to the tone that signaled the arrival of a new item in our inbox is long gone. As the volume of e-mail has grown and the percentage of it that could be considered junk-mail has risen, most of us have become reluctant to forward netlore to our friends unless we're pretty convinced that it will be worth their time to look at. In a review of *Send: The Essential Guide to Email for Home and Office* (Shipley and Schwalbe 2007), humor columnist Dave Barry, in his hyperbolic style, gives us a pretty good idea of the widespread scorn for "Internet sludge"—and the people who forward it:

> You received a message addressed to many recipients—often a much-recycled joke, story, list, urban myth, etc. There are millions of these floating around; many of us simply delete them unread. But you, the "Reply All" abuser, read it and decide to respond with some clever comment of your own (such as "LOL"). And instead of hitting "Reply," which would inflict your reply only on the sender, you hit "Reply All," thereby forcing everybody on the recipient list to receive, and delete, yet another useless piece of e-mail. Please do not take this personally, "Reply All" people, but: everybody hates you. We hate you almost as much as we hate the people who mass-mail this Internet sludge in the first place. (Barry 2007)

In other words, the same considerations that govern our decision to seize the floor in face-to-face conversations apply in cyberspace. Though we are not the creators of the material and our "delivery" is not at issue, our judgment is under scrutiny. We get mildly irritated at those who waste our time; we appreciate those who offer a welcome diversion from our labors—and who give us something good to pass along in turn, to our own credit.

The act of forwarding thus tells us one very important thing: that the forwarders had enough confidence in their audience's response to believe that forwarding would enhance their prestige or, at least, do it no harm. Note how many of the attached comments listed above assert that the recipient *will* appreciate the item in question (the more cautious senders tell recipients they *might* like it or append question marks: "a little laugh??"). The risks of forwarding may be slight compared to the risks of live performance, but forwarding is a choice. One makes it with the awareness that addressees might be either grateful or annoyed to receive the item in question.

Another advantage that studying forwarded jokes has over observing traditional joke-telling or monitoring newsgroups is that it may be easier to get a sense of which jokes are popular at any given time. With most of the jokes that get forwarded to me by friends or family, my name is one of many on a list of addressees who are linked only by our relationship with the sender. In some cases, the body of the e-mail includes lists of the addresses of multiple rounds of recipients. Some of the subject lines look like this: "Fw: Fwd: Fw: Fwd: FW: The Talking Parrot," the five forwards serving as a clear indication of how widely distributed these items were. In one instance, the e-mail that came to me preserved three previous generations of addressees. The first round went to 25 people, the second to 13 people, the third to 25 people and the one that came to me included 34 people. If those 97 people in turn forwarded the same joke to 25 of their closest friends and relations, and then that cohort of 2,425 recipients did the same, one can see how quickly we get into some pretty large numbers. From these glimpses at the history of any given item it is no great stretch to say that any folklore text that lands in my inbox must land in a lot of other people's inboxes as well. It would be much more difficult to gauge the popularity of an orally told joke.

Knowing that all the items that come one's way are popular is not the same as knowing that all the popular items are coming one's way, however. In my own work on topical jokes I have had to consider the possibility that I am out of the loop, relatively speaking—that I may be receiving only a fraction of the jokes that are in circulation at any given time. One obvious way to augment my certainly incomplete and possibly even woefully incomplete trove of material is to go to the overwhelmingly vast collections on various websites.

Elliott Oring puts the problem with this kind of website nicely: often, it's "more like an archive than a repertoire" (2003, 139). In other words, most webmasters don't see themselves as gatekeepers, deciding which material deserves a wider audience. In keeping with the democratic spirit that informs much of the Web, they would rather let site visitors rate the jokes than do it for them. Some of the sites keep lists of the most frequently e-mailed items; others tout their most popular categories. In January 2008, for example, About.com's political humor page (http://www.politicalhumor.about.com/) listed these links in its "Most Popular" box: "Political Miniclips, Bushisms, Democratic Loyalty Quiz, Funny George Bush Pictures, and Late Night Political Jokes." Thus there is overlap in the public world of the websites and the private world of personal e-mail recipient lists: a surfer can find a good joke on a website, copy and paste it into an e-mail, and let the forwarding begin. Websites

such as Jokes Gallery (http://www.jokesgallery.com/) make it even easier for us. The site enables one to compose a message and send a joke to
as many as ten friends. One can also subscribe and "receive hundreds of
jokes each week" via e-mail.

Finally, in keeping with the cyberspace mania for interactivity, many
of the jokelore websites invite visitor comments, which brings us back to
the cyber conversations I mentioned at the outset. In February 2007, the
Suburbarazzi website asked visitors whether jokes about Anna Nicole
Smith's death were inappropriate. More than half of the 300 respondents
said yes—a surprising number given that this is not a random sampling
of the population but people who choose to visit websites devoted to
jokes. Perhaps the most intriguing response was this one: "About her,
yes. About the media's insatiable, vulture-like coverage of her, no"
(http://www.answerbag.com/q_view/138725).

The distinction recalls studies of jokes about the Challenger disaster that proposed that the jokes were less expressions of insensitivity
about the tragedy than they were expressions of exasperation at media
coverage of the tragedy (Oring 1987; Smyth 1986). A modest amount
of coverage of a celebrity's life might prompt an appropriately modest
response to her death: perhaps some of us would feel a little bit sad.
Disproportionate coverage brings out the contrarian in many of us: we
don't feel *that* sad. The jokes are a form of folk-media criticism, a collective eyerolling over the news media's lack of restraint. They have
less to do with the foibles of the celebrities themselves than with the
unseemly level of news-media interest in them. There may be an element of self-mockery here as well: we who get caught up in the medi-
athon and thereby make it possible (which is to say, profitable) ought to
be ashamed of ourselves.

As it happens, I have found that much of the material on the humor
websites is pretty lame, from which I infer that it has not circulated as
much as the material I receive via e-mail or that made the lists of "most
e-mailed." The best site for my purposes has been Rec.Humor.Funny
(http://www.netfunny.com/rhf/), which subjects all submissions to
the site moderator's own critical eye, with a view toward keeping the
archive to a manageable size. Since the size issue is an important consideration for me also, I wound up relying on Rec.Humor.Funny as
my guide to the best topical jokes. I still prefer the way forwarding, by
approximating some of the risks of performance, winnows the supply
of jokes down to what might be thought of as a collective repertoire,
but the online discussion of jokes on the humor websites suggests how
forwarded jokes and electronic archives might be used in tandem: the

forwarded jokes give us a better sense of which jokes are in widest circulation at any given moment; the websites give us a better sense of what people think about the jokes.

Forwarded Joke Topics and Types

It is not entirely clear how the subject matter of online jokes differs from the subject matter of face-to-face jokes, if it differs at all, but my preliminary sense is that electronic communication is particularly well suited to topical folklore: just as the Internet lends itself to the reporting of news as soon as it happens, it lends itself to registering instantaneous responses to the news—including jokes. One way to test this proposition is to work with the Center for Media and Public Affairs' annual list of the most-joked-about topics by television's late-night comedians (http://www.cmpa.com/punchlines.html). It stands to reason that what those guys find jokeworthy is fodder for amateur jokesters as well, especially when we factor in the likelihood that the late-night comedians (Jay Leno, David Letterman, Conan O'Brian, et al.) set the joking agenda for the country. (When Dan Quayle's name surfaced as a possible presidential candidate in 2000, a joke suggested that the late-night comedians would be glad to have him back in public life: "I recently saw a poll on the news showing that Dan Quale [*sic*] had 7% of the Republican support. I found this very disturbing—I had not realized that such a large majority of our nations [*sic*] comedians were Republicans.") The CMPA's 2006 list—1. President Bush, 2. Dick Cheney, 3. Bill Clinton, 4. Mark Foley, 5. Hillary Clinton—tracks fairly well with my week's worth of forwards, with the exception of Florida Congressman Foley, whose sexual overtures to congressional pages came to light later in the year. The Enron/Arthur Andersen scandal was five years old by them, so it's no surprise that it was no longer fodder for the TV comedians.

Looking at ten years' worth of CMPA lists reveals several distinct patterns. First, unlike the Associated Press's annual list of the top ten stories of the year, with which it overlaps, all the CMPA entries are people, not topics such as the economy or oil prices. Second, most of the people are politicians. (They are also mostly men, but that follows from their being mostly politicians.) Third, as Oring (2003, 129–40) has also noted, Bill Clinton has had remarkable staying power as a joke target, remaining at or near the top of the list even after he left the White House and before he became more visible during his wife's presidential campaign. Here is my own composite list of top joke targets based on number of years on the CMPA list from 1997 to 2006:

1.   Bill Clinton (10 for 10)
2.   George W. Bush, Hillary Clinton, and Al Gore (8 for 10)
3.   Dick Cheney (7 for 10)
4.   Saddam Hussein (4 for 10)
5.   O. J. Simpson, Janet Reno, Monica Lewinsky, Martha Stewart, Osama bin Laden, Arnold Schwarzenegger (3 for 10).[3]

Armed with the CMPA lists, one can then go to the humor websites and search for particular joke topics. This raises one of the thorniest problems in dealing with Internet humor, the problem of professionalism and copyright. As broad as the definition of folklore has become, we stop short of saying that the jokes Jay Leno tells on the *Tonight Show* or the news story parodies that appear on the Onion website are folklore, at least initially. But netizens are notoriously casual when it comes to attribution. If people see or hear a joke they like, they pass it on, usually without bothering to say where they got it. So one thing that troubles me as I grapple with this material is what would happen if I traced an oft-e-mailed joke back to a professional source.

The list of "Top Ten Cheney Excuses" for accidentally shooting his hunting companion, for example, was unattributed to any source. "Top Ten" lists are a regular feature of the Letterman show, but they also inspire people to compose their own. Was this a Letterman list or a Letterman-like "folk" list? It was easy to find out it was from Letterman. Does this disqualify it from consideration as folklore even though it may closely resemble a joke whose provenance cannot be determined? Is known authorship or payment for services rendered a meaningful disqualifier? Tracing a joke to its source is a practical matter. Should we make the success or failure of this sort of detective work determinative of whether the joke is folklore or something else? If we make circulation a criterion, provenance ceases to matter. Whatever its source, a forwarded and refor-warded joke becomes folklore by virtue of its wide circulation. Its creator, even if he wants to sue for copyright infringement, should be flattered.

One obvious limitation to working with the CMPA lists is that jokes on television, even late-night television, are going to be much tamer than the "folk" jokes on the Internet. This means that not only are we going to see different jokes on the same topics, we will also see jokes on different topics. Dead celebrities are a prime example of a topic that might be off-limits on television but not in cyberspace, where anything goes, even if, as we have seen, one can find arguments between defenders of the harmlessness of sick jokes and those who are censorious of them. Interestingly, I have found far nastier jokes on humor websites than in my inbox, which again suggests that forwarding is more subject to the constraints of face-to-face interaction than posting, anonymously and invisibly, to a website.

In any case, my week's worth of forwarded jokes from early 2006 tracks pretty well with the CMPA lists. The task before me was to trace the individual items back to the news that precipitated them and then ask Elliott Oring's open-ended question of each: "What does this joke communicate?" (1992, 17). Such a question did not bind me to a single, invariably reductive theory, but the idea I return to again and again in my own work is that topical jokes are subversive. They violate the rules of deference and discretion when it comes to authority figures, bodily functions, and social conflict in a way that may appear anarchic, even nihilistic, but that is, at bottom, quite moralistic: their target is hypocrisy. Their mood is grimly amused exasperation with false piety, with speaking respectfully of those who deserve no respect, with euphemism, with all attempts to ignore the 800-pound gorillas in the room. In Mary Douglas's words, the joke "is an image of the leveling of hierarchy, the triumph of intimacy over formality, of unofficial values over official ones" (1991, 297). Orwell wrote that "every joke is a tiny revolution" (quoted in Powell and Paton 1988, 40). I will offer an example of how one might analyze a topical joke a little later in this chapter, but first let's take a quick look at which joke *types* are most popular online.

Whether one is sitting down to compose a poem or a song or a joke, the easiest way to go about it is to find a tried-and-true form and fill it with (slightly) new content. Most jokes are either riddles or stories with punch lines. Riddles are questions with unexpected answers. Look at enough of them and, as with "What was the last thing to go through X's mind?" or "What's the difference between X and Y?"[4] (or the flip side, "What do X and Y have in common?"), you see variations on several questions:

- What does/did X say to Y?
  Q: What did the Zen Buddhist say to the hot dog vendor?
  A: "Make me one with everything."

- What does X (if it were an acronym) stand for?
  Q: What does WACO stand for?
  A: We aren't coming out/We all cremated ourselves, etc.

- How many Xs does it take to screw in a light bulb?
  Q: How many bureaucrats does it take to screw in a light bulb ?
  A: Two. One to screw it in and one to screw it up.[5]

The story jokes are more varied. One persistent motif is the presence of three or more characters who engage in some form of one-upmanship. In a common subtype, the three characters have arrived at the pearly gates. Another story-joke type involves a magic lamp, a genie, and three wishes. A third joke type, as we have seen, is the Top Ten list. A fourth type is the parody, with a wide assortment of subtypes—parodies of Dear Abby letters, of newspaper stories and television news reports, of press releases, of chain letters, of commercials, of movie posters, of office memoranda, of instruction manuals in general and frequently asked questions (FAQs) in particular. Here's a widely circulated mock chain letter that parodies many of the popular rumors and legends circulating online. I found this version at Anvari.org:

> To all my friends, thanks to you sending me chain letters in 2003, the following occurred:
>
> I stopped drinking Coca Cola after I found out that it's good for removing toilet stains.
>
> I stopped going to the movies for fear of sitting on a needle infected with AIDS.
>
> I smell like a wet dog since I stopped using deodorants because they cause cancer.
>
> I don't leave my car in the parking lot or any other place and some-times I even have to walk about 7 blocks for fear that someone will drug me with a perfume sample and try to rob me.
>
> I also stopped answering the phone for fear that they ask me to dial a stupid number and then I get a phone bill from hell with calls to Uganda, Singapore, and Tokyo.
>
> I stopped consuming several foods for fear that the estrogens they contain may turn me gay.
>
> I also stopped eating chicken and hamburgers because they are noth-ing other than horrible mutant freaks with no eyes or feathers that are bred in a lab so that places like McDonalds can sell them Big Macs.
>
> I also stopped drinking anything out of a can for fear that I will get sick from the rat feces and urine.

I think I'm turning gay because when I go to parties, I don't look at any babe no matter how hot she is, for fear that she will take my kidneys and leave me taking a nap in a bathtub full of ice.

I also donated all my savings to the Amy Bruce account, a sick girl that was about to die in the hospital about 7,000 times. Funny that girl, she's been 7 since 1993. . . . .

I went bankrupt from bounced checks that I made expecting the $150,000 total that Microsoft and AOL were supposed to send me when I participated in their special e-mail program.

But I am positive that all this is the cause of a stinking chain that I broke or forgot to follow and I got a curse from Satan himself.

IMPORTANT NOTE: If you send this e-mail to at least 1200 people in the next 10 seconds, a bird will crap on you today.

Visual Joke Genres

While it was certainly possibly to craft photographic and videographic jokes and parodies before the digital age, computers have made them far cheaper and easier to produce and distribute. The "virtual Niagara of lore flowing over the electronic grapevine" (Brunvand 2001, 65) includes *photoshops*, or digitally altered photos; *mash-ups*, which are clips made from extant commercials, films or news footage; folk animations; and parodies of print advertisements or movie posters. There are a number of fairly obvious reasons for the popularity of commercial parodies and jokes: our lives are saturated with these messages so they spring readily to mind for the creator of a parody and are readily recognized by the receiver of the parody. Plus, they cry out for parody because they are so inherently cynical. Whatever they purport to be about, they are always ultimately about one thing: selling goods or services. The more "warm and fuzzy" they are, the more cynical they seem to be. MasterCard's "priceless" campaign, which debuted in 1998, is among the warmest and fuzziest. Therefore, it is among the most oft-parodied.

The "priceless" commercials show people having a delightful time and the prices of the various goods and service they are enjoying. What it all adds up to, though, is not the sum of the costs, but the pricelessness of the experiences. "There are some things money can't buy," says the voiceover. "For everything else, there's MasterCard." The verbal/visual parodies hinge on the dual meaning of the word priceless. MasterCard uses it to mean "worth more than money can buy." As parodists use it, it's an all-purpose superlative, as in "too funny" or "too perfect." A Google search for "priceless parodies" yields dozens of sites. Their messages are consistent with what Oring (1987) found in the Challenger joke cycle, with its plays on well-known TV spots for beer (Bud Lite), shampoo (Head and Shoulders) and soft drinks (7UP). Paraphrasing Dorst (1990), Ellis, who includes the credit-card spoof in his study of 9/11 humor, writes that topical jokes appropriate "mass media imagery in order to challenge official definitions of reality" (2002, 2). Here are a few news-related examples from my collection:

1. Elian

The photo, which is untouched, shows two armed men in helmets, goggles, and olive-drab uniforms. The one in the foreground appears to be confronting a frightened-looking civilian who is holding a young boy in his arms.

> A Rubber Inner Tube and Trip to America: $17.38
> A Plane Ticket from Cuba for Dad: $325.00
> A FULL SWAT Team w/ Automatics: $75,000
> The look on the little bastard's face: Priceless

The back story: The photo, taken in April 2000, would be recognizable to most people. It appeared on the front page of many newspapers as the culminating moment in a long tug-o'-war over a six-year-old Cuban boy named Elian Gonzalez. Elian had fled Cuba in a motorboat with his mother, who died en route to Florida. The boy, found floating on an inner tube, then went to stay with his relatives in Miami. The boy's father wanted him to return to Cuba. On one side were those who thought Elian should be reunited with his father; on the other were those who thought the boy would be better off remaining in the United States. Finally, Immigration and Naturalization Service agents were ordered to seize the boy from his Miami relatives and take him to his father. This was one of those mediathons where coverage of the story was out of all proportion to the importance of the story. The parody put the boy—but really, the story—in its place. This was not the final battle in the great twentieth-century war between communism and democracy. It was a custody battle.

2. Bush/NASCAR

The news photo shows President Bush shaking hands with a man in a jumpsuit emblazoned with patches from makers of various automobiles and automotive parts. A number of similarly attired men look on. A crowded grandstand is in the background.

> Air Force One Flight: $1,000,000
> Extra Secret Service: $200,000
> Having the Taxpayers Foot the Cost of Your
>   Campaign Stop: Priceless

The back story: NASCAR dads—white men who tended to be culturally conservative but receptive to Democratic appeals on economic issues—were identified as "the election cycle's hottest new constituency" during the 2004 presidential race. President Bush dropped in on the Daytona 500 in February 2004, greeted the 180,000 spectators and said, "Gentlemen, start your engines." Both engines and spectators roared.

One of the marvels of Bush's career is that an Ivy-League-educated scion of a wealthy New England family succeeded in representing himself as a regular guy from West Texas. The creator of this parody wasn't buying it. The parody could have served as an illustration of Ellen Goodman's column in the *Boston Globe*: "All this was billed—and I do mean billed—as a presidential, not a political, visit" (2004). The purpose of Bush's drop-in, Marc Cooper wrote in the *Nation*, was "to burnish the Everyman cultural pose that Bush has so successfully honed, and this was a ripe audience" (2004).

3. Bush/Cocaine

The photo shows a smiling President Bush in the cabin of an airplane, presumably Air Force One, with a plastic water-pipe in his hand. The wording on the familiar overlapping red and gold circles of the MasterCard logo has been changed to read MasterRace.

> New Bong: $50
> Cocaine Habit: $300
> Finding Out that the Good-Old-Boy Network Can
>   Still Rig an Election in the Deep South: Priceless
> For the rest of us, there's honesty.

The back story: When reporters asked candidate Bush in the summer of 1999 whether he had ever used cocaine, he declined to answer, apart from alluding to his "irresponsible youth." Many drew their own conclusions. The rest of the parody links Bush's lack of candor about drug use with the way he allegedly stole the election by stealing votes in Florida.

4. Bin Laden

These next three examples are similar. One shows Osama bin Laden in the crosshairs.[6]

> Trip to Afghanistan: $800
> High-Powered Sniper Rifle: $1,000
> Hotel Stay with Accessible Roof: $100
> Scoring a Head Shot on Osama bin Laden: Priceless
> For everyone else, there's cruise missiles.

The next version shows photos of a bullet, a rifle, a commercial jet, and a head shot of Osama bin Laden.

> Ammunition: $12
> New Rifle: $385
> Airline Travel to Afghanistan: $1,349
> Clear Line of Sight: Priceless

The third photo shows a bomb.

> Gross Weight: 15,000 lbs.
> Aluminum Powder Explosive: 12,000 lbs.
> Unit Cost: $27,318
> The Look on Their Faces When This Ugly
>   Motherfucker Falls into Their Tent: Priceless

The back story: These parodies come across as criticisms of the Bush administration's failure to bring Osama bin Laden to justice, though that may not have been the intent of the creators. The fake ads suggest that getting bin Laden is so clearly desirable and should be a very simple matter, in terms of both logistics and expense: Why, then, is he still at large? Perhaps, the parodists did not believe Bush's tough talk about wanting bin Laden "dead or alive." The more typical American approach would be to capture and try him in a court of law, as was done with Saddam Hussein. Seizing someone, which can only happen with troops laying hands on him, is a lot more complicated than killing him, which can be accomplished at a distance.

5. Hillary Clinton

The photo shows Hillary Clinton shaking the right hand of a soldier who has crossed the middle and index fingers of his left hand, signifying that he is not as pleased to be meeting the senator as it would appear.

Haircut: $8
BDUs: $100
Knowing You Just Mocked the "Smartest Woman
On Earth" Right Under Her Fat Elitist Nose:
PRICELESS!!!

The back story: According to Snopes.com, the photo, taken in Iraq in 2003, has not been altered. An alternative version, sans the Priceless parody, offers this explanation:

> Picture shows that this guy has been thru Survival School. He's giving the sign of "coercion" with his left hand. These hand signs are taught in survival school to be used by future POW's to send messages back to our intelligence services viewing the photo or video. This guy was being coerced to holding hands with Hillary. Little did she know that he would tell us.

The Snopes site says there is no evidence of outright coercion (http://www.snopes.com/photos/military/crossed.asp). Oh, and BDUs means "battle dress uniforms" (I had to look it up).

I have only begun to look at live-action and animated creations, so I will devote the remainder of this discussion to photoshops. The apparent verisimilitude of the photographic image drew pranksters right from the start. Photos could be faked before the film was exposed—by arranging a tableau—and after—by cutting out one image and pasting it onto another. Folklorists have been interested in two types of hoax photographs: spirit photographs, which purport to capture ghosts and other otherworldly manifestations on film (Wojcik 1996), and tall-tale photographs, which typically show a gigantic fruit or vegetable on a farm wagon or railroad flatcar, or a chimerical beast like the jackalope—half jackrabbit and half antelope (Welsch 1974). As the name implies, the tall-tale postcard is offered as real; gullible souls like I was at age twelve when I saw my first jackalope card might even believe it.

The best of these images are pretty seamless: if you disbelieve them, it isn't because the cutting-and-pasting was poorly executed, but because you know enough about the world to doubt the existence of supersized potatoes or antlered rabbits. But when the cutting-and-pasting involved real scissors or knives and real paste, it took considerable skill. And there was still the problem of the slightly raised surface of the superimposed image, resolved only by taking a photograph of the photograph. At that point, the project became not just labor intensive, but costly. Computers, then, don't allow us to do what could not be done before as much as they allow us to do it better, more easily, and, aside from the initial outlay for hardware or software—presumably purchased for purposes other than doctoring photographs—less expensively. This, logically, makes it more likely that people with a modicum of skill will alter photographs just for the fun of it.

In his survey of what he refers to as World Trade Center humor, Ellis expresses surprise at "the proliferation of 'computer-generated cybercartoons' . . . a phenomenon that will need much closer study in the future" (2002, 13). *Cybercartoons* is a good name, to the extent that the closest analog for most of this material is the political cartoon, but I prefer the term *photoshops* to *cybercartoons* or *computer-generated art* for two reasons. First, most of these images are digitally altered photographs rather than cartoons, which I think of as drawings, whether they are drawn by hand or with the aid of the computer. Second, *photoshops* is the preferred (emic) term among people who create, upload, and archive the images.[7]

Evidence of the robustness of the culture of photoshopping is found on websites like the aptly named Worth1000.com, where aficionados offer step-by-step instruction in how to achieve such effects as "zombifying, gender bending, face swapping, fattening, and aging." Also included are guides to the making of a specific image:

- How I turned a stack of pancakes into something you probably wouldn't want to find on your plate
- How I puppetized Charlize [Theron]
- How to turn Tom Cruise into an alien ("Photoshop Tutorials")

Worth1000.com hosts what it calls a "daily manipulation contest." Those who would enter photoshopped images involving Britney Spears, President Bush, "scantily clad women (i.e. in bikinis) for no practical reason," "Star Wars references," the Statue of Liberty, the World Trade Center, Hitler "or Nazi references," or Osama bin Laden "or terrorist references" are advised that these are "annoying overused entries (clichés)" and therefore are unlikely to win ("Entering Contests"). Here, too, the best material seems to be forwarded.

As with verbal jokes, photoshopping lends itself to commentary on the news, for the simple reason that news photographs constitute a readily available supply of images to play with. Consider this e-mailed photo, which bore the subject line "Got Fish?" and was accompanied by this comment: "Disgusting. But funny." The photo showed the two presidents Bush on what appears to be the deck of a sportfishing boat. George Bush the elder, smiling in cap and windbreaker, is holding a fishing rod. George Bush the younger, grinning in leather jacket and sunglasses, is holding a striped bass. That's the foreground. In the background we see nine or ten people, most of whom, if not all, appear to be African Americans, wading through waist-high water on a city street.

Here is some of what one needed to know to understand why the photograph was disgusting but funny. The Bushes are members of the leisure class, which likes to do things like sportfishing. The streets of New Orleans had flooded when Hurricane Katrina made landfall the week before. Many African American citizens of New Orleans are poor and therefore lacked the ways and means to heed the order to evacuate the city. They were trapped. Then-president Bush in particular and authorities at all levels of government in general were perceived as being catastrophically and criminally slow to respond to the gravity of the situation. The message of the photo: the Bushes are so out of touch with the plight of the poor, especially poor blacks, that they saw the flooding of New Orleans as nothing more than an opportunity to do a little fishing. The name of the file is BushVaca.jpg—an abbreviated version of Bush vacation. The subject line "Got Fish?" refers to the long-running (and much-parodied) "Got Milk?" advertising campaign.[8]

Thus far, the meanings I have teased out of this photo explain only why it's disgusting. To understand why it's funny, you have to know that the photograph is a fake, which is to say you have to know that it is possible to digitally alter or combine photographs in ways that make the altered photo almost indistinguishable from a photograph of a scene as it appeared to the photographer through the camera's viewfinder. Snopes.com says it received many "Is this real?" inquiries about "Got Fish?" and displayed the original photos from which the spoof version was made (http://snopes.com/katrina/photos/recreate.asp).

That some people believed these images to be true tells us two things: (1) even though we are routinely exposed to and aware of realistic digital images, our kneejerk response to the physically plausible image (as opposed to, say, a horse's head on a man's body, which would be a physically implausible image) is to accept it at face value; and (2) we are likelier to believe a physically plausible image if the content accords with beliefs we already hold. In the present instance, I suspect the believers are those whose boundless contempt for George W. Bush makes them susceptible to almost any calumny. The fact that "Got Fish?" hadn't appeared in any newspapers wouldn't surprise them. If you believe "Got Fish?" it's no stretch to believe in conspiracies to suppress news. Presumably, these people did not find the photograph amusing.

Those who laughed at "Got Fish?" didn't recognize it as a fake because they were able to spot the telltale signs of a cut-and-paste job, but because the conduct depicted in the photo was so breathtakingly inappropriate to the situation. Borrowing Elliott Oring's language (1992), "Got Fish?" is appropriately incongruous in multiple ways. Although digitally altered photographs have become commonplace, we continue to marvel at how realistic a fake can look. The disconnect between the visual plausibility of the image and the implausibility of the conduct is startling, but it would not be funny if the conduct, though literally false, did not express a figurative truth. If we laugh at "Got Fish?" we laugh because someone has cleverly brought together these disparate scenes to craft a false, yet maliciously apt representation of the Bushes' perceived insensitivity and disengagement.

Summary

This overview barely scratches the surface of the world of forwarded jokes, but I hope I have made several points. First, e-mail may be the most popular medium we have at the moment for the transmission of jokes. Second, though forwarding lacks most of the elements of a real-time performance, it may be a more naturalistic medium than humor websites—to the extent that receiving a joke via e-mail is more like hearing a good one from a colleague who pops his head in your office door, whereas going to a website is more like going to a comedy club or watching a comedy show on television. Third, it offers almost a daily snapshot of which joke types and topics are popular. Fourth, it lends itself to a genre of humor—the visual joke—that is barely possible in face-to-face joke telling. And fifth, as I tried to show in my brief discussions of the "Priceless" parodies and the "Got Fish?" photoshop, we needn't be stymied by the dearth of social-contextual information, given the abundance of cultural-contextual information. By going back to the news-media sources of the jokes and to the humor websites that register reactions to the jokes, we can begin to understand what they have to tell us about how computer jockeys across the land are reacting to the news of the day.

Appendix: A Week in the Life of My Inbox

Here is a sampling of the jokes that poured into my inbox during the week of 12 February 2006:

Sunday, 12 February:

- Two digitally altered photos under the subject line "German Pope Makes Changes in Mass." The first shows Pope Benedict XVI raising a glass of beer instead of a chalice of wine. The second shows him bearing a pretzel where the eucharist would be.
- A joke letter to the IRS, in which the taxpayer encloses "four toilet seats (value $2,400) and six hammers (value $1,029), bringing my total remitted to $3,429," to pay a $3,407 tax bill. (Citing a *USA Today* story, the taxpayer proposes sending the $22 overpayment to the Presidential Election Fund in the form of one 1.5-inch Phillips-head screw.

Monday, 13 February:

- An outsourcing joke. The doctored photo shows a man pedaling a stationary-bicycle-like generator that he is using to power up his laptop, the lid of which is labeled, "Microsoft Tech Support Center #25 Bombay."
- Two jokes about President Bush:
  1. "Never Underestimate the Power of Makeup." This joke features a series of before-and-after photos of women who look plain before, then glamorous after. The last pair shows a horse's rear end before and the face of George W. Bush after.
  2. "This just in: In an attempt to thwart the spread of bird flu, George W. Bush has just ordered the bombing of the Canary Islands."[9]

Tuesday, 14 February :

- Two more Bush jokes. One is lyrics to "The Kennebunkport Hillbilly," sung to the tune of the "Beverly Hillbillies" theme song. The other is a journalism ethics joke. While taking pictures of a flood you [a photojournalist] see President Bush hanging on to a tree limb for dear life. "You can either put down your camera and save him, or take a Pulitzer Prize winning photograph of him as he loses his grip on the limb. So, here's the question and think carefully before you answer the question below: Which lens would you use?"
- A Bill and Hillary joke dated 7 February 2001. Hillary asks Bill why he keeps a box under their bed containing three beer cans and $81,000 in cash. "Whenever I was unfaithful to you," Bill says, "I put an empty beer can in the box under the bed to

remind myself not to do it again." Hillary figures three infideli-
ties in thirty years of marriage isn't bad. Then she asks about
the cash. "Well," Bill says, "whenever the box filled up with
empty cans, I took them to the recycling center and redeemed
them for cash."

- A Bush-as-numbskull joke dated 9 February 2001. During a visit
  to the White House, President-elect Bush uses the bathroom.
  Later, he tells Laura how impressed he was with President
  Clinton's solid gold urinal. Laura shares this story with Hillary.
  That evening, Hillary says to Bill: "Well, I found out who peed
  in your saxophone."[10]

Wednesday, 15 February:

- A parody of the White House's handling of Cheney's hunting accident in the form of a transcript from "Ye Olde Briefing
  Room," in which a presidential spokesman stonewalls questions
  about Vice President Aaron Burr's role in the death of Alexander
  Hamilton (attributed to Salon.com).

Thursday, 16 February:

- Three Bush jokes, including this one:
  While suturing a laceration on the hand of a ninety-year-old
  man, a doctor and the old man were discussing Bush's health-
  care-reform ideas.
  The old man said, "Well, ya know, old Bush is a post turtle."
  Not knowing what he meant, the doctor asked him what a
  "post turtle" was.
  And he said, "When you're driving down a country road,
  and you come across a fence post with a turtle balanced on top,
  that's a post turtle. You know he didn't get there by himself, he
  doesn't belong there, he can't get anything done while he's up
  there, and you just want to help the poor thing down."
- A Cheney hunting joke in the form of an animated game. Cheney
  raises his shotgun. A covey of quail flies up from the trees. One
  is instructed to click one's mouse when one wants Cheney to
  shoot. I do so. Cheney spins and shoots one of the three people
  standing off to the side.

Friday, 17 February:

- "Unconfirmed Urban Myth (1/19/02): Hard Laughter." A female
  news anchor in Michigan, the day after it was supposed to have

snowed and didn't, turned to the weatherman and asked, "So, Bob, where's that eight inches you promised me last night?" Not only did the weatherman have to leave the set, but half the crew did too, because they were laughing so hard.

- Five Enron / Arthur Andersen jokes:
    1. "How to Explain Enron to Your Children": facetious explanations of feudalism, fascism, communism, totalitarianism, capitalism, and finally Enron venture capitalism follow.
    2. The second is a parody appeal to adopt, for only $20,835 a month, an Enron executive who is "living at, or just below the seven-figure salary level."
    3. The third consists of a series of sample math problems from 1950, 1960, 1970, 1980, 1990, and 2000. In the 2000 problem a businessman's costs exceed his sales receipts, yet he makes a substantial profit. "This is verified by his auditing firm, Arthur Andersen . . ."
    4. A teacher asks her pupils what their fathers do for a living. When it's Jimmy's turn, he says his dad is a striptease dancer in a cabaret for gay men. Later, the teacher asks Jimmy privately if what he said was true. Jimmy blushes and says, "I'm sorry, but my dad is an auditor for Arthur Andersen and I was just too embarrassed to say so."
    5. The fifth joke is a first-person account of an encounter with a ragged twelve-year-old boy who is holding a one-hundred-dollar bill. The boy tells a sad tale of his impoverished family and about being deprived of his other hundred-dollar bill by an older boy. The writer asks him why he didn't cry for help. The boy says he did, in vain. "How loud did you scream?" the writer asks. The boy whispers, "Help me!" The writer grabs the other hundred and flees. The account is signed "Kenneth Lay, Enron CEO."

- Two unattributed political jokes (one of which is a metajoke):
    1. I don't approve of political jokes . . . I've seen too many of them get elected.
    2. How come we choose from just two people for President and fifty for Miss America?

- A Social Security joke:
    Kathy and Suzy are having a conversation during their lunch break.
    Kathy asks, "So, Suzy, how's your sex life these days?"

Suzy replies, "Oh, you know. It's the usual, Social Security kind."

"Social Security?" Kathy asked quizzically.

"Yeah, you get a little each month, but it's not really enough to live on."

- A couple of Bill Clinton jokes:

  1. Clinton is in the supermarket picking up some things for the new office in New York when a stock boy accidentally bumps into him. "Pardon me," the stock boy says. "Sure," Clinton replies, "but it'll cost you."

  2. The second is a letter from Clinton to the "Federal Aviation Agency" suggesting that strippers be employed as flight attendants to prevent hijackings. "Muslims would be afraid to get on the planes for fear of seeing a naked woman, and of course, everyone in this country would start flying again in hopes of seeing a naked woman. We would have no more hijackings, and the airline industry would have record sales."

- A joke about three fallen religious leaders. "Jesse Jackson, Jim Baker [sic], and Jimmy Swaggert have written an impressive new book . . . It's called: *Ministers Do More Than Lay People*."
- A Bush-as-numbskull joke in which he eats his first bowl of matzoh ball soup and asks, "Do the Jews eat any other parts of the matzoh, or just the balls?"
- The Cheney joke of the day is a two-panel photo cartoon. In the first panel, Dick Cheney is on the phone; in the second, Bill Clinton is on the phone. Cheney is saying, "Bill—interested in doing a little quail hunting next weekend?? Bring the wife!"

Saturday, 18 February:

- A joke about a new Japanese student in an American school who incurs the wrath of his classmates by being the only one to correctly identify the sources of some famous quotes from American history. As the classmates mutter imprecations, Suzuki mistakenly thinks that these, too, are quotes, so he continues to name incorrect, but humorously apt sources: Lee Iacocca, George Bush, Bill Clinton, Gary Condit. Seeing how the teacher is reacting to this little scene, one of the students says, "Oh shit, now we're in BIG trouble!" To which Suzuki responds, "Arthur Andersen, 2001."

- Two more Bush-as-numbskull jokes and a Bush administration light bulb joke:

  1. Bush is on a plane that is about to crash. There are five passengers on board but only four parachutes. Bush is the third passenger to grab a pack and jump out of the plane. That leaves the Pope and a twelve-year-old boy. The Pope, citing his advanced age, offers the last parachute to the boy. The boy assures him there are still two parachutes left: the president took his schoolbag.

  2. Bush, Einstein, and Picasso arrive at the Pearly Gates at the same time. Each must prove to St. Peter that he is who he says he is. Einstein does so by filling a blackboard with the theory of relativity, Picasso by sketching a mural. When it's Bush's turn he asks, "Who are Einstein and Picasso?" St. Peter says, "Come on in, George."

  3. "How many members of the Bush administration does it take to change a light bulb?" The answer is ten [I include only the three best of these ten]:
      - One to tell the nations of the world that they are either for changing the light bulb or for eternal darkness;
      - One to give a billion dollar no-bid contract to Halliburton for the new light bulb;
      - One to arrange a photograph of Bush, dressed as a janitor, standing on a stepladder under the banner "Bulb Accomplished."

Notes

1. Oring (2003), on the other hand, argues that it is possible to learn as much or more about the webmasters who traffic in jokes as we learn about a casual acquaintance who tells us a joke in the "real world."
2. Web cameras and Internet telephony have introduced the possibility of using voice, gesture, and facial expression and, therefore, variation, in online joke telling.
3. The only other surprise on this list, apart from Bill Clinton's dominance, is former U.S. Attorney General Janet Reno. My suspicion, soon confirmed, was that most of the jokes had to do with her central role in the protracted battle over custody of six-year-old Cuban refugee Elian Gonzalez in 2000. But I was also reminded that she ran (unsuccessfully) for governor of Florida in 2002 and that she took some of the blame for the FBI's disastrous raid on the Branch Davidian compound in Waco, Texas, in 1993.

4. A subtype of the "What's the difference" riddle involves a spoonerism:
    Q: "What's the difference between a rooster and a lawyer?
    A: A rooster wakes up in the morning and clucks defiance . . ."
5. For a discussion of light bulb jokes, see Dundes (1981).
6. The image recalls a photocopied cartoon of the Ayatollah Khomeini's face appearing in a gun sight's crosshairs that circulated via fax machine in 1979 (Dundes 1991a).
7. See, for example, Choe (2001) or Park (2002).
8. Another "Got Milk?" parody aimed at George W. Bush shows him with a bag of cocaine and a bit of white powder on his nose. The tag line is "Got Coke?"
9. This joke is reminiscent of a joke about the 1989 Loma Prieta earthquake in California: after the earthquake struck, President Bush dispatched Vice President Quayle to the epicenter. The vice president flew to Orlando. According to the Rec.Humor.Funny website, Julian Bond originally made a similar joke about Dan Quayle during a speech at the University of Colorado in 1989. The site says Bond was quoted in the *Boulder Daily Camera* as having said, "He thinks *Roe v. Wade* are options for crossing the Potomac."
10. President Clinton's saxophone playing became famous when he appeared on the *Arsenio Hall* late-night television show during the 1992 campaign.

Chapter 5

Epistemology, the Sociology of Knowledge, and the *Wikipedia* Userbox Controversy

WILLIAM WESTERMAN

All knowledge is folk knowledge. Whether we are concerned with the scientific findings by a Nobel laureate published in an academic journal, the report of the destructive power of a hurricane reported in a local newspaper, gossip about a neighbor spread via the rumor mill, or a local legend, all knowledge is produced within the communication conventions of a particular community and disseminated in ways that are acceptable or trustworthy to a degree held customary by that same group. The Nobel laureate is published through a process of peer-review, a form of group approval, and speaks to other specialists who read that scientific journal. The local newspaper reports as quickly as possible on the storm's damage and its effects to readers who are familiar with a particular locale and who may know the affected individuals. The rumor mill circulates among people who know one another, if not first hand, then separated by no more than two or three degrees. What distinguishes these forms of knowledge is not, as most academics outside the field of folkloristics[1] would argue, a level of accuracy and truth or the professionally trained academic expertise involved in their production, but the verifiability of the statements, the strength of the evidence, and the transparency with which such knowledge is generated.

This is what makes the field of folkloristics epistemologically radical: not that we folklorists reject in a postmodern way the notion of a single "truth," but that we see all forms of knowledge communication as essentially similar, including our own, and the degrees of "truth" and of "belief" are questions which, while relevant, are measured along different axes.[2] All communication, then, whether academic or interpersonal, exists in the contexts of groups of insiders, usually a smaller set than the set of outsiders in the world at large. Knowledge can be conveyed among groups of insiders (for example, ophthalmologists speaking to other ophthalmologists at a medical conference who have a shared methodology and body of knowledge in the field), or it can be produced by insiders for the consumption of those outside of that particular world (such as doctors writing a health column in a newspaper or website). Folklorists, then, judge validity not on the basis of academic prestige or credentials—again, including our own—but on verifiability, trustworthiness, honesty, use-value, transparency, context, and a range of other criteria we have not yet fully articulated. This is why bias bothers us so little. We know it is there, in everyone, because everyone is a member of some groups (class, gender, educational level, region, and so on) and not others. In the advancement of knowledge, the issue that can be useful beyond group borders is how to filter for bias, since bias is adjunct to knowledge, like white on rice.

Specifically, this chapter concerns knowledge construction and community formation among the editors of the largest encyclopedia the world has ever known, the *Wikipedia* project. If indeed individuals who share at least one common factor become part of a folk group, then it follows that those who contribute to a common Internet-based project, such as *Wikipedia*, will share their own folk traditions. That such contributors would develop folklore content consisting of folk speech, argot, and customs is a given.

What makes *Wikipedia* more interesting—like social networking sites (which its editors adamantly assert it is not[3])—is the formation of a large group of editors and writers and, within that, smaller communities organized around interest areas or administrative tasks. But what is most significant is that a mutually understood system of knowledge production has emerged within a few years, along with an evolving epistemology—or epistemological methodology—that is shaped by the community and that has been archived in the continually-being-edited pages of the site. This provides contemporary corroborating evidence for Steven Shapin's observation that

> what we know about the world is arrived at, sustained, and recognized through collective action . . . no single individual can constitute

knowledge; all the individual can do is offer claims, with evidence, arguments, and inducements, to the community for its assessment. Knowledge is the result of the community's evaluations and actions . . . Since the acts of knowledge-making and knowledge-protecting capture so much of communal life, communities may be effectively described through their economies of truth. (1995, 6)[4]

We cannot be present at the earliest editorial meetings of the *Oxford English Dictionary* or the *Encyclopedia Britannica* except through historical reconstruction,[5] but we can observe and eavesdrop on the conversations among groups of otherwise total strangers across the globe who have come together to collaboratively produce an encyclopedia that will eventually dwarf the aforementioned two projects. To pick up on a question asked by Barbara Kirshenblatt-Gimblett over ten years ago, "What is produced socially when strangers communicate instantaneously with one another across vast distances with little or no prospect of ever meeting face to face?" (1996, 23), I ask, What happens not only when those strangers communicate, but when they try to write an encyclopedia together?

Within five short years—time being drastically foreshortened as it has been throughout the development of the Internet—not only was there a functioning argot, a community code of behavior, and organized subgroups within the larger community, there was also a discussion of how to handle bias and political affiliation in the project itself. Even more specifically, this debate revolved around the right of contributors to post their political and social affiliations in the form of little graphic banners, called *userboxes*, in their own biographical profiles. The community's aesthetic—that is, establishing what comprises quality in the crafting of explanatory articles—was openly debated. This became a fascinating folk discourse on how bias shapes scholarship. All of these shared behaviors, from slang to aesthetics to ethics, are of central concern to folklorists and are key to developing a sociology of knowledge construction.

Wikipedia is an online, Internet-based encyclopedia that was launched on 15 January 2001 by founders Jimmy Wales (sometimes referred to in the community as "Jimbo" Wales) and Larry Sanger as an open-source encyclopedia, a medium that the Internet can accommodate but printed matter effectively cannot ("Wikipedia"). The idea of a *wiki*—originally a term from the Hawai'ian language meaning "quick"—is that anyone with an Internet connection can enter the site and have the ability to change its content through its existing programming language ("Wiki"). This builds on the relatively new tradition of *open-source* software (such as, most famously, Linux), meaning anyone can have access to changing the code, because the program is not covered by typical legalistic conceptions of exclusive intellectual property, and such changes are usually made by volunteers working in community.[6] In other words, anyone at any time can use a computer to change, delete, or add text to, in this case, any entry in the encyclopedia, or even create a new entry. The computer technology to do this has only been available since 1995 ("History of Wikis"). This is what is and remains radically different about *Wikipedia* relative to the history of print encyclopaediae. It is remarkable that to this day many of the users of *Wikipedia* are unaware that anyone can edit or change the information written therein.[7]

As of 1 April 2008, *Wikipedia* consisted of 10 million articles in over 250 languages, including 2.3 million entries in the English-language edition, and more than 50,000 entries in each of 31 other languages, including two artificial languages, Esperanto and Volapük.[8] There are also additional websites in the *Wikipedia* family, including dictionary sites, news sites, and media sites. The media sites, such as Mediawiki.org, provide free software packages and templates for people to start their own wiki projects, including their own encyclopedias. So, for example, in addition to the Punjabi-language *Wikipedia* (http://pa.wikipedia.org/) which at 300 articles is relatively small,[9] there is also SikhiWiki, which bills itself as an English-language "Encyclomedia of the Sikhs" ("you don't have to be a scholar, a pundit or a gyani to contribute"), with nearly 4,000 articles thus far.[10] This chapter chiefly concerns a debate that took place during the editing of the English-language and German-language *Wikipedias*, but some of these other sources may be referred to in the notes.

For anyone who uses the Internet, *Wikipedia* is well known because the major search engines will refer any user to it among the top hits they offer. The English-language edition receives hundreds of thousands if not millions of hits daily. In February 2008, for example, the Main Page was accessed 136 million times, while "Barack Obama" was viewed 2.25 million times and "Hillary Clinton" a mere 475,000 ("Wikipedia Article Traffic Statistics"). As of September 2006, the last month for which English-language statistics were maintained, there were over 43,000 contributors (also known as writers or editors, but within the group known as *Wikipedians*), making at least five edits per month ("Wikipedia Statistics"), out of more than 6 million registered users worldwide (which includes individuals using duplicate names). In addition, there are approximately 1,500 editors elected to have additional administrative privileges, known as *admins* (or, alternatively, *sysops*—system operators), an important part of the system of social organization of this knowledge community ("Wikipedia: Administrators"; "Wikipedia: Special Statistics").

A brief overview of what *Wikipedia* sites look like and how they function is necessary in order to understand the debate featured here.[11] One who accesses a *Wikipedia* article page sees black print in a sans serif font on a white background. This background is surrounded on the top and left-hand sides with a grey background and the *Wikipedia* logo in the upper left-hand corner; there is also the pale silhouette of an open book spread across the top of the page. Words in the text that are hyperlinked are in blue, meaning a viewer can click on these terms and be taken to the article about that concept (the links are red if there is not yet a corresponding entry). For example, someone viewing the "Barack Obama" page can click on such terms as "Illinois," "Harvard Law School," or a related article, "United States Senate career of Barack Obama," and be taken to those pages. This is an article page, which is headed in large boldface type with the title of the article. All *Wikipedia* articles are alphabetized by the first word or name in the entry title.

Each such page has four tabs along the top, marked "article," "discussion," "edit this page," and "history."[12] Clicking on the "discussion" tab takes one to a page that may include commentary on the article itself, including evaluations by various editors who review other articles, questions or errors that need to be addressed, or criticisms of the articles or the work of the writers. The "edit" tab takes one to another sort of page, where the text of the article is now in an editable format, written in Courier font. Any reader can change this text, then can click on one tab which will present a preview in "article" format for viewing and proofreading or click on another to "Save page" in its new format. Hyperlinking in the text is activated by typing double brackets before and after the term.[13] The "history" tab is a list of all changes and edits to the article since it was initially created, with each prior version available in an archived form; comparative views are possible, showing changes during a given period or between revisions.

Contrary to what many believe, the editing process is not unsigned and is rarely, if ever, truly anonymous.[14] Editors can make changes either logged in to the system or not. If not logged in, the IP address of the computer from which the changes were made will be recorded; this is how changes have been traced back, for example, to a number of Congressional offices ("USA Congressional Staff Edits"). If one is logged in as a registered user, then the author's user name will be recorded. The user name, like an e-mail I.D., can be as real or as fanciful as one wants. Some are more obvious than others, or can be deduced. For example, User:Kbandersen and User:Sbronner[15] who have edited the articles "Kurt Andersen" and "Simon J. Bronner," respectively, are likely, though not certainly, to be

Kurt Andersen and Simon J. Bronner themselves ("Revision History of Kurt Andersen"; "Revision History of Simon J. Bronner"). We know less about User:68.83.74.246, except that since thirteen of his sixteen edits are of the article "Simon J. Bronner" and the fourteenth is the addition of Bronner's works to the article bibliography for "Folkloristics," it is reasonable to assume (barring an IP search) that this too is Bronner himself, or perhaps a very devoted student ("User Contributions"). In theory, at least, this editing history will be accessible to scholars forever. On the other hand, the real name of User:Darwinek, an editor with an interest in African American culture, folklore, and history who had started hundreds of articles and currently is thirty-third on the list of most active Wikipedians ("Wikipedia: List of Wikipedians," 2 April 2008)—including "American Folklife Center," "Archive of Folk Culture," "Alan Jabbour," and "Sharpe James"—remains unknown. Every registered user gets a *user page* ("Wikipedia: User Page"), and if we are to believe User:Darwinek's page, he is a student born in 1985, of Polish nationality, who resides somewhere in Central Europe ("User: Darwinek," 6 October 2007).[16]

The anonymity, or pseudonymity factor, rankles scholars in much the same way that anonymity in folk arts could be used by fine arts scholars to demean the artistic value of craft. The situation is not completely analogous, but it is significant for folklorists. One of the critiques of the reliability of *Wikipedia* is that the academic credentials of the contributors can never really be known. Though there is a general guideline against posting original, unverifiable research on *Wikipedia*, and a strong, in fact growing, demand to cite all information posted to it, the possibility that an author could be a Harvard professor or a fourteen-year-old in a public library in Oshkosh[17] bothers academic purists and makes the encyclopedia inherently unreliable. Of course, an entry in the *Encyclopedia Britannica* is not innately reliable either, because any scholar writes with bias, and academic conventions and the hypereducated have their own biases as well, usually related to class. As a university lecturer, I can oppose the use of all general encyclopedias as unreliable sources. Where I do appreciate *Wikipedia*, particularly as a folklorist, is in the fact that peer review by the community will be almost instantaneous. The folk community in this case is self-defined; those who think, for example, they know something about Euclidian geometry are more likely to scrutinize an edit to the article on "orthants," but in theory anyone could change the text to make it nonsensical or simply inaccurate. Where I am critical, though, is in knowing that the context of the author is elided, except to the extent that the author willingly and truthfully self-reports. Identity may not matter as much to folklorists as do the circumstances of knowledge production.

The question of accuracy becomes particularly charged when politics is involved. As one can well imagine, any entry on any aspect of current events, as well as historical events, is subject to political interpretation. So how, then, to write about the administration of George W. Bush? In a standard print encyclopedia, the author and a board of editors appointed by a publisher are given canonical authority to provide the interpretation that will become the standard until the next edition is published—if ever. In an online, open-source encyclopedia, such changes can take place minute by minute and can be made by anyone. On the other hand, because it is open source, anyone can *add* anything as well, and as long as this new material is documented by a reputable source, no one is going to object and argue that something should not be there. This is knowledge by accumulation and never needs to be edited for reasons of space. As a result, for example, *Wikipedia* has the most complete and easily accessible list of current and past detainees at Guantánamo Bay and the up-to-date status of their legal cases ("List of Guantánamo Bay Detainees").[18]

At this point it is important to take a step back and consider the philosophy behind *Wikipedia* and its family of wikis. Without digressing into an abstract philosophical discussion of the open-source movement, several aspects of *Wikipedia*'s founding philosophy and structure need to be framed here for the reader who may be unfamiliar with them. First, with a few exceptions, the administrative structure of the enterprise is decentralized. Jimmy Wales, although acknowledged as the leader and thereby having some moral authority, does not maintain editorial control over the content or technological control over the hardware and software.[19] His philosophy is what others describe as a form of intellectual libertarianism inspired by the work of Ayn Rand.[20] The resulting enterprise is decentralized, governed by a community of thousands of editors and a smaller set of admins, who together have developed and refined certain policies and guidelines ("Wikipedia: Policies and Guidelines").[21] Among these are the *five pillars*, or basic principles of the project ("Wikipedia: Five Pillars"),[22] the second of which is a "neutral point of view," abbreviated NPOV (a term used among Wikipedians as an adjective; conversely, an article, section, or sentence that is biased is "POV") and codified by Jimbo Wales himself in April 2001 ("History of Wikipedia"). Through the policy guidelines, which have been adopted through consensus, community members are advised that in articles where there may be disagreement, "the policy is simply that we should *describe* disputes, not *engage* in them" ("Wikipedia: Neutral Point of View/FAQ"; emphasis in original).[23] An effective, self-referential example of this can be found in a page responding to common objections surrounding *Wikipedia*, which lists multiple points of view in response to these objections ("Wikipedia: Replies to Common Objections") and presents all as if each could legitimately be considered valid.

As mentioned above, each user is entitled to one user page,[24] which consists, as do the article pages, of a main page, a talk page, an editing page, and a history page, as well as any subpages for reference or future use, such as material for undeveloped articles or archived talk pages. Editors are requested to include only such biographical data as might be relevant to their *Wikipedia* work, not personal characteristics for the purposes of dating or other social networking ("Wikipedia: User Page"). *Wikipedia*'s own guideline on this, developed by consensus and in principle editable (but in fact locked as of the time of this writing), is to

> think of it as a way of organizing the work that you are doing on the articles in Wikipedia, and also a way of helping other editors to understand with whom they are working.
>
> Some people add information about themselves as well, possibly including contact information (e-mail, instant messaging, etc.), a photograph, their real name, their location, information about their areas of expertise and interest, likes and dislikes, homepages, and so forth. ("Wikipedia: User Page")

It is this added information that gave rise to the controversy concerning political allegiances.

This guideline does not make mention of *userboxes*, small (generally 45px by 238px) graphic banners, with the shape and proportion of bumper stickers,[25] created in HTML in the editing software and distributed by the copy-and-paste method through which much *Wikipedia* (and indeed open source in general) content and programming are propagated.

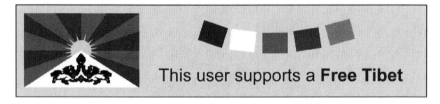

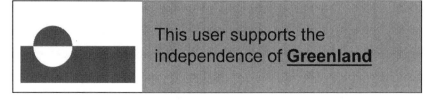

This user is **left-handed**

Copy-and-paste is greatly simplified by the use of *templates*, or programming shortcuts that are edited on one site and then reproduced in their shorter format through a process known as *transclusion*.[26] Thus, to choose a very neutral example, one user could type {{user recorder}} on his editing page, and a white userbox stating "This user plays the recorder" (underlined here to represent a hyperlink) would appear on his user page, along with a small photo of, in this case, a recorder (and the word itself is hyperlinked). Another user could see this, and she could go into the edit page of that first user's user page, copy {{user recorder}} onto her edit page, and the userbox would show up in her user page. Or she could go to the source of that template, change the program text to, say, saxophone, change the graphic image, and then paste that newly designed userbox code onto her page. All of this is folk transmission.

The first userboxes, known as *babel boxes*, were developed so that users could indicate what language(s) they could speak and, more importantly, write and edit in and at what level (indicated by a number from 0 to 5, plus native ability). This appears to have first been codified on the Wikimedia Commons site on 9 April 2005 ("Commons: Babel"),[27] with the native-English-speaker userbox already posted on the pages of over 540 *Wikipedia* users as of 29 March 2005 (the actual date of its creation is harder to uncover; see "Category: User En-N").

Having established the need to know what languages contributors speak, other userboxes with other affiliations developed, including those pertaining to hobbies, interests, locale, popular culture, sexual orientation, and political affiliation. In an abortive essay on the topic, User:MailerDiablo suggests the first variant from a babel box was proposed jokingly on 27 August 2005 ("User: Mailer Diablo"). Originally, when the first guideline page was created on 18 November 2005, userboxes were described by User:Cedrus-Libani in an almost lighthearted manner:

> A userbox is a small coloured box which allow [*sic*] users to add small messages on their user page. It is an extension of the babel-boxes used for user's language abilities. Feel free to use these on your user page. The Wikimedia Commons has a large range of icons for use within boxes.

Common uses for boxes include user interests, user skills, technical information, Wikipedia activities, or just for fun. ("Wikipedia:
Userboxes," 18 November 2005)[28]

The remainder of the page was filled with sample userboxes, none of
which were political.

Over the next few years, registered users created hundreds of userboxes, as only a rudimentary knowledge of programming—which
could really be picked up from copying, pasting, and adapting other
code—is necessary to do so. They circulate as folklore; as one user
noted: "Userboxes are so 'unofficial' and there are so many of them,
anyone can create more, and some of them are disputed but still very
difficult to delete" ("User: Rhanyeia"). Current categories for userboxes ("Wikipedia: Userboxes") include languages spoken (including
Klingon), programming languages, religion, interests (including sports,
cars, favorite colors, foods, etc.), media and popular culture (including
favorite books), locations, time zones, health, professions, military background, educational background, habits, handedness, even *Wikipedia*
use (such as numbers of edits). A fair number of these are self-referential
or even metafolkloristic, in the sense that they make use of in-jokes that
would only be comprehensible to aficionados of the same television
series, adherents to a particular religion, or experienced Wikipedians.
So, for example, a userbox with a picture of Humphrey Bogart and the
quotation "This user is the stuff that dreams are made of," when clicked,
redirects to the article for "The Maltese Falcon" ("User: Mtmelendez").

A prime example of a political userbox whose meaning hinged on
folklore—and one that proved so controversial that its template shortcut
was deleted—had a small photo graphic of Bush on the left side of the box.

This user believes that George W. Bush's edits to the constitution need to be reverted

The meaning of this userbox depends on folk knowledge of multiple
categories. The terminology is familiar to any Wikipedian; *reverting* is
the term used to refer to going back to a prior version of an article when
an unacceptable edit, most commonly vandalism, has been made (and
it can be accomplished with a single click), and this article suggests that
the U.S. Constitution has, under Bush, become some kind of wiki that

can be easily edited. (There's a subtle, implicit criticism here, too, that the Constitution is not being *amended*, which of course is part of civic practice, but that it is, like a wiki, being edited by a single, rogue user.) What gives this userbox such extra punch is that clicking on "edits to the constitution" would direct one to the article on the U.S.A. PATRIOT Act, while clicking on "reverted" does not lead to a *Wikipedia* policy page about reverting, as one might expect, but to the article titled "Movement to Impeach George W. Bush." Unfortunately, as with a few other pointed userboxes during the controversy, the template for this one was taken down for reasons of divisiveness. However, several users committed to userboxes and the free expression of political opinion rewrote their own code to produce this box, and then distributed that via Javascript and automated programs called *bots* ("Wikipedia: Bot Policy").[29]

More complicated, self-referential userboxes concern those dealing with *Wikipedia* customs or, more controversially, with the very usage of userboxes. As of the writing of this chapter, there are over eighty-five userboxes on the official *Wikipedia* page containing userbox templates referring to userboxes and their use, which does not include other userboxes other users may have created on their own user pages ("Wikipedia: Userboxes/Userboxes"). New userboxes are also being created all the time ("Wikipedia: Userboxes/Userboxes"), and there are even new guidelines in order to improve their overall quality ("Wikipedia: WikiProject Userboxes"). In short, userboxes are distributed within the group via observation and imitation (in the form of copying); they make reference to in-group understandings of culture, including the subculture of *Wikipedia* itself; and they serve to mark off subcommunities within the overall larger Wikipedian community ("Wikipedia: WikiProject").[30] All these factors naturally are the stuff of folklore.

By early 2008, the policy governing userboxes had become more serious (thanks to 1,046 edits carried out by 300 different Wikipedians) and included the following proscriptions in the English-language *Wikipedia*:

Content restrictions

- All userboxes are governed by the <u>civility</u> policy.
- Userboxes **must not** include <u>incivility</u> or <u>personal attacks</u>.
- Userboxes **must not** be inflammatory or divisive.
- <u>Wikipedia is not</u> an appropriate place for propaganda, advocacy, or recruitment of any kind, commercial, political, religious, or otherwise, opinion pieces on current affairs or politics, self-promotion, or advertising.
- Simply: If content is not appropriate on a <u>user page</u>, it is not appropriate within userboxes.

Potentially divisive words

- Avoid verbs which may be used to suggest negative comparison,
  and would thus be potentially divisive, such as:
      believes, considers, favors, finds, knows, prefers, thinks, and
      wishes.
- Avoid negative verb phrases which can be potentially divisive,
  such as:
      dislikes, despises, hates, loathes
- Also avoid compound sentences which are positive and negative,
  such as:
      This user likes <noun phrase>, but does not like <another
      noun phrase>.
- Essentially: Express what you like, rather than what you
  don't like. Express who you are, rather than who you aren't.
  Express what you do, rather than what you don't. ("Wikipedia:
  Userboxes")

So what exactly happened to make the policy so much more restrictive
and serious?

The answer is that during the period from late 2005 through early
2006, and coming to a head in February 2006 (when several admins uni-
laterally starting deleting templates for political userboxes), a debate
arose on the English- and German-language *Wikipedias* concerning
whether or not userboxes[31] that espoused a particular political view
could legitimately appear on a user page. The debate, known within the
community as the "Userbox Wars," concerned the question of whether
posting one's political beliefs on one's user page made that user's contributions more suspect for political bias. This represented an epistemological debate taking place among those who had assumed the mantle
of writing an encyclopedia on a voluntary basis. About one policy there
was consensus: that encyclopedia articles should reflect an NPOV, and
that it was better to represent all sides of the debate and describe each
one in as unbiased a way as possible. One can only begin to imagine
how difficult this can be in articles such as those that describe the history of the Israeli-Palestinian conflict, or even the Armenian genocide.
New users, those not yet socialized into the community, often do log on
and record POV statements, particularly on hot-button topics such as
illegal immigration. Thus the question arose during the project's early
years of whether one's own personal political beliefs—or for that matter another social group membership, such as gender or sexual orientation—could be openly stated while contributing to articles that met the
NPOV ideal.

In a way this comes back to a question posed by the British art critic John Berger in his famous television program and book, *Ways of Seeing,* in which he presents an image of a painting by Van Gogh and asks the reader if its meaning changes if the caption below were to read: "This is the last picture that Van Gogh painted before he killed himself" (1977, 27–28). With userboxes, the question was essentially—and it could just as well be asked of this or any article—would a reader's opinion of its reliability or truthfulness be changed if there appeared a box at the end that said, "This author of this article is secretly an anarchist"?

 This user is secretly an **anarchist**

Or, more directly, would an editor's contribution to the article on, say, "Illegal Immigration," be intellectually suspect if that contributor had the following userbox on his page?

 This user is does not begrudge <u>illegal inmigrants</u> and supports their right to inmigrate undocumentedly

For some reason, this was deemed an issue only if the userbox were posted at the end of an article or on the userpage of an editor. But if an author has a bumper sticker on her car (or if she marches in a demonstration), not only would no one know, but on the road the driver of the car would be equally anonymous. The issue then was only partly an issue of bias, and more significantly an issue of the *proximity* of that bias to the actual text of the article. The question implicitly being asked was whether one who is claiming partisanship elsewhere on the same website can be trusted to write prose that treats multiple points of view equitably.

There were two schools of thought that negotiated a compromise, although the compromise was more consistently implemented on the German page. On the one hand, there were those who felt that the point of an encyclopedia was to present knowledge without bias, and that allowing—or even encouraging—authors to state their political biases would inevitably produce not only more biased entries, but a less

credible encyclopedia overall. Such commentary on the talk pages read
like this post by one of the most prominent of the anti-userbox camp:

> Those buttons expressing beliefs or support for poltical [*sic*] or reli-
> gious causes would be fit for a blog or forum, but this is neither. It's
> an encyclopedia, and those buttons threaten its identity. It doesn't
> matter what the community thinks, we must act in the interests of the
> encyclopedia at all times.—Tony Sidaway I Talk 10:34, 3 January 2006.
> ("User Talk: Tony Sidaway")

Wales himself weighed in several times on the issue as being against
userboxes, with his strongest statement coming on 20 February in a mis-
sive from the top (such as it is, in a decentralized world):

> I think it is somewhat problematic to have users pasting bits of cruft
> on their userpage which make them seem to be engaged in Wikipedia
> as activists for a particular POV. I think users should realize that hav-
> ing that sort of cruft on their userpage will quite rightly diminish
> other people's respect for you and your work. But, whatever, if peo-
> ple want to do it, I see no reason to get absolutely draconian about it.
> However.
>
> The current situation with these things being in the main Template
> namespace, and promoted as if healthy and normal in the Wikipedia
> namespace, is that they are damaging to our culture. They are attract-
> ing the wrong sort of people, and giving newcomers the wrong idea
> of what it means to be a Wikipedian.
>
> That's why they need to go. Not to censor people's self-expression,
> but to make it clear that _as a whole_ the community considers these
> things to be divisive and inappropriate. (Wales 2006)

The other side, the pro-userbox people felt that by admitting to bias contributors can be held more accountable, and that it would be easy for the
discerning reader to try to filter for that bias. In the most basic terms, that
sentiment was expressed in this way by User:Imjustmatthew:

> **In terms of factionalism**: A userbox is just a template for insert-
> ing Wiki markup quickly and synonymously accross [*sic*] pages, it
> is no different then [*sic*] saying the same thing or writing the Wiki
> markup on your page itself. I do not believe that identifying your-
> self—your language, your passions, your beliefs—causes factional-
> ism within a professional project. I do not read a person's user page
> before reading their edits, rather I read their edits and perhaps their
> user page. Even in disputes I do not think that we judge based upon
> who a user is. Understanding each other clearly, where we came
> from and what we believe, often makes it **much** easier to resolve

disputes. Many conflicts both in our day to day lives and globally would be much easier to resolve if the parties truly understood each other. ("Wikipedia Talk: Proposed Policy on Userboxes"; see also the archived talk pages that come before it)

This is the more conventional argument in favor of allowing userboxes.

But closer research among the archived materials reveals a second objection, related to the notion that it is better to reveal overt diversity of opinion: diversity is not only inevitable, it is ideal. Oddly enough, it was in the discussion of sometimes seemingly politically insignificant (yet eminently folkloric) userboxes that the pro-userbox faction most vocally expressed their rationale, going beyond the notion that individual POV reflected allowable diversity to suggest that the negotiation of difference in POV produces a stronger intellectual community. In the following discussion of whether or not to delete a userbox stating that the user did not believe in Santa Claus, which a user spuriously named User:Santa on Sleigh nominated for deletion, User:Ian[13], located in the U.K., wrote the following on the debate page:

Userboxes are supposed to display a POV or an aspect of a user. They are designed for **userpages**, a place where users are supposed to tell people about themselves, and usually where POV is not taken into account since it is considered that a user can do what they want there, providing its [sic] not breaking any of the wiki laws . . . If userboxes are to be restricted to language only—then it destroys part of the culture of wikipedia, and I feel that would be a great regression in wikipedia status, as well as holding no full reasoning. Also, I feel the template is not POV in many aspects, it mearly [sic] shows what the user believes: it does not say it is wrong, or that he [Santa Claus] doesn't exist. I feel this template's removal would do a great injustice to the wiki, and where would the line be drawn—would userboxes and babel [those userboxes that refer to language competence] be altogether removed, or would Wikipedia just lose its sence [sic] of community? Should this template be removed, it will only complicate the managment [sic] of userboxes (I for one certainly have enougth [sic] to do) and members would be forced to use Template:Userbox to create the desired effect, or would Template:Userbox have to go, and users will have to waste even more of their encyclopedic writing time fiddling with div's—and yes that would lead to less server strain, but is it really worth it for that work and effort? Oh, and the nominator will have to be banned for a POV username, which is far more noticeable. I also notice how the nominator is using the Template:User Santa on their userpage—is this nomination to promote his/her point of view? Ian[13]_{ID:540053} 19:21, 28 December 2005 (UTC). ("Wikipedia: Templates for Deletion," 31 December 2005)

This provoked the following metacommentary/conspiratorial dialogue on his talk page between Ian[13] and User:Larix, a native Dutch
speaker who was a self-described member of "Users in Defense of
Userboxes and Individuality on Wikipedia" ("User: Larix"):

Free expression on user pages
Hi Ian! I saw your comment at Wikipedia:Templates for
deletion#Template:User_NoSanta and thought you might be interested in this template {{user freedom}}. I made it since a growing
number of users seems to be opposed to every possible form of free
expression on user pages. Regards, Larix13:02, 31 December 2005
(UTC)
> Oh cool, so we fight back their userbox removal with another user-
> box! That'll annoy them :D Ian[13]ID:540053 13:45, 31 December 2005
> (UTC)
>> It should illustrate a point :) Larix 14:02, 31 December 2005 (UTC)
>>> And if they try and delete it, just say they are of the opos-
>>> ing [sic] point of view, and breaking WP:POINT,[32] sorted!
>>> Ian[13]ID:540053 14:04, 31 December 2005 (UTC)
>>>> So you're going to use it? :) Larix14:05, 31 December 2005
>>>> (UTC)
>>>>> Do you mind if I shorten in abit [sic] /rephrase so it
>>>>> will be the average userbox size? Ian[13]ID:540053 14:14, 31
>>>>> December 2005 (UTC)
>>>>>> It depends on how you rephrase it—I'd like all the
>>>>>> links to remain in there, if possible. Larix 14:18, 31
>>>>>> December 2005 (UTC)
>>>>>>> Okay. I'll be bold[33] and give it a blast, it can always
>>>>>>> be reverted. Ian[13]ID:540053 14:19, 31 December 2005
>>>>>>> (UTC)
>>>>>>>> Hows [sic] that? It's only a tiny big bigger than
>>>>>>>> normal now . . . Ian[13]ID:540053 14:46, 31 December
>>>>>>>> 2005 (UTC)

Perfect, many thanks! You just earned yourself a barnstar[34] :) If you
don't mind, I'd like to contact you later about this as the dispute goes
on. Larix14:53, 31 December 2005 (UTC)
> No problem, and thanks! Where's this barnstar! :D. And yes, the
> userbox issue is becoming quite big. One [sic] the one side we have
> the Userbox WikiProject members, and on the other all those people
> opposed to liberty, humour and just plain userboxes. Ian[13]ID:540053
> 14:58, 31 December 2005 (UTC)
>> There it is! (and we've got the people in religious or political cat-
>> egories on our side, too) Larix 15:02, 31 December 2005 (UTC).
>> ("User Talk: Ian[13]")

At an even deeper level, though, a few users objected to the proposed ban on userboxes out of an intellectual libertarianism. Some of the strongest rhetoric in the pro-userbox camp came from User:John Reid, who explained his position in extensive terms on 19 and 21 February 2006. What is noteworthy here is that his argument operates on several levels of both political and folkloric interest. He writes of the importance of protecting intellectual diversity within groups while staking out a libertarianism that is, in a way, diametrically opposed to that of Wales. User:John Reid's worldview is that more points of view, not the absence of any point of view, are valuable for community and democracy. In other words, libertarianism is not the absence of another political point of view, as Wales might suggest, but the possibility that all perspectives can be accommodated in a community:

> It's human nature to form groups of all sizes and for all sorts of purposes. It's also our nature to *signify* our membership in groups by wearing and displaying symbols. Each of us tends to belong to more than one group and some groups themselves belong to larger ones; thus each of us bears many marks of membership.
>
> Group purposes vary and are oftimes at odds with other groups; sometimes they are destructive to all of us. Signs and symbols all are harmless in themselves; but people invest them with meaning, making them powerful. It is not possible to conceive of a human society that does not engage in group behavior or the display of symbols.
>
> Every society suppresses subgroups that threaten the larger group; and so their symbols. It has occurred to many great leaders that their positions and agendas would be secure if only *all* competing groups and subgroups could be eliminated; and all symbols replaced with a single standard behind which all must march.
>
> This political system is called *fascism*. John Reid 05:37, 19 February 2006 (UTC)
>
> > What, you didn't get the memo? Wikipedia is now under the direct control of the Wikipedia Fascist Directing Committee. Any expression of individuality is verboten. For these thugs, Wikipedia is everything, the Wikipedians are nothing.
> >
> > MSTCrow 10:53, 19 February 2006 (UTC)
> >
> > > I have to agree that i see no point in this mass destruction of userboxes. Their [*sic*] is nothing wrong with them. I agree wikipedia should not be *my space* but userboxes just make it more enjoyable to have a user page and to display random

> information regarding yourself. Isnt their [sic] such a thing as freedom of expession [sic] anymore or is Wikipedia the online China? Tutmosis 17:22, 19 February 2006 (UTC)
>> There's no need to raise the spooks of Goebbles [sic] &co here. Fascism is the technical term for a system of social organization that attempts to suppress all subgroups and their symbols and uphold a single group and symbol: *Fascism exalts the nation, state, or race as superior to the individuals, institutions, or groups composing it.* It's notable that fascist movements invariable [sic] concentrate heavily on *symbols.* So do other political movements; but fascists are remarkable for the degree to which they exclude *all* competing symbols.
>>> I do not begin to suggest that anyone is in danger of brownshirts in the night. But it is clear that many UBX opponents feel their worst effect is to permit users to identify themselves as members of groups which are *not* The Group; to display symbols which are not The Symbol.[35] . . . John Reid 23:35, 21 February 2006 (UTC) ("Wikipedia Talk: Proposed Policy on Userboxes"; emphasis in original)

This led to the formation of several groups within *Wikipedia*, including the Users in Defense of Userboxes and Individuality on Wikipedia (UDUIW), founded by two Wikipedians who have since ceased to be active, and the Association of Inclusionist Wikipedians ("Association of Inclusionist Wikipedians").[36] It appears that such criticisms of userboxes and their unilateral deletion by some admins led some of the more libertarian Wikipedians to actually leave the community.

There is no way to do justice to the discussion between the two camps itself. It is voluminous as well as fascinating in people's attempts to protect their own position while working out a compromise. There have even been userboxes about the use of userboxes.

	This user believes that only articles need reflect a NPOV, and that displaying political, religious, or other beliefs using userboxes and user categories should not be banned.

This user is interested in the belief that displaying <u>userboxes</u> does not divide the <u>Wikipedia community</u> but rather emphasises its <u>diversity</u>.

User:MailerDiablo provides a wonderful parody infobox (i.e., a sidebar), based on the {{Infobox Military Conflict}} template, summarizing the "Userbox Wars" as a *Wikipedia* article might address an actual battle.

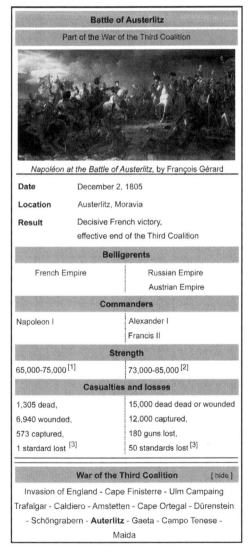

Battle of Austerlitz

Part of the War of the Third Coalition

Napoléon at the Battle of Austerlitz, by François Gérard

Date	December 2, 1805
Location	Austerlitz, Moravia
Result	Decisive French victory, effective end of the Third Coalition

Belligerents	
French Empire	Russian Empire Austrian Empire

Commanders	
Napoleon I	Alexander I Francis II

Strength	
65,000-75,000 [1]	73,000-85,000 [2]

Casualties and losses	
1,305 dead, 6,940 wounded, 573 captured, 1 stardard lost [3]	15,000 dead dead or wounded, 12,000 captured, 180 guns lost, 50 standards lost [3]

War of the Third Coalition   [hide]
Invasion of England - Cape Finisterre - Ulm Campaing Trafalgar - Caldiero - Amstetten - Cape Ortegal - Dürenstein - Schöngrabern - **Auterlitz** - Gaeta - Campo Tenese - Maida

Battle of Austerlitz	
Date	January 2008 to October 2006
Location	English Wikipedia
Result	German Usebox Solution
Belligerents	
Anti Userbox Camp	Pro Userbox Camp
Sysop 1, ⚑	Sysop A †
Sysop 2, ⚑	Sysop B †,
Sysop 3	Sysop C
Sysops and some editors	Editors and some sysops
Few wounded, some missing, Exact unknown	Some dead, many wounded, Exact unknown.

The material is also compelling quite simply because the diction is so wrapped up in an argot that only experienced Wikipedians can follow without clicking on various hyperlinks that direct the reader to obscure policy and guideline pages. Here are a few examples:

> I think (one of the few) positions which we can all agree on is that the level of contentiousness on this issue is unhealthy for the project. I'm sure both sides would like to see the divisiveness on this issue go away, but (perhaps not unexpectedly) each side wants the issue resolved on their own terms with minimal concessions. I've seen pro-userboxers who have argued that anti-userboxers want to take away their freedoms,[37] and that we wouldn't have all this dispute and disruption of the project if anti-userboxers would just leave userboxes alone, and instead focused on the encyclopedia. On the other hand,

some of the anti-userboxers (and I think <u>Jimbo's note</u> might be an
example of this) argue that the existence of POV userboxes is what's
fueling the conflict and causing much of the discord, and that removal
of the POV boxes (either voluntary or compulsory) is what's needed
to resolve this conflict . . . Of course, if both sides essentially argue,
"Division is bad for the project. However, if we can put our disagreements aside and accept my position as the best one, then we can put
this divisiveness behind us—wouldn't that be nice?", then we're
probably not going to make much progress toward a solution or anything resembling consensus ;-). If the userboxer wars (if they can be
so called) continue as is, I fear that the long-term status of userboxes
will be unduly influenced by which side has the greater tolerance of
incivility, the boldness to <u>flaunt process</u>[38] [sic] and to maintain reverts,
and the willingness to hit the other side harder with <u>the mop</u>.[39] We
cannot have a <u>war of attrition</u>[40] on Wikipedia, and so the userboxer
conflict cannot be sustained in its current state. Ultimately, it won't
be. . . .— Jeff | (talk) | 10:11, 7 February 2006 (UTC)

> Wikipedians need to have some identity. Jimbo's definition of a
> Wikipedian, just my impression, is someone who contributes a
> ton of information with no emotional leanings whatsoever. While
> Buddhists all over the world are celebrating this ideal, I just don't
> think it's a realistic goal. We're all living breathing human beings
> with thoughts, beliefs, opinions, passions, hopes and dreams
> firmly rooted in our personalities. We can't just ignore them.
> It's a physical impossibility. Humans are by nature POV. All we
> can do is turn the volume down on the POV and give it anger
> management. Denying users a certain level of induviduality [sic]
> actually hurts the community in my opinion. It's like taking all
> the hollidays [sic] out the school year. Sure, the kids may learn
> more and retain more but they are also miserable. Stick the fun in
> there and work is of higher quality and they tend to care more. I
> think the same holds true for Wikipedia or any other community
> of human beings. —§HurricaneERIC§Damagesarchive 06:22, 19
> February 2006 (UTC)

>> On the contrary, I would say, based on his comments on
>> the wikien mailing list, that Jimbo is quite appreciative of
>> the individual differences of Wikipedians. His concern, as
>> I understand him, is the way in which userboxes are being
>> used to express, not individual differences, but group soli-
>> darity for POV positions. —Donald Albury (Dalbury[(Talk)])
>> 11:47, 19 February 2006 (UTC)

>>> And he is, not to put too fine a point on it, wrong.
>>> Voluntary disclosure of the POVs of as many editors
>>> as possible helps the encyclopedia maintain NPOV by

> keeping biases in the open and therefore easily countered.
> Rogue 9 14:11, 23 February 2006 (UTC) ("Wikipedia Talk:
> Userboxes/Archive 4")

Keep in mind that all the while this policy is being discussed, everyone
involved is free to go online and make whatever edits he or she wants,
whether it is deleting objectionable or divisive userboxes or making
changes to the policy, until the policy gets hammered out to a point at
which it is an acceptable compromise.

What ultimately happened was that the contentiousness of February
died down, and by April, editors—those that remained—were having a
more measured discussion about how to change the policy. In the interim,
the German *Wikipedia* had come up with a solution, which editors on
the English-language *Wikipedia* site noticed by the end of May. The solution basically allowed for userboxes, but their code and the templates
could not be stored on common template space (within *Wikipedia*'s slice
of cyberspace); instead they had to be stored on individual user pages.
The final policy was written up, the editors created the necessary pages
on their own, and a few offered postmortems, predictably filled with
Wikipedia folk speech:

> Created Wikipedia:The German solution, go ahead and improve as
> you see fit . . . —Ashley Y 00:05, 1 June 2006 (UTC)
> Mumble. This still seems to me to be not very much of a compro-
> mise . . . but, OTOH,[41] if the existing userbox directory pages will
> be maintained and simply updated to point to the userboxes in user
> space, and the admins who have been deleting userboxes when-
> ever they get half an excuse will not do so if the userbox in question
> is in user space (except for things that are obviously against some
> other policy—I'm not proposing to waive Wikipedia policy entirely
> for userboxes, and never have), then it might work. Without either
> of these two conditions, however, it's not a compromise—it's a total
> capitulation. Jay Maynard 01:08, 1 June 2006 (UTC)
> > It works like this: All "nonstandard" (i.e. almost all except Babel
> > boxes) are migrated into userspace. Either a central repository
> > is created or (more likely) individual users adopt them in their
> > (to be created) userbox archive pages (which sould [*sic*] be
> > interlinked). They still can be used like templates, just that they
> > are in userspace now and outside the encyclopedic content.
> > Standard Wiki policy apply [*sic*] (i.e. WP:NPA, WP:CIVIL, etc.)
> > but besides that they only have to follow WP:USER—i.e. they
> > are allowed to be POV or controversial, [*sic*] and are not subject
> > to T1 (T2) speedy-deletion rules. Check my (small) repository to
> > see how it looks like (too tired to expand it right now) CharonX

<u>talk Userboxes</u> 02:06, 1 June 2006 (UTC). ("Wikipedia Talk: T1 and T2 debates")[42]

Those most invested in maintaining the idea of userboxes formed their own WikiProject—basically a team of editors devoted to writing and improving articles on related topics, such as WikiProject New Jersey, WikiProject Sociology, or even WikiProject Lace ("Wikipedia: WikiProject Council/ Directory/Geographical/Americas"; "Wikipedia: WikiProject Council/ Directory/Culture"). This new WikiProject, WikiProject Userboxes, "aims to organise, expand and improve all Wikipedia's userboxes." In the first two days it was formed, thirty-two users joined ("Wikipedia: WikiProject Userboxes"). A compromise seems to have been reached, and deletions are rare except in the case of openly divisive userboxes. However the controversy still smolders, and as recently as 4 November 2008, User:Ezhiki, an admin who self-identifies as "a male Russian American," added the following banner, in boldface type and a bright yellow background across the top of the page "Wikipedia: Userboxes/Politics":

> When considering placement of any of the userboxes from this page on your user page, please consider avoiding the boxes that suggest your support for a secessionist movement (even if democratic or by democratic means), a pro-fascist or a pro-communist ideology, or proclaiming any polemical view not strictly related to Wikipedia and the editing process.
>
> This recommendation aims to remove one instance of disputes about settling a precise line of division between <u>allowed and nonallowed content in userspaces</u>. Although you are not required to follow this recommendation, if you do follow, you will be part of a large group of people (one day encompassing, hopefully, the entire contingent of Wikipedia editors) that renounced posting similar content on their userpages for the sake of building a better environment. *By refusing to post such userboxes you in no way renounce your right to hold an opinion.* ("Wikipedia: Userboxes/Politics"; emphasis in original)[43]

The war, then, is not yet over. ˙

In the universe of wikis—at least that universe governed by Western Enlightenment ideals of neutral (if not objective) scholarship, as opposed to, say, theocratic ones—this kind of debate will arise again and again whenever a new encyclopedia project develops, because it is in the nature of wikis to define their own rules and guidelines and thus to define what is knowledge and what is opinion. In fact, the potential for this conflict has already been noticed on the aforementioned *SikhiWiki*, which has the following warning on its introductory page:

The basis of a WIKI is trust and respect for each other. The beauty of a good WIKI is that it is self-regulating and self-cleansing. You can post anything of value that you wish to contribute, but all contributions will need to be in good taste. If you want to stand on a soapbox and lecture, preach, advocate your personal or political view—this isn't the place to do that. If your stuff gets erased, that's probably why.

Those who want to use SikhiWIKI to advance their personal agenda will not be allowed to participate. ("SikhiWiki: Introduction")

I suggest that as knowledge communities—which is what wikis are—grow, a debate over how to accommodate bias is inevitably revisited anew. The only reason the issue does not come up in printed works is that the ground rules have been established by the academic community long ago and are seldom challenged. But wikis operate under house rules, not ground rules, and the former must be determined through negotiation in every folk community. (In fact, cleverly, if one goes to the *Wikipedia* entry "House rules" (http://en.wikipedia.org/wiki/House_rules), at the top of the page one finds a prefatory line indicating, "*For guide lines on Wikipedia, see* Wikipedia: List of guidelines *or* Wikipedia: Policies and guidelines.")

What *Wikipedia* represents, and what can be seen even more specifically in the userbox controversy and the development of its policy, is the social activity of knowledge production and how a community of knowledge-producers jointly developed effective practice while schooling new members in the ways of the community.[44] In the simplest terms, Wikipedians qualify as a "folk group," using Alan Dundes's famous definition of this as "any group of people whatsoever who share at least one linking factor" (1973, 1). But how Wikipedians are a folk group is more richly illustrated in Dorothy Noyes's contention that "group" emerges in the dialogue between a "community of the social imaginary that occasionally emerges in performance" (the group of registered Wikipedians themselves) and "the empirical network of interactions in which culture is created" (the activity of not only writing an encyclopedia but of formulating the policy and an epistemology of how that encyclopedia is to be created) (1995, 452). In this case, perhaps a more appropriate conception of the group would actually be what has been called a *wikiculture*, given that people's membership, participation, entry into, and departure from the group and its negotiation process is ad hoc, without formal rules, and governed by no one.[45] In fact, Duke University professor Cathy N. Davidson (2007) goes one step further in a defense of *Wikipedia*, contending that *Wikipedia* is not just the thing itself, but the community that produces it—in other words, not only the product *and* the process, *but also* the producers.[46]

Furthermore, I would go so far as to state that the construction of *Wikipedia* has given rise to an *occupational* folklife, following Robert McCarl's observation that "there are traditional ways of doing things in the workplace which workers themselves create, evaluate, and protect." He continues:

> The *canon of work technique* refers to this body of informal knowledge used to get the job done; at the same time, it establishes a hierarchy of skilled workers based on their individual abilities to exhibit that knowledge. The canon of work technique is not a law or written set of rules but a standard that workers themselves create and control. (1986, 71–72; emphasis in original)

This is exactly what the worker bees of *Wikipedia*, editors and admins alike, have taken on for themselves. The compilation of this encyclopedia—not its content—is completely based on a semiformal knowledge of what makes a public reference work *work*—meaning what makes it "labor" (n.) as well as what makes it "tick" (v.). There may be an ever-evolving set of written "guidelines" (while the only "rules" are the five pillars), but these guidelines are unfixed, ever-changing, and not dictated by an authority with any more than a rudimentary ability to fire writers or quash contributions; the guidelines have been "created and controlled" by the workers themselves.[47] This is one of the ways in which the Wikimedia projects, in the words of the Wikimania 2008 theme itself, "change the shape of wisdom" ("Wikimania 2008 Main Page").

The philosophical problem of wikis is that they sustain themselves on the force of trust, and trust in wiki communities does not depend on academic credentials. Where *Wikipedia* is epistemologically most radical and most like folklore—and, to many, frightening—is in the de-centering of authority away from those *necessarily* having academic credentials and prestige and in the elevation of trust as a social basis for epistemology.[48] Both of these are concepts of interest to the folklorist, but until now only the former has generated any comment. Typically, though, as historian of science Steven Shapin points out, "much modern epistemology has systematically argued that legitimate knowledge is defined precisely by its rejection of trust" (1995, 16).[49]

Some folklorists of the last quarter century working in the field of folk belief have openly questioned that rejection. In a series of articles that led to the development of belief scholarship within the field of folklore, David J. Hufford famously challenged scientific (or what he occasionally called "scientistic") ideology and its attempts to discredit folk knowledge and supernatural and folk medical-belief systems. As he observed, polemically (his term):

The academic world uses systems of ideas to explain and legitimate its practices. This includes not only those practices that are central to explicit academic goals, but also those that involve the special interests of academic individuals and guilds, although the rhetoric used primarily refers to a combination of academic goals and 'the public good.' . . . [T]he academic enterprise presents itself today as the basic source of authentic knowledge about what is useful and good, and even more fundamentally, about what is *real*. At the center of this assertion is the success of the physical sciences in recent centuries, especially as measured by their associated technologies, and the bonding of these activities to the universities. These developments account for a great deal of the academic world's success in establishing its members as a methodological and epistemological elite . . . Today one's claim to be modern and progressive is largely measured by the ability to establish connections with academic science . . .

The consequences of this hierarchy are partly political and involve the division of academic spoils, from salaries to prestige. But there are also profound consequences for the shape and direction of scholarship. (1983, 22–23; emphasis in original)

Fifteen years later Hufford again picks up this argument in ways that are more directly applicable to *Wikipedia*:

It is no accident, of course, that medical and scholarly views converge in a tendency to dismiss the knowledge claims of ordinary people. Both professional communities are faced with similar situations: each makes a claim to expert knowledge about the world, and alternative claims from nonexperts—whether informants or patients—are a potential threat to professional authority. (1998, 301)

Hufford then recommends a "methodological populism" that does not dismiss unofficial knowledges and explanations as *a priori* misguided and observes that in the history of medicine and science, "disagreements have often been rooted in inappropriate notions about the boundaries of expert knowledge and authority" (1998, 302). The issue here, then, is not that the writings of the self-appointed scholars of *Wikipedia* are more accurate, rather that the assumption that published, printed works by named, credentialed scholars are inherently more accurate, or are even remotely NPOV (if I may use that term). I argue that while the critics of *Wikipedia* draw the boundaries of expert knowledge in different places from where the contributors *might*, the folk process of defining expertise and accuracy while rooting out bias is a major —and growing —part of Wikipedian communication. This populism is an integral component of the ideology and practice of the open-source movement.[50]

Theologian Rubén Rosario Rodríguez takes that a step further in a specific discussion of the Wikipedia, which, he observes, "has evolved organically into a cross-cultural, crosscontextual, interdisciplinary conversation that can help liberate epistemology—especially theological epistemology—from the stranglehold of Enlightenment foundationalism." He compares the Wikipedia's implicit critique of what counts as authority to the approach of Latin American liberation theology and its critical response to the official Church; both utilize "an interactive philosophy that nurtures community" (2007, 175, 176). Granted, Rosario Rodríguez is less concerned than Wikipedians with bias and neutrality because liberation theology calls on the church to show "a preferential option for the poor." But in this context it is the interpretive and discussion-based form of theology which has taken place in the Christian base communities and grassroots communities that has its counterpart in Wikipedia's challenge to "authoritarian" (his term) scholarly orthodoxy. This religion,

> provides an alternative to the dominant epistemological perspective within the academy that is in many ways analogous to the organic, conversational epistemology embodied by the Wikipedia online community... This unique method of doing theology characteristic of Latino/a church communities, whereby theologians, pastors, and lay people (often in ecumenical conversation) gather together to reflect on the beliefs and practices of the people they serve, produces a theology that truly belongs to, and is validated by, the faith community. (Rodríguez 2007, 175–76)

For him, the potential exists for both religion and the Wikipedia to "liberate epistemology" in such a way that it can become "a more effective model for navigating differences in specific fields of knowledge—namely political, theological, and moral discourse." (2007, 176)

Although Hufford himself largely confines the scope of his argument to defending claims of supernatural, religious, and medical belief, the critiques by both Hufford and Rosario Rodríguez are also applicable not only to political belief-systems but also to the process of a folk construction of encyclopedic knowledge. One reason for the harsh criticism of *Wikipedia* as failing to be legitimate and reliable has to do with the pervasive academic ideology about claims regarding knowledge construction. The critique also has to do with what counts as knowledge itself (or valid methodologies and sociologies of knowledge).[51] Beyond (or within) that, *Wikipedia*'s self-critique in regard to userboxes hinges on whether editors who acknowledge their own political bias can jointly construct texts that are fair to multiple points of view.

Hufford's work in particular (1995c), influenced by the writings of Karl Mannheim (1952) and Paul Feyerabend (1988), among others, anticipated or perhaps paralleled the development of a field known as social epistemology that emerged in the late 1980s within the discipline of philosophy. I have neither the space nor the expertise to discuss the connection of folklore to social epistemology (and to the production of *Wikipedia*), except to say that at best this article is a prologue to that discussion, which I hope can follow. Nonetheless, what is relevant here is that only a few short years before a new knowledge industry exploded across the World Wide Web in the late 1990s, there emerged a field of inquiry that looks at the philosophical rules and social conditions under which the authority of scientific knowledge production is established. Specific critics, notably Steve Fuller, have observed that "a 'truly social epistemology' [is] an exercise in constitution-making" and that the question to be asked is, "How does one set up the forums for deciding science's research and teaching agenda, given the patently biased and otherwise limited nature of the participants?" (2002, xix). These are political and ethical questions that, in turn, anticipated the debates around knowledge (and I would add belief) provoked by the development of wikis as well as message boards.

Where Fuller's work is synchronous with Wales's vision is best expressed in Fuller's ingenious framework that "there are two ways of understanding the knowledge = power equation. One supposes that more knowledge helps *concentrate* power, the other that it helps *distribute* power" (2002, xix; emphasis in original). Fuller, who is largely an adherent of the latter view, cites the concentration of power that, for example, massive civil-engineering projects have historically abetted while appearing to benefit a public that foots the bill; at the same time, liberation theology has been criticized for distributing too much power and theological authority to lay people as opposed to the church hierarchy (2002, xix–xx). Yet wikis and open-source networks may prove to be equally powerful examples of the distributive power of knowledge (as long as there is open access to computers and the Internet—which, given the human history of literacy, access to technology, electricity, and education, is unlikely in practical terms).

But the potential of *Wikipedia* to distribute knowledge as power, and the fact that its creative structure is decentralized, and thus different from all prior encyclopedias, has not been lost on astute observers of the Internet phenomenon. One of the most eloquent analyses of the significance of this sociological/epistemological shift was posted by science-fiction novelist and blogger Cory Doctorow (and, in fact,

User:Doctorow) in response to a critique of *Wikipedia* as a form of collective-dominated "digital Maoism" in which the voices of individuals are lost behind a kind of groupthink that washes out their individual contributions (Lanier 2006) (a critique I find ironic, given the contentious nature of editors' conflicting brands of libertarianism). In much the same way that folklore is often dismissed, the Lanier essay sneers: "The hive mind is for the most part stupid and boring. Why pay attention to it?" Doctorow (2006) counters that by looking at the significance of *Wikipedia* as an opus being organized in a structurally revolutionary way. One difference is that, unlike an edited work that speaks with one authoritative voice, the fact that *Wikipedia* is "free, brawling, universal, and instantaneous" means that it can be "a noble experiment in defining a protocol for organizing the individual efforts of disparate authors with conflicting agendas." There are no gatekeepers, because "if you need to convince a gatekeeper that your contribution is worthy before you're allowed to make it, you'd better hope the gatekeeper has superhuman prescience. (Gatekeepers don't have superhuman prescience.) Historically, the best way to keep the important things rolling off the lines is to reduce the barriers to entry."[52] Thus *Wikipedia* is not Maoist, but at once communitarian, because it depends on the ability of individual scholars to negotiate their differences and come to an expansive consensus, and anarchistic, because there is no central powerful authority to prevent anyone from contributing. Doctorow also makes the point that *Wikipedia* must literally be read at different levels of discourse, much the way a folklorist reads a text within a tradition and a context:

> if you want to really navigate the truth via Wikipedia, you have to dig into those "history" and "discuss" pages hanging off of every entry. That's where the real action is, the tidily organized palimpsest of the flamewar that lurks beneath any definition of "truth."
>
> The *Britannica* tells you what dead white men agreed upon, Wikipedia tells you what live Internet users are fighting over.
>
> The *Britannica* truth is an illusion, anyway. There's more than one approach to any issue, and being able to see multiple versions of them, organized with argument and counterargument, will do a better job of equipping you to figure out which truth suits you best.
>
> True, reading Wikipedia is a media literacy exercise. You need to acquire new skill-sets to parse out the palimpsest. That's what makes is genuinely novel. Reading Wikipedia like *Britannica* stinks. Reading Wikipedia like Wikipedia is mind-opening. (Doctorow 2006)

I suggest that the userboxes were and remain among the most provocative catalysts in that intellectual negotiation. Ultimately, though, it is not a folklorist but, of all people, the Silicon Valley bureau chief of *Forbes Magazine*, Quentin Hardy, who makes an important observation about *Wikipedia* and other Internet intellectual resources: "Our new tool for communication and computation may take us away from distinct individualism, and towards something closer to the tender nuance of folk art" (2006). This is true because, after all, the wisdom of folklore operates with that same decentralized logic. This is not lost on Doctorow, Hufford, Rosario Rodríguez, or Fuller, who realize that knowledge construction and belief are tightly bound up with questions of authority and authoritarianism and with a politics of expertise and the laity,[53] as well as with texts where some (or some parts) are spoken while others are submerged.

Growing out of this is the question of trust and whom we believe in our social network. The question of trust has long been implicit in folkloristics, but it is a concept we need to interrogate more deeply and politically. We talk about trust in fieldwork and about establishing trust so that we can believe that what an informant shares with us is somehow fuller, richer, and closer to what he or she honestly believes to be true.[54] We also talk about trust in folk knowledge networks, whether serious—as in the case of folk healing—or perhaps more fanciful, as in the "friend of a friend" in urban legends (Brunvand, 1990, 23ff). So the question of criteria for determining trust and verifiable knowledge is a particularly interesting one for encyclopedias, given that *Wikipedia* presents us with one that may be written by nonacademic experts (not a problem for folklorists) who are anonymous (the problem here for folklorists is that no context is provided).[55]

But projects like *Wikipedia* force us to articulate a theory of trust. Philosopher Gloria Origgi, who agrees with Shapin, maintains: "Traditionally, epistemology had banned from genuine knowledge beliefs acquired by trusting others" (2004, 1). If so, then folk epistemology argues the contrary. Yet, Origgi points out, there are examples in social life when we defer to trusted authority—such as medical authority—and this has political implications:

> Political philosophy is a source of insight for social epistemology. In political philosophy, trust is seen as a key component of the authority relation, in which a person desists from demanding justification of the thing she is being asked to do or to believe as a condition of her doing or believing. Something of this kind seems at play when the lay person blindly defers to a recognised authority, be it an expert, a "wise man" (or woman), or a religious leader. We are all familiar with such cases of blind deference. (2004, 3)

The fascinating asymmetry of *Wikipedia* is that millions of (mostly young) users defer to its authority, giving power to its political decentralization; (many) academics are skeptical or dismissive of its authority; while its thousands of writers and admins scramble to bolster its authority with footnotes, references, and independent verification, a process fostered only by their essential trust in one another as a community that is unified in its pursuit of mission.

Folklore, of course, is all about belief and trust. So the reliability (a loaded term in the field of social epistemology, deserving further discussion in a separate essay) of a source is everything. We have long known that the legend hinges on its believability,[56] as does alternative medicine.[57] Both function within systems of epistemology that are different from academic epistemology, but the fallacious assumption is that the folk system is, by definition, more flawed. The other ancillary logical fallacy here is that a person who maintains one epistemological belief system—in this case a political one—is unable to accommodate the possible validity or even the existence of others, and thus is incapable of representing specific and multiple points of view in ways that are at once persuasive and NPOV. That is full of paradox and possibility. But the essential optimism espoused by *Wikipedia* is that political power is broadened by the accumulation and dissemination of that knowledge, and that the most creative folk groups may be open and not exclusive.

Notes

Acknowledgments

My initial thinking about the culture of the *Wikipedia* benefited early on from conversations with Dorothy Noyes, Kathy Condon, and Lee Haring. I want to express my deep appreciation to David J. Hufford, whose approach has been so instrumental to my analysis here. I belatedly thank Susan Garfinkel, whose attempts to drag me, kicking and screaming, into cyberspace were fruitless (other than e-mail) until I discovered that the Wikimedia projects were for me the "killer app" of the Internet (although of course I recognize that they are not an application). I also want to thank Adam Krumnikl and Jessica Jinju Pottenger for helpful readings of the draft, Francisco Sáenz for his assistance with illustrations, Trevor J. Blank for his patience, Paolo Sirotto and Jen Ross, and this volume's anonymous reviewers for useful references, and finally Wayne Bivens-Tatum, Sandy Rosenstock, Audrey Welber, and Rubén Rosario Rodríguez for help in tracking down the latter's article. All errors remain my own.

1.   Throughout this chapter I am going to use the term *folkloristics* to refer to the discipline, in order to distinguish it from *folklore*, which will refer to the subject matter or the textual material itself.

2. In a fascinating and significant work-in-progress, anthropologist Rena Lederman has been writing on the subject of what counts for and as knowledge in different disciplines. Her claim is that disciplines are defined not only by the area of study, but more significantly by what counts as moral practice in the production of knowledge: "Whatever else they are, disciplines are moral orders. Disciplines constitute themselves in implicit and explicit dialogue, or contest, with one another (as well as with extra-disciplinary modes of knowing the world) not simply as substantively *distinctive* but also as *better* or *worse*, even proper or improper—that is, morally weighted—knowledges" (2004, 62; emphasis in original).

3. "Wikipedia: What Wikipedia Is Not." See especially http://en.wikipedia. org/wiki/Wikipedia:NOT#SOCIALNET (accessed 6 April 2008).

4. This is one of the best examples I have seen of a sociology of collective knowledge production.

5. One example is Simon Winchester's (2003) study of the making of the *Oxford English Dictionary*.

6. For further explanation, see Weber (2004). Folklore, of course, is by definition open source.

7. When I polled the ninety-four students who had been enrolled in my classes at Princeton University, 2006–2008, only two responded that they had ever edited entries, and some reported having "used" the encyclopedia while misunderstanding I was asking how many people had *written* or *edited* it.

8. There's another article to be written on the impact that *Wikipedia* has had in the survival and revival of certain languages that do not have the status of official languages in their nations. It should be no surprise that there is a Basque version, for example, but the fact that the Catalan *Wikipedia* is the fifteenth largest worldwide as of this writing might be more noteworthy. Consider that there also exist a Galician *Wikipedia* (with 37,000 articles) and a Breton *Wikipedia* (20,000 articles), or the fact that in a little over two years, Piedmontese speakers have posted 15,000 articles (that's an average of about nineteen articles per day, every day), and one gets an idea of the potential impact on relatively small but culturally-charged linguistic communities. Since by definition *Wikipedia* and its related family of wikis can be changed instantly, unless otherwise specified this article refers to the current version at the time of writing this chapter. Most, if not all, of the cited entries will have changed by the time this book is published. In some cases I am choosing to cite a particular past version of an article, especially because this chapter is mostly concerned with a historical debate that took place during the editing process. In those cases, I specify the date of the *version* (not my date of access) since that is an archived version and cannot be changed without record. I cite this version date so that any reader who is interested can go back and find the identical version to the one I cite, even if it has been revised and edited many times since.

9. Especially compared to such other South Asian languages as Newari and Telugu (40,000 articles each), Bishnupriya (23,000 articles), Hindi (over 18,500), Bengali and Marathi (17,000+ each), and Tamil (13,000+) as of 1 May 2008 ("List of Wikipedias").

10. In fact, not only is it in English, but the contact telephone number for the administrator listed on the introductory page is a U.S. number with a New Mexico area code ("SikhiWiki Homepage" and "SikhiWiki: Introduction").

11. Obviously this is an oversimplification, for reasons of space. There's also a contradiction here. Those familiar with *Wikipedia* will find this superfluous, whereas those who are not interested probably will not read this, but I think it's necessary to provide some of the basics, especially given that the editing process itself is not universally understood, even among all those who use it as a reference work.

12. Despite being open source, some pages can be temporarily "locked" if there has been a great deal of vandalism posted on them recently. In that case "edit this page" is replaced with "view source," and only people with certain editing privileges may edit it. That is largely irrelevant to this article, except that the Obama example is, at the time of this writing, locked.

13. Thus, for example, "Barack Obama is a [[U.S.]] [[Senator]] from [[Illinois]]" would produce hyperlinked words leading to the articles for the United States, Illinois, and the U.S. Senate (in general, the U.S. Senate would have to be further specified in the editing stage by bracketing [[U.S. Senate]] and then perhaps showing onscreen only the word "Senate" by use of the typographic symbol " | " (referred to among Wikipedians as the *pipestem*): thus, [[U.S. Senate | Senate]] would produce the word "Senate" in blue in the article page, but clicking on that would redirect the viewer to the article "United States Senate."

14. As stated in the *Wikipedia* article on "Pseudonymity" itself, "true anonymity requires unlinkability," whereas there is a "continuum of unlinkability" on computer networks (and in literary circles)—from those contributions for which a user's true identity can never be discerned to those that are thinly disguised or even openly known.

15. To distinguish users from articles, I am adopting and adapting the format of referring to editors' user names as "User:——" for clarity's sake.

16. His year of birth disappeared from the page after this date. He confirmed some of this to me in a personal communication, but noted that he removed his nationality from the page because people accused him of writing with bias.

17. One is tempted to add to this list, "a native in a rain forest, a Tierra del Fuegan, an Eskimo . . ." See, of course, Guare (1990).

18. The level of detail and investigation, despite *Wikipedia*'s reputation among its detractors, is astonishing. Ultimately, I predict, it will come to be appreciated for being an almanac of record that puts information in public hands. To see an astonishing example of detail related to current affairs, see the *Wikipedia* entry "Casio F91W." No print encyclopedia or almanac could ever do anything like this, let alone keep it current.

19. A discussion of decentralized organizations, with specific reference to Wales and *Wikipedia*, can be found in Brafman and Beckstrom (2006). Their book is more of a leadership guide for businesses and organizations than an analysis of how *Wikipedia* works, but it is a useful introduction to this philosophy that points out its strengths, and it draws on an interview with Wales.

20. Wales himself rejects the term "libertarian" but acknowledges that other people see him this way. See Lamb (2005).
21. But see also "Wikipedia: Etiquette."
22. See also "Wikipedia: Neutral Point of View."
23. FAQ is an Internet abbreviation for "Frequently Asked Questions."
24. For various reasons, some users have registered multiple identities, usually because they have been blocked under a previous user name for violating *Wikipedia* policy. Those who set up registered identities for the deliberate purpose of deception are known on *Wikipedia*, as elsewhere on the Internet, as *sockpuppets* ("Sockpuppet (Internet)").
25. The similarity to bumper stickers may be intentional, and it is one of the grounds on which anti-userbox critics deride them as trivial. But bumper stickers are themselves folkloric, both in their content and in their positioning, and in the resultant dialogue and debate which may be carried out through the medium of stickers. Folklorist Hagar Salamon writes that bumper stickers are "arenas of complex covert and overt struggles between various groups representing competing political and even cosmological perspectives" (2001, 278). For a detailed analysis of this, see his full article.
26. For a fuller explanation, see "Wikipedia: Transclusion."
27. The notes, though, indicate that this page was copied from the *Meta-Wiki* site.
28. As of 2008, this page has equivalents among *Wikipedias* in forty other languages, including Yiddish and Nahuatl.
29. For examples of the work and explanations among those who converted deleted userboxes into usable Javascript programming, see, for example, "User Talk: Ilmari Karonen/archive2."
30. There were also interesting internal debates about the nature of community within *Wikipedia*. While this is a topic of folkloristic interest in and of itself, it goes beyond the scope of this chapter. But see "Wikipedia Talk: Esperanza."
31. Partly because of the German *Wikipedia* connection, there was an attempt, perhaps tongue-in-cheek, to make the official English plural "userboxen," along with a userbox campaigning for this change.
32. This links to the guideline "Wikipedia: Do Not Disrupt Wikipedia to Illustrate a Point."
33. This does not specifically link, but it does refer to the guideline "Wikipedia: Be Bold," which is not to be confused with "Wikipedia: Ignore All Rules" or "Wikipedia: If It Ain't Broke, Don't Fix It."
34. An award that can be inserted by a sysop on the user page of a fellow Wikipedian who has done something outstanding for the encyclopedia.
35. Here "The Group" refers to Wikipedians, as described on the page "Wikipedia: Wikipedians," and "The Symbol" refers to the .png image of the *Wikipedia* logo.
36. While outside the scope of this chapter, there have also been other organizations (subcommunities) within Wikipedia, including the now-defunct Esperanza (http://en.wikipedia.org/wiki/Wikipedia:Esperanza) and Concordia (http://en.wikipedia.org/wiki/Wikipedia:Concordia).
37. This directs to "Wikipedia: Free Speech."
38. This directs to "Wikipedia: Ignore All Rules," a little-known but important libertarian-anarchist *Wikipedia* policy.

39. This directs to "Wikipedia: Administrators."

40. This redirects to "Attrition Warfare," an actual entry in the encyclopedia itself. It's a nice touch that in the middle of the debate, this experienced editor hyperlinks to an actual concept that some passing reader might want to delve into.

41. This stands for "on the other hand."

42. T1 and T2 are shorthand for two of the criteria under which editors are allowed to delete certain pages quickly.

43. As of 17 December 2008 it was still there. See also "User: Ezhiki."

44. Although here the discussion is on producing knowledge, and not epic songs, the process of group review and refinement is not that far afield from the Parry-Lord theory of epic composition and performance (see Lord 1960). Among others, Roger Abrahams, in a number of articles, discusses the role of the speech community, performers, and audiences in shaping public performance. While he is talking about performance *events*, his description is equally apt for the construction of an encyclopedia in this fashion. Specifically, he refers to "the intensity of involvement in common carried by the participants into the encounter [and] their special rule-regulated behaviors, their manner of coordinating and regularizing the activity" (1983, 160).

45. Wikiculture is the human chemical bond of the open-source age ("Wikiculture").

46. "Wikipedia is not just an encyclopedia. It is a knowledge community, uniting anonymous readers all over the world who edit and correct grammar, style, interpretations, and facts. It is a community devoted to a common good—the life of the intellect. Isn't that what we educators want to model for our students?" (Davidson 2007, B20).

47. There is also a self-referential and satirical understanding of these traditions, manifested in the page "Wikipedia: Wikipediholic" and diagnosed at "Wikipedia: Wikipediholism Test," but this is funny only when one has amassed experience in *Wikipedia* editing.

48. Some have argued that this reconfiguration of trust is not only necessary to the *Wikipedia* but is the basis for what has become known as "Web 2.0" (see Fichter 2006).

49. See also Trudy Govier, who describes the web of "contending double standards of trust and distrust" in the creation of knowledge (1997, viii).

50. See Noyes (2006, 51 n. 41) and Weber (2004).

51. By this I refer to our potential ability as folklorists to create entries on the field of folkloristics, to link these topics as equals to equivalent entries in other fields, and—most significantly—to place our own definitions, methods, and interpretations on a par alongside those of more widely recognized disciplines in an NPOV way and allow the reader to choose among these as if at an even freer marketplace of ideas. As I gushed elsewhere upon discovering this: "For once we have an opportunity as a field to script our own entries and insert them as part of the canon of academic discourse, without an outside editor or committee to stipulate our field is a minor discipline which cannot be included for reasons of space" (Westerman 2006, 7). This also means, however, being perpetually vigilant against POV demotions of

folklore and oral literature as unimportant or trivial by other editors not versed in the field of folkloristics.

52. Doctorow also raises the issue of the GNU license, and the copyright/copyleft distinction, which are beyond the scope of this chapter, but these topics offer something to investigate further for those folklorists interested in intellectual property.

53. See Fuller (2002, 77–87), as well as Rosario Rodríguez's (2007) discussion of liberation theology in this context.

54. See, for example, Shopes (2003, 105).

55. Trust is a question for social networks on the Internet. For openers, see Golbeck, Parsia, and Hendler (2003, 238–49).

56. See Tangherlini (1990). I am happy to note that some in the field of social epistemology take the study of folklore seriously in this regard. See also Webb (2004).

57. See, for example, Goldstein (2004) and O'Connor (1995).

Chapter 6

Crusading on the Vernacular Web: The Folk Beliefs and Practices of Online Spiritual Warfare

ROBERT GLENN HOWARD

A Spiritual Wrong Turn

Amateur website builders and evangelists "Dean" and "Susan" of Hillsboro, Oregon, believe that directly palpable, evil, spiritual entities act in the world today. They describe seeing strange eyes, white fogs, and dark shapes, hearing loud breathing, and even feeling sudden changes in temperature. While these are common elements in folk tradition (Ellis 2000), Dean and Susan place these experiences into their conservative evangelical Christian worldview. Compelled by a radical certainty imparted by these experiences, they participate in an online vernacular web of communication with others who share this certainty (Howard 2008a, 2008b). In this vernacular web, communicating about their direct experiences with spirits authorizes a shared belief in a literal reading of the Bible. For the participants in this online web of communication, those who do not accepted their literal readings of the Bible are believed to be under the influence of demons.

Since at least the 1970s, small-scale evangelical Christian media publications have developed a set of beliefs, based on the folk traditions surrounding demons and Satan, under the term *spiritual warfare*. Interpreting his personal experiences with these evil beings in terms of spiritual warfare, Dean interacts with others who share his beliefs by building amateur web pages. These pages then contribute to a vernacular web of online discourse espousing the most conservative form of what has been termed "vernacular Christian fundamentalism" (Howard forthcoming a; Howard forthcoming b). This discourse occurs at the online nexus between vernacular fundamentalism and Christian folk traditions about demons, and two of its particular qualities result from the easy access to other people made possible by the Internet. First, because the Internet makes it simpler for Dean to locate many individuals with similar beliefs, online communication supports their interpretations of specific real-world experiences as demonic attacks. Second, because the Internet also makes it easier to locate people with ideas they consider to be inspired by Satan and his demons, spiritual warfare can proceed across the Internet itself to engage more (and more distant) targets.

Recounting his decision to begin to share his experiences with demons through the Internet, Dean recalled how "God said: 'I want you to write about this!' The new [web page] I just posted up there is called 'Demon Domains and Christian Fortresses.' That was something God wanted me to put up as fast as possible because . . . well, maybe he had somebody he wanted to see that" (Dean and Susan 1999). After putting up web pages like this, Dean receives supportive e-mails, and such e-mail exchanges often direct him to the pages and online postings of others who have undergone demonic assaults. Exchanging stories that are felt to demonstrate the veracity of their beliefs about demons, Dean and his fellow participants in this dialogue develop a radical certainty that they have attained a special understanding of demons and Satan.

Their use of the Internet, which enables them to locate geographically dispersed individuals who share this understanding, creates an insular enclave where repeated exposure to their shared ideas reinforces their beliefs. Because they view many ideas that diverge, challenge, or conflict with their own beliefs as deceptions created by Satan and his demons, the Internet functions not only to support their convictions but also to give them greater access to individuals whom they believe deserve to be the targets of their spiritual attacks. By allowing them to find these potential targets, the Internet seems to enable a particularly active kind of intolerance (Howard forthcoming b).

For Dean this intolerance has become particularly strong, a result of the ferocity of the attacks to which demons have subjected him and his family. He feels that demons single him out because he first invited their attention by getting involved in "occult" practices when he was a young man serving in the Navy. He later spurned these demons after he had a "spiritual rebirth" experience that precipitated his conversion to evangelical Christianity. As a result, Satan and his servants have a personal vendetta against Dean and his family. During an interview, Dean showed me his "warlock" tattoo as proof he once was "into the occult." In fact, he was so deeply involved that he came to believe that a demonic spirit had entered his body and "possessed" him. His personality changed. He became distant and emotionless, and he felt that he gained minor supernatural powers: mind reading, seeing the future, and partial control of the weather. Because of these powers, he told me that he developed quite a reputation on board ship.

One night, having trouble sleeping, Dean went to a part of the ship's living quarters where there was enough light to read and met another sailor there. When the latter saw Dean's warlock tattoo, he stated he was a Christian and confronted Dean : "'God's given me the ability to tell when a person's possessed.'" As he looked at Dean, Dean felt that "something shrank into a cold hard knot in my chest and started moving around like it was trying to hide." Dean believes the demon was fleeing from the Christian and "flipping out." Shortly after this experience, God came to Dean and gave him an ultimatum: "God told me. He said: 'Now. Decide who you want to follow.' And He has since told me if I was to continue to follow Satan, I would be dead." Because of his rejection of Satan, however, Dean has regularly experienced demonic attacks ever since. The devils attack him, they attack his wife, and they have attacked his son and daughter. He and Susan take these episodes very seriously (Dean and Susan 1999).

As is common in Christian folk traditions, Susan and Dean believe that Satan was once one of God's angels. Among these conservative Christians, Satan is thought to be a master of deception who has spawned non-Christian religious belief systems throughout the world in order to lead humans into error. For them, occult practices—including witchcraft, ESP, and even ghost beliefs—are all potentially demonically inspired errors. Ghosts contacted through Ouija boards or in séances are actually demons. Even UFOs are considered to be demons masquerading as aliens in an attempt to lead humans astray.

Demons, however, are not all-powerful. They must be invited into an individual's life. They can gain that invitation when people explore non-Christian religious beliefs and practices, like Dean did when he was young. New Age religions, American Indian spirituality, and even some forms of Christianity are termed *cults* and thought to bring their followers under the influence of demons. Once initial contacts are made between these forces and specific individuals, the demons can begin to manifest themselves in more directly destructive ways. Because Dean initially invited demons into his life but then became a true Christian, he and his family suffer particularly ferocious demonic onslaughts by them.

Dean and Susan reported having many physical demonic attacks while living in a particular apartment when they were first married. After the regular attacks had stopped, they learned from the landowner that their upstairs neighbor had been evicted and was discovered to have enacted strange occult rituals. The proximity of the apartments, Dean contended, allowed the demons his neighbor was contacting to enter into Dean and Susan's apartment as well. From Dean and Susan's perspective, anything they view as a cult can function this way. One well-known group Dean considers a cult is the Church of Jesus Christ of Latter-day Saints.

During our interview, Dean gave an example of how a spiritual attack can originate from a real-world wrong turn. One afternoon Susan was walking home from the local store. She choose to take a shortcut through a "Mormon church's" parking lot that was just across the street from their home:

> As soon as she walked in the door [at home] she became violently sick. And just for it to come on that suddenly? I had a feeling . . . As soon as I mentioned it, she turned around and saw the church [through the window]. I said, "That's it!" So what we did was I took and bound and got rid of the demons that were causing the sickness. As soon as I did it she stopped being sick. And what God told us was that even unwittingly she had invaded their territory, which gave them [the Mormon demons] the right to attack her! And I was really worried about that . . . I says, "God? My daughter has to pass by the church every day when she goes on her way to school." What he told us was: "Their authority ends at the street. As long as you don't go on their parking lot, they can't touch you." (Dean and Susan 1999)

In addition to the testimony of Dean and Susan, this chapter documents other participants in the online vernacular web of expression that has emerged among fundamentalist Christians who believe they are engaged in an ongoing war against demon spirits. In the case of this particular vernacular web, the access it creates functions to encourage particular forms of intolerance. Out of a perceived need to share strategies for combating evil spirits, many educated and skilled amateur website builders see themselves as crusaders in a world led astray by the homosexual rights movement, government conspiracies against Christians, New Age spirituality, and other belief systems (Howard 1997, 2000; Wojcik 1997). Creating a vernacular web of online discourse, these individuals can communicate within a discursive enclave that reinforces their extreme views. At the same time, access to the diversity of people and ideas that is possible online has led some of these individuals to engage in a spiritual warfare tactic of aggressive "witnessing." When their divine experiences are frequent and ongoing, both certainty and intolerance are forged into their most extreme forms. Alternate views are not merely considered to be wrong—they are perceived as Satanic and need to be actively combated. For these individuals, the Internet serves as an active battleground.

The Mass Media Discourse of Spiritual Warfare

The discourse of spiritual warfare is part of a vernacular belief tradition reaching back long before mass media. Historically, fears of witchcraft and demon visits in dreams pervade European and American folk traditions (Ellis 2000; Hufford 1982, 1995; Kelly 1968). With a surge in media attention to the subject in the 1970s and early 1980s, conservative evangelicals reached what appears to have been a new peak in concern about Satanic influence (Aranza 1983; Victor 1993).

Since that time, the idea of spiritual warfare has been linked to a Bible passage from the New Testament. In Ephesians 6:11–17, the early church leader Paul exhorts the followers of Christ to "Put on the whole armour of God, that ye may be able to stand against the wiles of the devil." Once saved, the believer was thought to have a responsibility to actively avoid sin and error. The "armour" aided in that struggle. Imagining demons and sin as terms for this internal struggle, Paul exhorts humans to rely on their faith in God to overcome both personal temptations and the worldly difficulties that sometimes exacerbate those temptations. Here, putting on "the armor of God" is an analogy for having complete faith in God's plan for one's life. In this benign form, spiritual warfare is an internal struggle between faith and temptation within the mind of each Christian (Dew 2008; White 1990).

A more extreme form of the spiritual warfare discourse, however, emerged in the evangelical mass media of the 1970s. One of the most influential media evangelists, Bob Larson, became famous for claiming that Satan and his demons are the sources of non-Christian religious systems. From Greek mythology to New Age beliefs, and from Native American religions to Mormonism, Larson defines over 3,000 non-Christian spiritual belief systems as cults in his well known books: *Bob Larson's Book of Cults* (1982) and *Bob Larson's New Book of Cults* (1989). The author of over thirty books and over one hundred DVDs and tapes, his other titles include *Talk Back with Bob Larson: Mormonism and Magic* (1988), *UFOs and the Alien Agenda* (1997), and *Larson's Book of Spiritual*

Warfare (1999). His website describes the association of non-Christian beliefs with demons, stating that "those who give themselves to the occult" have "demon-induced visions" ("What is a Demon?" 2003).

In addition to the books written by Larson, numerous other popular-press books describe how individual Christians can engage and defeat the influence of demons. Sometimes referred to as "deliverance ministries," this discourse takes as its premise the idea that demons exist and that lay ministers can call upon the Holy Spirit to confront and defeat them. In his influential 1973 volume, *Using Your Spiritual Authority*, Pat Brooks argues that all individuals who have experienced spiritual rebirth are authorized by the Holy Spirit to combat demons: "In other words, because I am *in Christ*, His authority is mine to use here on earth. His Holy Spirit makes available to each believer the power to use His authority" (19; italics in original).

One of the most well-known and still widely read texts is another 1973 book, *Pigs in the Parlor: A Practical Guide to Deliverance* by Frank and Ida Mae Hammond. The authors describe demonic attacks as the physical manifestations that have long been associated with ghosts or hauntings in European folk traditions, and they associate these phenomena with "sinful" activities. "Many have told of hearing voices or sounds in their houses. Such manifestations are sometimes called 'poltergeist,' a German word meaning "knocking or noisy ghosts" (Hammond and Hammond 1973, 141). In this text, the authors assert that "demon spirits can invade and indwell human bodies. It is their objective to do so" (Hammond and Hammond 1973, 1). Through references to the New Testament, the authors argue that individual Christians have been given the power to throw out these demons through the Holy Spirit: "Demons are spiritual enemies and it is the responsibility of each Christian to deal with them directly in spiritual warfare . . . the Bible shows us how the Christian can put pressure upon the demons and defeat them! He must learn the practical ways in which this is done" (Hammond and Hammond 1973, 5). The authors then describe various techniques for engaging demons directly. These techniques are common in the discourse and include the "binding and loosing" of demons, commanding demons "aloud," and the "laying of hands," among many others.

In this form of spiritual warfare, the belief that actively evil forces are seeking to have an impact on the lives of real people requires true Christians to act against the individuals who are influenced by such demons. Dean and Susan described this sort of spiritual warfare in their stories of the shortcut through the parking lot of a Mormon church and of being attacked by demons from a neighbor's apartment.

In recounting another case of direct demonic attack, Dean explains how his use of the Internet brought him in to dangerous contact with these evil spirits:

I had gotten a letter from a Christian and her sister had just been hammered by a coven [of witches] and I guess they were just attacking her from [sic] some reason. I didn't really find out what exactly she did, but I guess they were really hammering her hard. And she told me about it. One night I was driving to work and maybe it's Ecclesiastes that talks about "hedges"—where you can put a hedge around something? So what I did was I commanded that a hedge be put around this coven. And just as I said that all of a sudden it was like I was looking into a dark place and saw this pair of yellow eyes swing around and look westward. Like it was trying to figure out where this hedge had come from. So I said, "OK. It's searching." Well . . . about a week later . . . two weeks later, just in downtown Hillsboro, right in front of the courthouse, we were stopped at a red light. And the light turned green. Somebody ran right out and smashed right into our jeep. Now the jeep's got plastic running boards which can't stop anything. This van, even though it hit straight on, somehow got jerked around so that it took almost the whole front side [of the jeep] off even though it hit originally right by the driver's side . . . by my door. Even the cop that investigated the accident says "That's not possible!" So . . . it was kinda funny 'cos a couple weeks later I got on the Internet and there's a Christian chat room called JCN Home. They have some people from the occult get on there. And I logged on and one of them says, "Feeling a little worse for wear?" And they put "smirk" in parentheses. And I says, "What do you mean?" And they said, "We heard about your accident." So basically it was a direct assault. And the only thing we could figure—because even the cop who investigated the accident said it couldn't possibly happen—was that when the van slammed into the running board something grabbed the other end and jerked it around so that it took off the front end of the jeep instead of plowing right through my door. So yeah. Angels do react. Especially with Christians. (Dean and Susan 1999)

As this story makes clear, the mass media discourse on spiritual warfare that focuses on demonic attacks and the need for Christians to combat those attacks now manifests itself online. In this environment, however, two new aspects of spiritual warfare have emerged. First, those who adhere to even the most extreme and intolerant understanding of spiritual warfare can find not just books to support and explore their beliefs, but can also interact with others who actively experience demons, much as they do. In this way, they create a vernacular web of expression that supports, extends, and encourages their intolerant beliefs and practices without publishers, editorial boards, or institutional religious figures to temper their intolerance. Secondly, intolerant discursive practices can now be enacted online. Because the Internet gives these individuals easy access to people with whom they disagree, acts of spiritual warfare can be actively waged online with very little potential for nonspiritual repercussions. For these two reasons, the online environment has proved a rich battleground for individuals who see themselves as engaged in this crusade against the demon world.

To document this vernacular web, a common search engine that organizes its results in a hierarchy by relevance was used. The first hundred websites that contained the words "spiritual" and "war" or "warfare" were cataloged. Any sites that were part of an institutional church or other website, as well as those built by individuals who were located outside of the United States or who were trained as professional ministers, were eliminated. Additionally, a messianic Jewish site and three Catholic sites were excluded. After these exclusions, forty sites created a sample set of the online discourse emerging from the practices and folk belief surrounding spiritual warfare.

The Vernacular Web of Spiritual Warfare

In my winnowed sample of forty web pages, there is one page that contains a devotional poem about spiritual warfare (Christy 2008). Six pages are on sites debating the theology of spiritual warfare. Twelve other sites focus on how individuals might engage in spiritual warfare in an effort to avoid personal temptation and sin. On these sites, demons are described as manifesting themselves in the daily challenges faced by many Christian believers, ranging from sexual temptations, to spousal abuse, to self-doubt. Because the sins these temptations can provoke are perceived as being outside of proper Christian action, believers assume that such desires or compulsions are the product of demonic influence. To overcome these internal devils, individuals can turn to Christ in personal prayer as a means of actively struggling against their personal weaknesses.

One such site portrays new converts to Christianity as particularly susceptible to the influence of Satan and his demons. Under the subheading "Once You Are Saved, There Is a Battle To Be Fought: It Is Called Spiritual Warfare," the website warns new converts: "Do not underestimate Satan and his powers of deception ("Spiritual Warfare Battle—Spiritual Warfare" 2008). Another site expands on a belief in the active influence of Satan: "Does the newspaper or some other form of entertainment keep you from obeying God, and take time that should be spent reading your Bible? You say, 'I don't see it that way.' Did you know these are Satan's words?" ("Spiritual Welfare: Cares, Worries, Pleasures" 2008).

Beyond the three forms of this discourse represented in these first nineteen sites, the twenty-one remaining sites in the sample are devoted to promoting the techniques and practices of aggressive spiritual warfare. These latter sites engage a variety of tactics common among the more internally focused sites previously discussed. However, they also include very different sorts of spiritual warfare tactics that focus on demons as external actors instead of internal manifestations of temptation. One of the most common of these specifically outward-looking tactics is called *mapping*. Based on the assumption that Satan and his minions are active forces in the world, creating error and sin, Christians discuss how to locate, or "map," and delineate both discursive and geographic places where demons are thought to be exerting their influence.

The website Battle Ax Brigade describes the technique of spiritual mapping at some length. The self-identifying mother and homemaker who built the site defines spiritual mapping as the first in a series of actions necessary to combat demonic influences on other people:

> Spiritual mapping is the process of collating and putting spiritual information concerning a region or people on a map . . . It allows us to see how the enemy is strategizing and exposes Satan's hidden agenda for that particular region or people group. ("Spiritual Mapping for Effective Spiritual Warfare" 2008)

Citing a passage from the Bible, Mark 4:22, the website builder goes on to describe mapping in more detail. She suggests that a team be formed of ten to twelve Christians and that this team should expect to spend two years on any mapping project for an average-sized city. The team members should collect information about a wide variety of groups of people in the area, including: "Cult and Occult Churches, Cult and Occult Establishments, Pornography, Freemasonry, Aborturaries, Homosexual Works, Prostitution Works." As the team locates places where demonic influence is strong, they should mark the locations in different-colored pens on a city map. She encourages establishing a post office box under an assumed name and requesting materials from organizations to discern if evil is present in them.

She even suggests that "a study of the history of land and its people" can be useful. In particular, "we must be able to understand the mind set, habits, and customs of the 'original people.'" To exemplify her point, she describes a case where she had a team mapping her own region. They "recognized that its earliest people were a particular tribe of Indians," so they "concentrated" their research on "finding out the unrighteous practices and beliefs of these people."

> Another mapping team discovered in their area that the original Indians of their community were fascinated with tattooing their whole bodies, and considered it to be their clothing. Today public nudity is a real problem in that community. Also, there are unusually large numbers of tattoo parlors there. These facts better equip them to target their warfare. ("Spiritual Mapping for Effective Spiritual Warfare" 2008)

From the perspective of this website builder, the traditions of Native Americans were born of Satanic and demonic influence, and the fact that Native Americans once lived in a specific location led this woman to assume that their influence was the root of current practices she considers sinful.

She goes on to suggest that team members might need to engage in "reconnaissance." She notes that this activity should "not to be done by one person—remember the enemy knows you are invading his territory." She even recounts a specific case from her own experience where two women attended a local political function, pretending to be a homosexual couple in order to "infiltrate" the local homosexual population. She notes that popular rock concerts, "psychic fairs," Nation of Islam meetings, and other public gatherings are all reasonable targets.

In addition to mapping, several of the websites exhibiting this form of discourse discuss tactics that target the evil spirits directly. This targeting is generally described as being done through prayer, and many sites offer a wide variety of examples to be used. Some of the most common prayers are those that call on God to establish a "hedge" between a person or place being attacked by demons and the demons themselves.

In addition to this sort of hedging, "binding" prayers are mentioned as being used to trap evil spirits in particular places. All of these tactics are usually described as "delivering" individuals from demonic attacks. Because these prayer-based tactics are enacted either by individual Christians in private or by small groups of Christians, they do not necessitate any direct discourse between Christian believers and their targets. Instead, they use the Internet primarily to focus on sharing practical information with like-minded Christians. However, a few sites discuss a more aggressive deployment of the Internet. Some sites, such as Battle Ax Brigade, call for "witnessing" or "prophesying" online.

In this specific usage, *prophesying*, or *witnessing*, is the aggressive public profession of one's faith in Christ to an audience of individuals under the influence of demons or Satan. Because this kind of witnessing, by definition, seeks non-Christians for its audience, it is the most overtly aggressive tactic commonly used in spiritual warfare. While it might be difficult or dangerous for these Christians to confront many of the groups they believe are demonic in the physical realm, the Internet provides easy access to them. Through this medium, these believers can aggressively witness to groups that would otherwise be out of reach, difficult to find, or present dangerous repercussions.

The aggressive nature of this sort of online witnessing is particularly plain on an amateur website featuring a bright yellow page with a heading reading simply "Spiritual Aggression." The website builder states that "we must first fight the War before we can plant the crops" ("Spiritual Aggression" 2003). On another site, the website builder is particularly concerned with warning his Christian audience that they themselves will certainly come under attack if they engage individuals with divergent ideas:

> If we are effectively spreading the gospel message, through word and deed, then we will become engaged in spiritual conflicts. There is no doubt about it. Satan will send his forces to try to prevent us from fulfilling our commission. We will be confronted with demonic influences. (Keys 2008)

This website builder goes so far as to state that if a Christian is doing a good job of "spreading the gospel message," then she or her will be attacked. If an aggressive Christian does not confront non-Christians in a way that causes the latter individuals to resist, then that Christian is simply not trying hard enough to engage non-Christians.

One of the most aggressive websites in the sample is titled Battle Focused Ministries. As a former United States Army infantry sergeant, this website builder fully engages the militaristic language of spiritual warfare in an effort to teach fellow Christians how to combat evil spirits. On his website, he describes in very systematically militaristic terms how Christians can form "battle groups" based in their church communities. These groups need to train to become "battle focused":

> The term "battle-focused" refers to a concept used in the US Army to determine peacetime training requirements based on wartime missions. For Christians, "spiritual warfare" should not be separated from our mission to make disciples of all nations. We are in a spiritual battle for the eternal souls of all humanity. (Sims 2008)

Clearly, this individual sees his role on the world stage as taking part in an aggressive, even mythic struggle for "the eternal souls of all humanity." He even claims that those Christians who disagree with his militaristic approach are themselves demonically controlled:

> Most popular spiritual warfare instruction focuses on the individual Christian's struggle against his own weaknesses and his individual fight against evil powers. That emphasis on self is a symptom of modern society's corruption of Christian thought. (Sims 2008)

In another particularly aggressive example, a website titled Apocalyptic Hope imagines spiritual warfare as part of a literal Christian martyrdom that will occur during an impending world war pitting true Christians against all others. This website builder argues that the approaching return of Christ renders it imperative that all Christians actively engage in spiritual warfare. Here, the main page is a simple yellow background bearing, in large green letters, the heading "SPIRITUAL WARFARE 'To live is Christ, to die is GAIN' Philippians 1:21." By suggesting that there is something to gain through one's own death, the site builder implies that there will be some Christian reward for martyrdom in the struggle against non-Christians. Under the quote, there is a small graphic that depicts a knight's armor, shield, sword, and ax. Below the image, the web page cites the now familiar verse from Ephesians about the armor of God : "Putting on the Whole Armor of God" (Good 2008).

This website includes informational pages on microchip implants thought to be the Mark of the Beast, the One World Government, Antichrist, and other typical End Times topics associated with the Tribulation Period. However, the site is particularly concerned about the Tribulation Period as an approaching historical era when true Christians will be persecuted by the forces of the Antichrist (Howard 1997, 2006; Wojcik 1997). Associating the Antichrist specifically with Satan or one of his chief demons, the spiritual warfare discourse takes on a new sense of urgency.

A good example of this can be found on the Whole Person Counseling website. Here, the website builder describes the need for immediate and ongoing spiritual combat in a personal-experience narrative about a wasps' nest. The story begins when the narrator was about to leave his office for the day. Heading out the door, he looked up above the door to see "a large wasp nest with live wasps crawling over it." He happened to have a glass of water in his hand, so he "decided to try a little experiment." Throwing the water on the wasps' nest, the wasps became "excited," but "with the cold water and cool air, they couldn't fly." So he took a mop, knocked down the nest, and stomped all the wasps to death. The next afternoon, he went back to see if the nest was still on the ground. He found one wasp still alive. "So, guess what? I also stepped upon him." The website builder then explained the meaning of his story: "The church of Satan is praying that Satan will destroy your home, your life, and the life of your church. Today I must give us a 'wake-up' call to spiritual warfare and prayer" (Frasure 2008).

In the vernacular web of online communication about spiritual warfare, these crushed wasps serve as just one of example of a "wake-up call" to engage in aggressive witnessing. In this form of the discourse, the websites overtly call on Christian believers to use the Internet for the explicit purpose of locating alternate or diverge beliefs. After locating such beliefs, these Christians confront them with the radical certainty that because they are alternate, they must also be inspired by Satan or his devils.

For some of these vernacular Christian fundamentalists, even UFOs are seen as demonic illusions that must be combated. Many of those involved in this discourse believe that demons sometimes take on the appearance of space aliens in order to discredit the Bible and lead humans astray. For them, the existence of beings other than humans in the cosmos would contradict their interpretation of the creation story told in the first book of the Bible. UFOs cannot be piloted by nonhuman extraterrestrials unless those beings are demons. Demons choose to masquerade as space aliens in an effort to provide apparent proof that the literal interpretation of the Bible that characterizes vernacular Christian fundamentalism is wrong (Howard forthcoming a), since this interpretation assumes that God created the Earth and heavens for humans to inhabit and "have dominion over" (Genesis 1:26).

In an excellent example of sustained online aggressive witnessing, one site systematically inserts this fundamentalist Christian view of demons into the broader secular discourse on aliens. The site titled Alien Resistance.Org makes the alien-demon connection in a way that suggests its builders are seeking to bring this message to an audience of non-Christians. Alien Resistance.Org is, at first glance, a typical amateur UFO website. It has a black background dotted with little white spots indicating stars, and its title is written in a white technology-inspired font. There is a photograph of its primary builder standing in front of a sign that includes a schematized alien face with a red circle and a band across it to indicate "no aliens." Overall, the website maintains the slightly humorous tone that is common among UFO sites.

Despite this humorous exterior, the website's topic is a serious one, and its motive is aggressive witnessing within the secular discourse of

UFO theory. Just beneath the title graphic, there is a single line reading: "Re: How to Stop Alien Abduction, UFOs & The Bible, Genesis 6,
The Nephilim, The Book of Enoch, UFO Cults, 1947 Roswell UFO Crash,
UFO News." According to their online statement, the website builders
originally entered the virtual community to "research" the UFO phenomenon: "[Our research group] began a systematic search of the UFO/
abduction community, through the Internet, and the published findings
of other researchers. The premise of spiritual warfare was beginning to
develop" (Malone 2008).

Then the builders of Alien Resistance.Org discovered an active
community of people who shared their belief in UFOs. However, unlike
most UFO researchers, these individuals also found fellow Christians
who had "invoked the name of Christ" to resist the alien attack. They
collected these stories and then distributed them into the general, non-
Christian, UFO discourse community. According to their own account,
"the resulting article drew a large number of responses within the local
area." Claiming that most of the individuals they found were Christians,
the website builders state that these people "didn't feel comfortable
discussing their experiences with UFO investigators due to the New
Age inclination of many UFOlogists." As the researchers found more
and more cases of Christians warding off aliens, "the data showed that
in every instance where the victim knew to invoke the name of Jesus
Christ, the event stopped. Period. The evidence was becoming increasingly difficult to ignore" (Clark 2008).

The discovery of these instances of spiritual warfare tactics warding off alien abductions led to the development of a website devoted
to resisting aliens as demonic spirits. The site includes personal tes-
timonies of demonic aliens as well as a variety of essays specifically
arguing that aliens are in fact demons and must be actively resisted by
Christians. It posits that aliens are not average "demons" but instead
are even more deadly and dangerous spiritual beings who seek to mate
and create offspring with humans, as well as torture them. In order to
prove this point, the website builders cite over seventy-five different
passages from the Bible.

The website creates personal authority by stating that its builders are members of the large UFO theorist research group MUFON. In
a bid to garner the attention of non-Christian UFO enthusiasts, they
premise their entire argument from scripture by countering a perceived, already-held assumption that the Bible contains "primitive"
and "superstitious" beliefs:

Modern UFO apologetics often make the argument that since the "primitive, superstitious people of Bible times" had no understanding of technologies which we take for granted today, they would see a UFO or an alien entity and—in ignorance—describe them as angels or gods. We believe the reverse is true—modern "sophisticated" man has little understanding of God. When we witness supernatural events, we super-impose our technological mindset to force a "scientific explanation," I.E., when God acts supernaturally in our realm, or when angels (good or bad) travel the skies, we rationalize away a biblical understanding of the phenomena, and force it to fit our chosen paradigm. In our modern efforts to reject the Bible, we instead embrace the UFO cult-inspired doctrine of "panspermia"—the idea that life was created or manipulated by aliens. ("Ephesians 6:12 in Relation" 2008)

The subsequent pages on the website then proceed to "witness" the message of the divine Word of God as presented in the Bible in support of their belief that aliens are actually extrapowerful demons.

Because these website builders specifically involve themselves in the online UFO discourse in an attempt to debunk what they perceive as "errors," the production of the web page itself can be considered a witnessing behavior. These individuals seek out secular UFO believers and communicate their Christian message to them. However, they do this with the powerful certainty that (despite the very idiosyncratic beliefs they hold) they are in fact right and, by virtue of that certainty, are obligated by their faith to share that knowledge (to "witness" it) to a community of nonbelievers.

The Mundane Casualties

In the vernacular web that has emerged from online communication about spiritual warfare, people's direct, real-world experiences of demons, spirits, and even UFO abductions seem to galvanize the faith of believers. When these episodes are supported by experiences of demonic attack, it seems that otherwise compassionate and well-meaning people are able to express intolerance for individuals whom they feel are under the control of Satan. With the Internet affording believers an increased ability to locate and communicate with other individuals on both sides of the issue, the problematic nature of the folk traditions associated with spiritual warfare seems to be exacerbated.

Publicly "demonizing" non-Christians on the Internet suggests that the people involved in this particular web of discourse contribute to an acceptance of intolerance in two ways. On the one hand, the vernacular web of like-minded believers made possible by the Internet creates an enclave of adherents who accept a literal demonization of non-Christians. On the other hand, the access to nonbelievers afforded by the Internet makes it possible to verbally attack others. When groups of believers engage in this action online, it enables highly intolerant behavior to appear to be reasonable or even devout.

A final example from the forty websites in my spiritual warfare sample most clearly demonstrates the danger of this possibility. It is the closest that any of these sites came to actually advocating physical violence, and it is the most extreme example of spiritual warfare I discovered in the course of my research. Describing an act of spiritual warfare, the Christian believer imagines that the mere resistance to the Christian message by an unbeliever caused that unbeliever very real personal injury. No longer just advocating spiritual violence and not merely the victim of demonically aided physical injury, this individual claims to have actually caused casualties in the mundane world through his invocation of the sacred:

> I personally know of a number of people who came against me, and met with terrible judgment from the Lord. One man use to make fun by saying frequently, "seen any demons lately?", with a laugh. He unexpectedly was fired from his job, his wife divorced him, he was in an auto wreck that almost killed him, he turned into an alcoholic, and had a massive heart attack. ("End Time Deliverance Ministry" 2008)

In his testimony, the website builder describes physical violence brought on through his invocation of the spirit world. In the end, he even offers his audience a prayer that they can use to bring this violence down upon non-Christians:

> If you are under a lot of attack, you may want to specifically pray these scriptures against someone . . . Pray—Father, in the name of JESUS I send the judgment of God to (name names). I pray Deuteronomy 30:7, Psalm 109 and 140, Isaiah 54:17, and any like Scriptures on them, and anyone else coming against us, in the name of JESUS. ("End Time Deliverance Ministry" 2008)

Chapter 7

Ghosts in the Machine: Mourning the MySpace Dead

ROBERT DOBLER

Social networking websites like MySpace.com have exploded in popularity over the last few years.[1] Teenagers use the Internet to join online communities of peers who share virtually every aspect of personal experience in the public arena of cyberspace. MySpace in particular has become a major facet of modern American youth culture. Bill Tancer, corporate analyst for Hitwise.com, reports that MySpace achieved a 4,300 percent increase in visits over the last two years and a 132 percent increase over last year's figures (2006). In the span of a few years MySpace has become familiar to an entire generation of American youth as an indispensable means of experiencing and communicating with the world. The events of everyday life are documented on MySpace profiles, from schoolyard gossip to weekend plans; it has become a forum for daily interaction with peers.

Unsurprisingly, life-changing events in the lives of MySpace users also are represented on user profile pages. Marriages, births, graduations, military service, and relocations are all incorporated into their user pages and assimilated within the context of the Internet through pictures, blogs, and user comments. Death is similarly represented online, often in striking ways. MySpace users continuously update their pages to reflect changes as they occur. When a user dies, however, the site remains unchanged—except for the message board. The deceased's online network of MySpace "friends" (composed of real-world friends

and people met *through* MySpace) continue to leave comments on the
message board of the dead user. These comments are generally personal expressions of grief and an attempt to mitigate the permanence
of the loss by keeping up a direct correspondence with the departed.
Communication with the dead via MySpace message boards functions
within a matrix of intermingled contexts: social, spatial, and temporal. It
involves a unique overlapping of several spheres of influence, including
the public and the private, the progressive and the static, and varying
patterns of grief and otherworldly belief.

While it is difficult to pinpoint the exact demographics of MySpace,
a report by owner and Fox media mogul Rupert Murdoch announced
the creation of the 100 millionth MySpace account on 9 August 2006
(Adest 2006). The site has experienced exponential growth since its
launch a few years ago, and it has become a byword in any discussion
of current youth culture (Tancer 2006). Teens use the site as a way to
create and perpetuate individual identity as well as a means of staying
in touch with one another outside of school. A typical MySpace page
includes pictures of the user, links to blogs written by the user, links to
the MySpace pages of the user's friends, and a comment board where
friends can post messages to the user that are visible to all visitors at
the site. Personal modifications can be added to this basic format, such
as the creation of unique web backgrounds and a feature that allows
the user to choose a song that will play whenever his or her page is
viewed. The result is an online representation of one's self over which
each user has complete control. And it is this very personal representation of self that gives a MySpace page increased importance when the
user dies.

I have observed that bereaved friends often continue to comment
upon a now-static MySpace page in the present tense on a wide variety
of topics: from the sharing of memories, to updates on daily life, to asking for guidance and signs from the deceased. In conducting a survey of
the types of comments left on the pages of dead MySpace users, I have
found that several trends seem to arise from this mass of communications. In this chapter I will provide an overview of some of the scholarship relating to the memorialization process; give a description of the
various trends found in the MySpace comments, with special attention
to the contexts in which these trends should be viewed; and conclude
with an analysis of this phenomenon as an important area of study in the
field of folk, or vernacular, religion.

Roadside Memorials

Given the recent emergence of social networking sites like MySpace, there is a dearth of scholarly literature examining the role the Internet can play in the expression of grief. However, the scholarship on road-side memorials[2] can be very useful in building an approach to the topic. Holly Everett discusses these in relation to the history of American death rituals, from the early tradition of funereal preparation occurring wholly within a private home to the modern and much-discussed "denial of death" where the preparations are performed in seclusion by the third-party, objective mortuary industry. Everett emphasizes the uniqueness of the roadside memorial as occupying "a space in the *public* landscape, and imagination, in between the home and the often geographically removed modern cemetery" (2002, 82; emphasis in original). It is just this interstitial nature that imbues the roadside memorial with such an affective charge. Public memorialization makes the act of mourning accessible to anyone in the vicinity of the shrine, personalizing this act while still separating the mourner from the physical corpse. Anyone who is affected by the death is free to visit the memorial and experience grief in his or her own private manner.

In addition to allowing for individual grief, roadside memorials place great emphasis upon the individuality of the deceased, affirming personal identity in the face of the anonymity of adolescent highway mortality, which made up 36 percent of all teenage deaths in America in 2006 (Centers for Disease Control and Prevention 2007). The sheer statistical prevalence of automobile deaths blurs the victim's personality and relegates the tragedy to the realm of cautionary tales and newspaper obituaries. Robert James Smith makes this point, describing a site maintained by a man to honor two victims of a fatal accident far from their own homes as "an attempt to declare and maintain a public grief against the seeming anonymity and erasure of most highway deaths" (1999, 103–04). Such shrines also "reflect a deeper unease about modern mobility, transience, the fragility of life, even the difficulty of identifying those responsible for the tragedies" (105). The American highway is symbolic of the modern high-speed world of the information superhighway, in which attention is always pushed forward to focus on the next thing. In a more literal sense, the highway system is maintained in such a way that the physical evidence of an auto wreck vanishes within weeks of its occurrence, effectively erasing the tragedy. As a result, the bereaved become determined to create and maintain a physical reminder to set the deceased apart from the mass of highway deaths that occur each year.

Public and Private

There is a sense of spiritual mystery about the roadside death site, as though something of the essence of the deceased might linger in the area, imparting a hierophantic aura to the physicality of the monument. The accident site becomes a publicly accessible space for interaction with and contemplation of the dead. It is an active process in that it is common for personal items to be left at the site, such as the crosses—covered with writing, engravings, and pictures—that Everett documents in her study (2002, 87). The public nature of these memorials allows anyone to mourn; the rights of grieving are not restricted to immediate friends and family. There is a communal aspect here, one that is not so obvious at the more sober and austere cemetery plot where the physical body rests. George Monger sees this as "an act of remembrance and of solidarity, a symbolic coming together of the community in mourning" (1997, 114). MySpace grief similarly involves active participation in the grieving process, although it is questionable whether or not the mourners who leave messages on these sites should be viewed as comprising a "community" in the normal sense of the word.

The act of posting a comment on the message board of the deceased is essential to this online grieving process. Because MySpace is usually a public forum, the profile of a deceased member can be viewed by anyone at any time, but the simple act of anonymously visiting a page does not appear to be enough for many mourners. A more direct and perceptible engagement with the deceased becomes necessary. This can be seen in the hesitancy that many posters show in their messages, as well as in the feeling that they are somehow obligated to express their feelings in a public forum. The following, pulled from the message boards of deceased teens, reveal the posters' struggle to understand tragic loss with emotional words to the departed. The first three are from the MySpace page of a young woman, Valerie, and clearly show that for some mourners, time was needed before they felt able to comment, an act that seems to signify the permanence of the loss:[3]

> Valerie—I have not been able to bring myself to comment because I do not want to believe this is even true.

> Valerie, Valerie, Valerie . . . this has taken me awhile to leave you a comment since you've been gone and I thought it was time that I really need to do this . . . I hope you will get this somehow, but I know that you can't reply back to me.

It's been a week since you've been gone and I think I really need to do this . . .

In the next message, a poster questions the public nature of the MySpace page:

Jason, I have trouble understanding why I would write to you for everyone to see, when I know you understand anyway, but, damn, sometimes I'm just compelled to. I miss you bro.

Similar themes are found in these comments posted to the page of a young woman:

Hey Kate!!! I'm sorry I haven't left you a message yet but I just couldn't bring myself to do it. I'm gonna try now but just thought of writing this to you knowing that you are gone makes me cry. It's not fair.

Hey baby girl just wanted to let you know that I am still thinkin of you and I visit your site all of the time it's just hard to always stay long enough to leave comments I love and miss you everyday.

For many mourners, posting a comment appears to be a step toward dealing with the loss. This seems similar to a loved one visiting and possibly speaking to a grave marker in the cemetery, only on MySpace, the act is done in a public sphere. Each comment will theoretically last as long as the site itself.

In an article in the *Miami Herald*, MySpace researcher Larry Rosen suggests that "when teens visit a crash site or grave marker they grieve alone. But at virtual memorials they meet an entire peer grieving community" (Bird 2006). Nonetheless, the existence of a "community" of grief online is debatable. Society's attitude toward the Internet seems to be that anything communicated online becomes public domain, independent of the scrambling legal networks that are constantly evolving around Internet usage. The much-publicized debates over the legality of music and movie piracy are evidence of this mindset. Anyone who expresses personal, private grief through a comment left on a MySpace message board knows that his or her message can potentially be viewed by anyone who wishes to look. The similarities in the types of comments left on the same pages show a congruity in grief, but I have found very little evidence of any of the bereaved acknowledging the sorrow of any other message-poster. Instead, the posters commonly express feelings of loneliness and abandonment in the absence of the departed, giving the impression that MySpace mourners grieve alone, together. Nothing can be inferred about the coping mechanisms in place outside of the cyber-world, of course, but in terms of virtual memorialization, the community

of mourners seems to be united in their isolation. For instance, these
comments left by three different female posters on the MySpace page of
a fifteen-year-old girl who died in a car crash indicate intense feelings of
forlornness and isolation in their experiences of grief:

> lisa i really need you right now things are going wrong . . . my life is
> so turned around and i am lost. i dont know what to do anymore.

> im beginning to hate life, once again . . . i know that i shouldnt, but
> what do you do when you feel like theres no one around to be there
> for you or even wonder whats wrong . . . i just want to leave, and be
> with you . . . it seems that you are the only person that i could rely on
> to love me and care about me.

> I miss you sooo much and I think about you everyday. I can't wait
> to be with you and see you again. I don't know if you know or
> not . . . but you were really the **only** person I could tell everything to.
> I could trust you . . . like no other person. I'm not afraid to die any-
> more, 'cuz I know . . . that when I do end this life here . . . I'll be with
> you. And I don't want to sound crazy, but that would make me soo
> happy . . . to be able to spend time with you again. But I'll write more
> sometime else . . . sometime soon. I love you! and I miss you terribly.
> I'll talk to you later. <3

It is possible that these messages function as cries for help, given
the public nature of MySpace, but it also seems quite likely that there
is a high level of teenage solipsism occurring in these comments. It is
hard, if not impossible, to determine to what extent these declarations of
grief are public posturing and to what extent they are genuine, personal
expressions of deep feeling.

As discussed above, a main feature of MySpace is the creation of
individual identities, or *profiles*, which serve as thoroughly constructed
personae to represent the essence of a personality. Every MySpace
interaction, then, is carried out along the lines of these public-oriented
expressions of the private. Because all MySpace identities are specifically manufactured, and since their representations of self may differ
from the reality of that self, the only means of truly sincere expression
must focus on the individual's *voice*, that is, on the text of a person's comments and messages. The amount of posturing involved in the construction of these identities makes it difficult to gauge sincerity, though the
undeniable presence of casual conversation, fraught with jarring slang
and mistaken grammar, grants a much clearer picture of a true personality reaching out from the manufactured profiles. The ideas conveyed
in these impromptu comments are often so heartbreakingly direct and

unselfconsciously fumbling that it leads me to believe that the expressions of grief communicated on these message boards are quite genuine. In most cases the posters seem to intend them to be very personal, private transmissions to the deceased, although it must be stressed that the public component is so thoroughly pervasive in Internet culture that the extent of its influence on communication, whether conscious or not, is impossible to delineate. As Montana Miller emphasizes in her work on the subject of web memorials, one never knows exactly which "frame" these teens are working in, and to further confuse the issue, the teens themselves do not know. "How are the performances keyed? The senses and sensibilities we used to use to gauge this no longer apply. It's like trying to apply the rules and ethics of friendship to your 387 MySpace 'friends'" (2007).

In some instances it seems that the public aspect becomes more important to the griever than the private one. This may be the case in the frequent postings by people who claim to have not really known the deceased well but are nonetheless struck by the loss. A feeling of being part of a group becomes especially important to these posters, both in the sense that they experienced the loss of the deceased on a community level—sudden death confronts the poster with the fact of his own fragile mortality—and in the sense that the act of expressing sorrow on a public page joins them to the supposed community of grievers. In this band of isolated mourners, the bereft acquaintance can easily enter the online grieving process, avoiding the awkwardness of interacting with the close friends and immediate family of the deceased, to whom this grief is socially supposed to belong. As could be expected, this seems especially prevalent in cases of particularly random deaths, such as that of a Wal-Mart employee who was killed in the parking lot by a stranger who began indiscriminately firing a gun. With car accidents and suicides, there is often some notion of personal responsibility—maybe the victim was driving too fast or going somewhere he should not have been—but in cases of random violence, the pure unpredictability of death is shocking:

> R.I.P. Billy! u will be missed buddy . . . Didnt no u that well but everytime we chilled or talked it was always something funny . . . u cracked me up . . . You are a caring person n dont no why such a thing would happen to u.

> This world is quite a scary place to live in at times.

> Even though i never met him he is part of my family, the walmart family, i along with him both work there, i a cashier and he a cart boy.

Billy,
Though we only hung out once this tragedy has really impacted me.
Why someone could do that to someone innocent is sick.

These posters can be seen struggling to understand violence in the world. They are expressing confusion and fear at the simple abruptness death can impose on anyone's life at any time. Although "Billy" was a peripheral character, or even a stranger, in their lives, the unpredictability of his death could just as easily happen to any one of the posters or to their own loved ones.

The idea of a supporting community of grief is often very apparent in the studies of roadside memorials. Everett (2002) writes of a memorial as a "gathering place" for friends of the deceased, and reports "groups of teens" congregating at a site to mourn. The parents of the deceased often end up taking an active role in the creation and maintenance of a memorial out of concern for the emotional health of the deceased's friends. While there is some direct evidence of parents communicating with friends of the deceased through MySpace, there is perhaps greater evidence that this is often not the case. Every profile lists the most recent login date for each user. Many accounts have not been accessed since the day of death, suggesting that there is no adult participation in the mourning process of the bereft adolescents.

Motion and Stasis

Roadside memorials have an existential resonance, in that they mark the point of departure from life into death, which is vitally important to the grieving friends of the deceased. The memorial, often a cross at the side of the road, can function as a physical representation of this transition. Visitors are confronted with the fact of a deep and long-lasting change; they come to the site because they feel that something of the deceased's spirit remains, but the irrevocability of the loss is symbolized in the cross, the traditional Christian representation of life transforming into death. Contemplating death's permanence, coupled with a belief in the persistence of the soul, can help in dealing with grief. A woman interviewed by Everett describes this occurrence at a memorial site for her daughter: "[Tara's] friends tell me all the time that when they're feeling down or they've got a problem or whatever that they'll go up there and sit at the cross. And then they'll feel better when they leave. So I feel like to them it's, it's a place to go, someplace that they feel like Tara's still there, you know, and I, it's hard to explain" (2002, 93).

There is a sense of progression, or at least of motion: a life was lived, and then it underwent a drastic and visible change into the form of a departed soul. This movement may be what lies behind the affectivity of a memorial over the actual gravesite. Everett quotes another woman who has lost a son: "Even though I go to the cemetery, I don't, it didn't seem like that was where I was drawn because he's not really at the cemetery. For some reason or another this location is where he was, so I would go there and so I wanted to put a cross there because that was where I went the most. And so I guess the symbolism is that that's kind of where I felt his spirit was last" (2002, 96). The mourners experience a feeling of the momentum of a life force that hangs about an accident site.

MySpace memorials lack this sense of movement for the most part, an aspect that is all the more striking in the context of the Internet, which is characterized by constant motion and fleeting temporality. Many MySpace users check their accounts at least once a day, visiting the profiles of their friends to see the latest posted pictures, comments, blogs, and music. If a profile does not experience steady change, it becomes increasingly less likely to be visited. The page of a dead MySpace user necessarily remains static. Comments accrue, especially on birthdays, holidays, and the anniversary of that individual's death, but the personal aspects of the deceased's constructed online identity are unaltered. The pictures stay the same, no blogs are added, and often the last login date remains painfully close to the date of death. The song picked to play for the visitor never changes, even though it has often significantly outlived its pop-chart expiration date. In an arena so dependent on fluid and constant motion, these sites possess an eerie stillness. On the surface this stasis seems to be appropriate for the funerary atmosphere of the message board; however, any representation of physical change—like the life-to-death progression of the roadside cross or even the solid finality of a granite slab—is wholly absent. The teens who visit a dead friend's site sometimes seem unnerved by this lack. They express distress at the tension between the invariability of the deceased's profile and the continuance of their own lives, now marred by the pain of loss. The following quotes, taken from several different message boards, all reflect the emotional turmoil of confronting the unchanging song choices and photos of their lost friends on the latter's MySpace pages:

This song makes me really sad . . .

I think cuz I listened too them ALL THE TIME in 8th/9th grade when we hung out so much . . . i hate how memories hurt so bad . . .
i love you.

Its so hard for me to come on here and see this.

damn girl i miss u sO much! when i lOok at ur pics. i think abOut ur smile, ur laigh . . . just everything n i miss it sO much! sO much has changed cOurt! so much! n it hurts.

fuck man im missin you! i look at your page still everyday n can't believe ur not around ne more. love ya man stay up n keep on ballin man! :'(

Everytime I look at this page, and your last login, it's almost as if I expect something to change, but it never does . . . a tear will always shed in my eye.

One result of this conflict between motion and stasis is the mourners' increasing desire for the deceased's page to be permanent. A great deal of this feeling is probably an extension of the same yearning shown by erecting roadside memorials—to protect the memory of the deceased from the anonymity of teenage death. Because there is no physical, real-world "space" involved in a MySpace page, the apparent possibility of forever losing traces of the deceased is intensified. Since its inception, MySpace has been plagued with persistent rumors that it will either be taken down or start charging members to maintain accounts. The increasing frequency of spamming, phishing, and other chronic e-mail and Internet hazards throughout the MySpace community may also be weakening users' general trust in the site. Many comments emphatically promise the deceased that they will not be forgotten, using all caps and bold type to stress phrases like "never forget" and "always remember," but there are also frequent examples of this fear of "losing" the deceased in specific relation to a MySpace profile:

does the pain ever go away angie? like a part of me wants it to bc im tired of hurting all the time, but another part doesnt want it to go away bc in a sence thats me forgetting a part of you and not remembering what happened and how much i fuckin love you! i really just hope you know how much i love you angie . . . and thats one thing that'll never die . . . i miss you and love you with all my heart!

i hate how your MySpace is deteriorating :/

Who ever is running Billy's profile now . . . plz NEVER delete it.

The idea that time erodes all traces of the departed seems to be especially poignant to MySpace grievers. There is evidence that many of these

MySpace dead have active roadside memorials and gravesites in addition
to their online profiles, but the motionlessness of the profile, in its static
depiction of the deceased at the time of his or her death, seems to possess more immediacy. Even more than a depiction, it represents an act of
creation by the deceased, who put something of himself into the construction of his online identity. While the palpable memorial sites manifest the
physical loss of the person, a MySpace profile holds the memory of the
deceased frozen in time and thus unchanged in the minds of mourners.
The transformative aspect of death is removed, and the deceased effectively becomes a "ghost" in a space that is not tangible and a time that is
arrested. This is not necessarily a hindrance to the healthy overcoming
of grief by the bereft, but it is something I believe to be unique to the
medium of the Internet. The passing of time in the "real" world affects
MySpace mourners, who are sometimes distressed, as above, and sometimes take a kind of comfort in the stability of the profile, though mindful
of the sense that it, too, could vanish. For some users, the act of checking
the deceased's MySpace page and commenting on it becomes ritualistic.
There is often a sense of disbelief in the amount of time that has passed
as well as the idea that the deceased can be held on to in some manner
through continued activity on his or her MySpace profile:

> every time i come in here, i always want to tell you the same thing.
> and that is, i love you. but i want to say something more than that
> this time.
> something like i think about you all the time and how i love to see
> your face everyday even though they're just pictures.
> i still love you tons and i miss you very very much.

> It sucks that its been 7 months today. Time has just been flying and I
> dont want it to. I wish it was like May 3rd when i was talking to u in
> class before i left for my game.

> heey tyler i was lookin at ur page like everytime im on here lol i cant
> believe its been almost a year. it seems like it was jus yesterday but
> then again it seems like 4ever its weird :[but i miss u just the same
> especially now that its summer. i keep thinkin about last year and
> how at this time we were havin so much fun* everyone Loves u &
> misses you down here *xoxo*

There is evidence that as time increases the distance between the mourners and the dead, the posters worry that the deceased will lose importance in their lives. These individuals express the fear that if they overcome their grief and "go on with their lives," the dead friend will cease to

exist altogether, and not just be lost in the physical, mortal sense. There is a belief that the passage of time lessens the importance of past friendships and events, and we can plainly see attempts on these MySpace pages at safeguarding memory against the steady sweep of time. The widening gap between the period when the deceased was alive and the mourner's present timeframe is especially visible on a MySpace profile, where the unchanging personality of the dead exists seemingly forever.

Grief Patterns

Certain trends emerge in the comments left on the pages of dead MySpace users. Some grievers exhibit a more intuitive, feeling-based connection to the spirit of the departed, while other mourners tend to focus on past memories and what they imagine the deceased might be up to in heaven. Some posters write of "sensing" the presence of the deceased and a certainty in the knowledge that the deceased is actively watching over them and participating in their lives. Others seem to focus on the continuation of past activities into the afterlife, often instructing their deceased friends to get the party in heaven ready for their own eventual arrivals. They experience the immediate presence of the dead much less frequently than do the intuitive grievers.

The patterns emerging on the MySpace message boards fit the descriptions of mourning trends discussed by Terry Martin and Kenneth Doka (2000), who write of *intuitive* and *instrumental* patterns of grieving that the authors stress are related to, but certainly not determined by, gender. The intuitive style is characterized by an intense, feeling-based, affective experience and generally occurs more often in female mourners, while males are more likely to be instrumental grievers, mourning on a more physical, cognitive level. Intuitive grievers find solace in an outward expression of anguish and in sharing their feelings with other mourners, while instrumental grievers are less affected on a gut level, transferring their energy into action, often in the form of physical or written dedications to the deceased. Again, the authors are careful to assert that both intuitive and instrumental patterns of grief are found among mourners of both sexes, and that the prevalence of the intuitive form among women and the instrumental one among men is almost certainly the result of the socialization of gender roles. The examples used in this chapter tend to fall along these gender lines, with female and male mourners often respectively exhibiting aspects of the intuitive and instrumental styles of grief; however, more data would need to be collected before this observation could be discussed conclusively.

These findings echo those of Gillian Bennett in her study of supernatural beliefs among women. She describes the commonality of the belief in the "good dead" among women, referring to spirits that are helpful and protective: "As they describe it, they are made aware of the souls of the good dead more often through sensing their presence than by seeing them in physical form" (1988, 30). Belief in the good dead reinforces the traditionally "feminine" intuitive notion that the world is an inherently benevolent and deeply meaningful place. "A traditional belief is accepted most readily if it depends upon the utilization of intuition, imagination, insight; if it is an involuntary experience rather than a chosen activity; if it enhances or extends personal relationships; and if it gives reassurance of the goodness of God and man" (31). Many female MySpace mourners comment very directly, thanking the deceased for protection that they seem certain has been provided:

> i got my license 2 days ago . . . i wore your necklace for good luck . . . a butterfly landed rite next to me and stayed there for like 5 mins before i went in the car . . . hmmm maybe it was you :) i miss you like crazyyy keep me safe while im driving. i love you and miss you so much
> 918 foreverr

> Kelly . . .
> You've been so heavy on heart the last few days. When I get into my car accident a few weeks ago, I know you were there to protect me, bcuz my accident coulda been way worse than what it was, and I think you were watching over me, not letting the air bags go off, bcuz everyone is shocked they didnt go off . . . but its a good thing they didnt bcuz I woulda got really hurt just from the air bags . . . Thank You for being my angel and always watching over me and every-one down here . . . I love you and miss you sooo much, I think of you everyday, every song on the radio makes me think of you, and I know you enjoy my kisses I blow you everyday when I drive by! I love you girl!
> ♥Nicole

> Hey Pete! Well I just wanted to thank you for being my angel today and making sure that my accident didn't end up much worse . . . I know you were there and everyone told me I was very lucky I didn't flip, and that I walked away unharmed . . . They all said that I must have had an angel looking out for me . . . And I knew it was you . . . I love you Pete!

Interestingly, these young women assume that because the deceased died in car accidents, the realm of automobile safety somehow falls under their personal jurisdiction, similar to the functions of Catholic saints.

Many intuitive grievers also express thanks to the deceased for the manifestation of certain "signs" to communicate their continued presence in the lives of the posters. This can range from the abovementioned appearance of a butterfly, to the playing of a certain song on the radio, or even significant formations in the clouds:

> The other day, you randomly came into my mind right when I felt alone . . . and then, for some reason, I turned around and immediately looked out the window and there was a sunstreaked sky just about to begin one of the most beautiful sunsets I've ever seen . . . it brought tears to my eyes. It was as if you took my chin and turned my head to show me that you are still with me and to show me how beautiful life can really be when put into it's simplest forms.

> I love you sweetheart and think about you EVERYDAY! Yesterday I saw that rainbow :) U knew exactly what I needed . . . Thank you!

There is even some evidence that the public nature of MySpace may influence how the living experience otherworldly communications. On the message board of a young girl who died in a car accident, many of her friends write of the same types of signs from the deceased. The quantity of these experiences on this one page may indicate that the mourners are taking cues from one another. Numerous examples are given by different posters of the popular Shakira song, "Hips Don't Lie," being used by the deceased to offer reassurance; and various phenomena in the sky are reported, including one girl who posted a photograph of a cloud formation roughly in the shape of the numeral 3, the uniform number of the deceased:

> hips dont lie has come on the radio like twice everyday when i'm listening to it . . . and right away i'm like yup, vals with us! i know it =) i love youuuu sooooooo much girl. i'll keep praying and i can't wait to see you again! ♥

> I was at rehab today and while I was doing my excercises doesn't hips don't lie come on. I had a big smile on my face because I knew you were telling me you were there with me. I miss you so much! I can't wait to see you again someday!

> Everytime I'm stressin over school or upset, your song comes on Val.

And I know it you, telling me to smile, and that I'll get through it.
Miss you. Love you.

Ashley and I went to Subway to eat today and as soon as we sat
down doesnt hips dont lie come on . . . we both looked at each other
and said thanks val for letting us know your with us . . . you just love
to do that to us . . . i miss you soo much . . . love you hun cant wait to
see u again!!!

the other day at field hockey it was soo shitty out and as soon as
michelle scored it got soo sunny out and we know it was you letting
haley know you were proud . . . me and ruth just looked at eachother
and we were like ahh VALERIE. and today for the first home game
everyone kept finding 4 leaf clovers . . . we know youre always with
us girl.

we lost to palmerton tonight.
how depressing is that.
i know you were watching.
@ the beginning of the game. i kept starring @ the clouds around the
moon . . .

then the letters L. A. V. appeared . . .
VAL . . . then a big heart formed around the moon.
that brought the biggest smile to my face . . . and i started to get teary
eyed.

I love you val . . . and i know your looking over all of us. I saw
another number 3 in the sky when me and my friends were going out
last week!! Love you girl. [left several weeks after the user posted a
photograph of a cloud formation to the site]

It is common for intuitive grievers to use the MySpace message boards
to confirm to the deceased that they are receiving their communications
from the afterlife. Due to the life-altering nature of the loss of a close friend,
naturally many teens find themselves dreaming frequently of the dead
person. They often seem to recognize this as a product of stress and grief,
but sometimes it becomes apparent that these posters are interpreting the
dreams as the deceased's attempts to make contact. As a result, comments
spring up assuring the dead friend that the attempt has been acknowledged and should be repeated. The subconscious nature of dreams, however, leaves these posters frustrated by their inability to control the situation or say the things they wish. MySpace message boards give them this
control, but it is only a one-sided conversation with the dead:

hi leah . . . i know we talked and u gave me a hug good bye the other
day in my dream.. i know it was real because even in my dream i was
crying to you telling u that u were gone n beggin u not to leave me,
but wen i turned to look at u again u were gone!

Baby girl, I'm trying, I had a dream of you the other night, thanks,
You know I need the visit!!! I Love You BH FOREVER & EVER

Call me again please !!! My dreams feel more real every time I have
them. I long to have them, that at times all I want to do is sleep all
day just to get close to you. I need you so bad right now. I want to
hear your voice and see new pics of you.

hey ant-man i love you so much i had a dream like a while ago that
you came down from heaven and all i said was i love you and good
bye then you went into the sky and i woke up crying i hope you
have seen courtney in her dreams like i asked you to well i love you
soo much!

Posters' comments on the MySpace pages of the dead that relate
experiences of otherworldly contact mostly fall under the rubric of the
intuitive style of grief. These individuals *feel* the dead as a continued presence in their lives and often readily interpret daily events and dreams as
communications from the beyond. There may even be something in the
general communicative nature of MySpace that readily lends itself to
these intuitive experiences.

Trends in the comments left by instrumental grievers are generally
more oriented toward the past and the future, focusing on old memories and looking forward to continuing the friendship in the afterlife.
These posters seem to view life and death as distinctly separate spheres,
with much less evidence of spirits actively interacting with the living,
although both they and intuitive grievers share the belief that the dead
are able to read the messages they are posting. The posts usually emphasize past memories and future reunions, with the present mentioned
only in the form of creative dedications. The following are examples of
future reunion posts:

so im thinkin a keg . . . a few kegs lots of food, im talkin like all the
snacks man. cookies chips dip crackers (not like the kind we are) an
island to party on (im sure theres a good one big enough to fit us all
on up there) fire wood guitars and the sax fa sho. i dont know how
long you have but it better be there when we get there brother because
its gonna be the biggest party youve ever seen!!!!!!! love ya bro

wutup my nigga, me dave n jimmy bout to visit u n smoke a blunt
with u
jus like old times

Hey bro i think about you all the time and everytime i do it brings
a tear to my eye how something so horrbile happened to some1 so
nice. i Miss you cant wait to see you once again but we all know you
are living it up where you are now. see ya when i get there.

made some pumpkin pies like we did last year . . .
make jesus one . . . tell him Shawn Carter taught me that bomb ass
recipe . . . =-)

And here are some creative dedications:

ill smoke my next blunt to you =/

r.i.p. i'll lay down a sweet ass happy hardcore set for ya at the next
party at the end of the month

happy birthday angela i still miss u so much u'll neva kno we haven
a party 2nite jus 4 u gurl

Instrumental expressions of grief on MySpace pages mostly fit this
pattern of viewing death as final and divisive. For these mourners,
communication with the dead appears to be a one-sided endeavor; the
deceased can hear them but cannot interact with them. Since this concept effectively removes the dead from the present realm of existence,
the comments of instrumental grievers more frequently focus on the
continuation of earthly activities "in the name of" the deceased, with
the idea that the dead appreciate this in the afterlife and even anticipate
a future reunion. These messages display a more cognitive approach to
grief, in that the mourners seem to accept that the loss is permanent and
begin to reshape their existence around it, dedicating their lives, songs,
and drugs to the deceased without the intensity of feeling exhibited by
intuitive mourners.

MySpace Mourning as Folk Religion

Communication with the dead via MySpace message boards recon-
textualizes the grieving process for the cyberoriented generation of
American youth. This virtual arena for the experiences of death and grief
exists at the intersection of the public and private lives of teenagers. On
an existential level, much of the emotional charge of dead users' profiles

arises from the dynamic contradictions of motion and stasis in Internet space-time. Active engagement and communication with the deceased can be described in terms of patterns of mourning. What emerges is a complex and multilayered depiction of teenage grief adapted to and influenced by the cyber medium.

Functionally, the phenomenon of MySpace mourning reclaims death from the clinical hands of highway statistics and the funerary industry, making it accessible on a very intimate level. Every poster to a MySpace profile is free to express grief in whatever way he or she feels best pertains to his or her personal experience of that death. Specific trends in MySpace comments indicate the possibility of a public-sphere influence on the poster (as may be the case when multiple posters relate nearly identical experiences of signs from the deceased), but the *sense* of allowing personal approaches to grief is still present. The casual, conversational tone of many of the messages abounds with individuals fumbling toward coming to terms with loss.

Folk religion, based on Don Yoder's definition (1974), is often conceived of as a set of beliefs existing apart from and alongside of "official" religious beliefs and practices. Leonard Primiano (1995) responded to this concept by placing more emphasis on the individual, personal aspect of religious belief. The act of commenting upon the profile of a dead MySpace user brings many of the folk-religious aspects of the creation and maintenance of roadside memorials into the digital age. Both phenomena can be viewed as a folk reaction to the objectivity of the modern American death industry. They personalize death, keeping the individual characteristics of the deceased alive and preserved in a space separate from memory and photographs. Any person who wishes to participate in the grieving process—including communication with the dead—may do so, whether it be talking to a cross at an accident site or via the medium of a MySpace message board. They are both unique approaches to mourning that offer alternatives to the traditional funerals and cemetery rituals that seem cold and impersonal by comparison.

The psychological aspects of Internet grieving, as compared to roadside memorialization, remain to be seen, but they could prove to function differently, since MySpace profiles lack motion, contrary to the transformative symbolism of roadside shrines. The oldest profiles of dead MySpace users are no more than a few years old, and they already possess a haunting stillness. A few of the sites, just a year after the user's death, have already experienced a dramatic decrease in the frequency of posted messages. Except for a few who post with regularity, many mourners post only on birthdays, anniversaries of death, and holidays.

And, of course, the deceased remains unaffected by time and space, frozen at the age of death for as long as the MySpace phenomenon maintains its popularity.

Only time will tell what effects the transition of grief into the digital world will have on the memorialization process. The ubiquitous presence of the Internet in today's society is still an emergent phenomenon in many ways, with new advances and trends appearing almost daily. The current popularity of MySpace and the movement of everyday life into the sphere of cyberspace effect youth interactions in a complex variety of ways. As traditions of grief are adapted to the new virtual world, many exciting vistas for folkloric study are opening up for the observant, and the rapidity of change makes the continued documentation of digital influences all the more important in understanding modern culture.

Notes

1. Versions of this chapter were presented at the 2007 meeting of the Western States Folklore Society and the 2007 meeting of the American Folklore Society, where it was awarded the Don Yoder Prize for the Best Student Paper in Folk Belief or Religious Folklife.
2. This chapter owes much to the work of Everett (2002), Santino (2006), and Miller (2007), as well as to the encouragement of Dr. Daniel Wojcik at the University of Oregon.
3. All names of MySpace users have been changed to protect the users' privacy. I have replicated the spelling and grammar of all comments in their original public syntax.

Chapter 8

Public Folklore in Cyberspace

GREGORY HANSEN

In 1985 I was working with the Kentucky Center for the Arts in Louisville as a fieldworker for the Kentucky Folk Project. The project was funded by a grant from the National Endowment for the Arts, and it consisted of a twelve-county survey of folk arts in north-central Kentucky. Four months of fieldwork resulted in presentations at the center's festival, the Kentucky Folklife Celebration. Additional activities included a traveling exhibit entitled "Patterns between the Rivers: Tradition in North-Central Kentucky." During the course of the project, fieldworkers documented a range of Kentucky folk arts, including blues music, quilt-making, old-time fiddling, johnboat building, tobacco twisting, weaving, woodcarving, beekeeping, and dozens of other forms of expressive culture. The project provided me with many firsts: the opportunity to work as a public folklorist, assist with a folklife festival, and see photographs that I had taken featured in an exhibit (Feintuch 1988, 1). It also was my first exposure to the use of computers in public programming. I open with this example to illustrate several of the activities of public folklorists, as well as to foreground some of the salient issues involved in using computers in public presentations of folklife.

This era of computing was pre-Internet. I had heard rumors of something akin to text messaging while I was taking courses on computing at the Pennsylvania State University. The instructor was teaching us to use BASIC as well as PLI computer languages, and I completed an independent study project in which I computerized Vladímir Propp's morphology using computer punchcards. The next semester our campus installed its first CRTs, and I learned to use existing software, create databases, clandestinely send messages on a nascent network confined only to small computer labs, and discovered a range of graphics programs that involved scanning images and using titles. These types of computer uses all became part of the Kentucky Center's exhibit, as the project director was able to secure support from the Wang Corporation to use its PCs and receive some technical assistance to enhance the presentation of fieldwork material.

During this time, public folklorists were using computers in their projects, but colleagues told me that they were mainly employing them as resources in the field. Word processors were beginning to replace electric typewriters, and folklorists were starting to assemble databases of material they had collected. When the Wang Corporation agreed to create a partnership with the Kentucky Center for the Arts, the idea was that computers would augment the panels of photographs and text by supplementing the primary material on display. These support materials mainly consisted of information available from a database that would allow viewers to find specific details about the folklife of a particular county within the survey area and see images scanned using Wang's Autocad program. Examples of items audiences could access from the database included weather beliefs, home remedies, and recipes. Our visual images were limited by the scanty storage of these early personal computers, so the computer screens showed a diagram of a tobacco plant, a drawing of a johnboat, images of quilt patterns, and other one-page representations. The results from the computerized component of the exhibit were mixed. On the one hand, viewers did interact with the computer, but they quickly lost interest; the relatively crude black-and-white images were not nearly as attractive as the exhibit's color photographs reproduced from 35mm slides. Emphasis on using the computer for images was often at the expense of content, as there was little opportunity to integrate interpretive text into the scanned images at this time. The databases had the potential to be more successful, but the grand plan of indexing collectanea to counties suffered because of limited data as well as the Byzantine system that was required to create this program. Furthermore, our plan to place the computers and their CPU into wooden cabinets failed within the first day of exhibit. The equipment overheated, and woodworkers had to redo the cabinets to create a ventilation system by cutting out large sections of the wood and installing small fans. Maintaining this computer technology became so labor intensive that eventually the traveling-exhibit version of the project became available without the support of the computers, and the older model of combining text and photographs on exhibit panels seemed to succeed just as well without access to scanned images and the database.

This somewhat nostalgic review of my first use of computers in public programming provides some historical context for employing them there. The Kentucky Folk Project was one of the first times computers were used in the presentation—rather than the researching—of folklore within the public sector. This brief account also provides specific examples of ways in which public folklore often differs from academic research. Our work was supported through a public institution, funded by a grant, designed for public viewing rather than academic review, and written for a nonacademic audience (Baron and Spitzer 2007, viii). The focus was less on advancing scholarship on folklore and more on using the concepts and methods of folklorists to address the interests and needs of the general public (Hufford 1994, 5). Our staff had to follow the basic principles of keeping exhibit labels and computer texts short and simple. Jargon and footnotes were an anathema. This particular experience with computers also showcases some of the central problems in using them in public folklore. Even with the subsequent great advances in hardware and software and the myriad resources of the Internet, public folklorists still face the same problems that we encountered. Using computers creates challenges in adapting fieldwork data to computer-friendly formats. Reshaping the material of folklore into graphic forms appropriate for computer displays can be difficult. There often is a surprising scarcity of appropriate field data that can be used in computer technology. It is also challenging to use this technology in an innovative way that doesn't duplicate what can be presented in non-computerized formats. Moreover, it is tempting to simply computerize folklore mainly for the sake of computerizing folklore, rather than recognizing that some aspects of folklife can be understood much more vividly, vibrantly, and viscerally outside of cyberspace. Lastly, the equipment tends to break down. Despite the drawbacks, public folklorists and folklorists coordinating applied folklore projects within academic institutions are creatively using the Web to build innovative and engaging presentations to teach the public about folklore outside of college and university classrooms.

Marshal McLuhan's shopworn mantra, "the medium is the message" (1964, 23), is sometimes juxtaposed with the adage that content is king in cyberspace. The widespread adoption of new media has changed the scale of human interaction, and the Internet itself—as a new medium—is a novel way of conveying information about social interaction and a shifting sense of what it means to be part of an audience for public-folklore programming. On the other hand, folklore —as content for this innovative media—also has important implications for thinking about ways in which public folklorists use the Internet. Collections were simply waiting to be digitized, and widespread preservation efforts to convert archives and other collections into this format easily lend themselves to online applications. In this respect, using the Internet blends together the importance of the medium with the message as it addresses the dual goals of preservation and dissemination.

Moreover, looking at public folklorists' use of computer technology from both poles can provide additional useful perspectives that are well worth further consideration. One major interest is in ways folklorists' use of various computerized media shape the users' interactions both with the material of folklore and with a community of users. The sense of "public" in public folklore is very different in cyberspace. An audience of one person who is staring at a computer screen to view the work of public folklorists is in sharp contrast to an audience of hundreds, thousands, even millions, who attend concerts and folk festivals. It would be well worth researching how this different sense of audience is related to major themes in folklore, such as the place of public presentations within community life, the role of folklore in cultural conservation, and the potential use of folklore as cultural intervention (Hufford 1994, 3–4; Kurin 1997; Baron and Spitzer 2007, viii; Whisnant 1983, 13–14). In contrast to the metafolkloric issues that pertain to the use of media in general, what of the relationships between folklore as content and the use of computers to present information about our discipline? It is easy to access the Internet to discover a wealth of data and commentary about specific folk traditions, and folklore has an intrinsic appeal to many computer users. The content of folklore is evident in some of the most popular activities in cyberspace, from the presence of motifs, tale types, and folkloric themes in fantasy games to the websites of folklore enthusiasts who may specialize in highly esoteric forms of folk music, traditional art, vernacular architecture, or virtually any other genre.

A specific argument to weigh out one side or the other in this dichotomy, however, seems less relevant than looking at the ways public folklorists are using the Internet. Public folklorists are culture brokers (Kurin 1997, 13). They must mediate an understanding about folklore that engages both the intellectual history of folklore studies as a discipline and the needs of various interested publics. To comprehend how public folklorists use the computer to broker folk culture, it could be useful to explore these implications further by examining the tension between the importance of the medium versus the place of content in the use of computer technology. But, taking a different stance, leaping outside of this dichotomy provides a more useful way of understanding how folklorists are using cyberspace. Looking at specific genres and modes of representation gives a clearer idea of some ways in which folklorists are using computer technology to teach the public about folklore.

Sharon Sherman (1998) provides a useful entry point for looking at the modes of public presentations of folklore in cyberspace. Adapting ideas from film theorist Bill Nichols, Sherman analyzes folklorists' documentary films and videos and places them into five characteristic modes of presentation. These modes consist of the following ways to structure websites: expository, observational, interactive, reflexive, and performative. This chapter will later explore in greater detail specific websites examined in relation to these modes, but it is important to begin with basic definitions and the distinctions between them. In the *expository mode*, the website's builder typically poses a problem and then develops the content to establish conclusions about the initial situation. In the *observational mode*, the designers provide less mediation and typically use web cameras and synchronized sound to show events either unfolding in real time or video recordings of previous events. The *interactive mode* is especially well suited to the Internet. In this form of presentation, the website focuses on ways in which the user interacts with the content and forms of presentation. In contrast to an interactive documentary film, which highlights the director's choices, an interactive website places its emphasis on ways that computer users make choices as they navigate a specific site. The *reflexive mode* takes a different approach to this type of interaction. Whereas the previous mode stresses the users' interactions within the website, the reflexive mode emphasizes various problems involved in the presentation of its content. Rather than building a Brechtian fourth wall in cyberspace, reflexive website designers bring their own presence into the form and content of the presentation. The website builder is unmasked, and his or her choices and sense of subjectivity are included in the presentation of the material placed into cyberspace. Content frequently forms the emphasis of such modes as the expository and the interactive. In contrast, the fifth representational form, the *performative mode*, opens enormous resources for creatively using new technologies. In this style, the website foregrounds the artistic, poetic, and rhetorical aspects of what is presented, thereby forcing viewers to fill in the material itself. The focus is less on didactic content and more on aesthetic appeal. Finely crafted performative websites unite techniques from documentary filmmaking with principles of website design to create a highly mediated feel for the experience of a folkloric performance. Sherman's typology undoubtedly can be extended into additional modes of presentation, and most websites embody elements of each of the five modes in their own presentations. There are, however, numerous websites designed, created, and maintained by public folklorists that predominantly use one of these particular styles in their presentation. The subject is so vast that doing full justice to all of the work of public folklorists is beyond the scope of this chapter. Rather, it will explore exemplary sites that typify each mode of representation.

By necessity, much of work in public folklore involves exposition. Exposition is part of all websites, although the mode is often presented implicitly as webmasters guide viewers through their sites by blending contextual information together with content. For public-folklore sites, the explicit problem often is simply and explicitly stated as providing those who view the website with an understanding of the nature of folklore and folklife studies. Most public folklorists use the definition of *folklore*, formulated largely by Archie Green in Public Law (P.L.) 105-275, to explain that folklife is "the traditional expressive, shared culture of various groups in the United States: familial, ethnic, occupational, religious, and regional" (Bartis 2002, 1). P.L. 105-275 lists specific forms of folk culture to provide examples of genres and activities that encompass the nature and scope of folklife studies, and these, in turn, allow public folklorists to dramatically use the resources of computer technology to show denizens of the Internet how the folklorists identify and present various forms of traditional expressive culture. They offer the results of their fieldwork and public presentations of folklore through visual images, sound bytes, and written text in ways that broker a vivid perception of folklore to an audience whose understanding of it ranges widely—from those having virtually no information to experts in the field. Public folklorists recognize that a major part of their exposition is to resolve problems with misconceptions about folklore, and they frequently expand on the narrow popular conceptions of folklore by integrating a diverse array of folk traditions and folk groups within their websites. In this respect, the challenges created by a limited public understanding of folklore become opportunities for using the Internet to teach about folklore in a direct and meaningful manner.

One of the most successful sites for accomplishing this type of exposition is the Mississippi Arts Commission's "Crossroads of the Heart." After entering the site through an attractive home page, viewers come to the crossroads, graphically illustrated in a vivid black-and-white photograph at the top of the site. Scrolling down, viewers can read a succinctly written text that introduces the website and explains the essentials of folklife studies that are supported by Mississippi's public folklore program. Themes relevant to community life and traditional expressive culture are then vibrantly explored in specific subject areas that viewers can access through five thumbnails on the right of the page: music, handmade objects, maritime traditions, quilting, and narrative. This page also includes links to an excellent teacher's guide for use in the public schools plus a resource guide for additional information on the folklife program, its artists, and its resources.

Each thumbnail's link is well worth a mouse click. They all use a similar template in which genres or forms are linked via additional thumbnails. For example, clicking on the general subject of music, viewers find more expository text that introduces them to Mississippi's folk music traditions as well as four additional thumbnails that direct them to genres that are characteristic of the state's musical traditions: blues, gospel, fiddling, and Sacred Harp singing. Each of these thumbnails, in turn, provides a biographical sketch of a folk musician or musical community, an audio sample, and a link to additional text written by folk music scholars such as David Evans, Kip Lornell, Jay Orr, and David Warren Steel. The blues link provides an excellent introduction to the Mississippi blues of Johnnie Billington, and the fiddling link allows viewers to learn about the old-time fiddle tunes of Charles Smith, including an audio sample of his spirited rendition of "Andy's Tune." This format also shows up in each of the additional subject areas, and the engaging introductions to the wide array of Mississippi folklife reach not only residents of the state but also aficionados of southern folklife who live outside of the region.

"Crossroads of the Heart" uses the expository mode to introduce viewers to Mississippi folklore with the implicit purpose of encouraging additional fieldwork and programming on the state's folk culture. Other sites employing the expository mode take different approaches. One common method is to allow viewers to access an archival collection of preexisting fieldwork. Some of the most extensive and interesting websites to take this approach are the American Folklife Center's "American Memory" projects. One valuable collection, one of the first to be placed online, is the Center's "Florida Folklife from the WPA Collections: 1937–1942." This collection is now housed within the Library of Congress and Florida's State Archives, and it contains irreplaceable field recordings by researchers including Stetson Kennedy (the project's director), Herbert Halpert, Alan Lomax, and Zora Neale Hurston. This site's exposition involves a less-direct explanation of key terms in folklife studies and more emphasis on ways to locate the important recordings and field documentation that are now available in digitized form through this site. The indexing and cross-indexing is impressively arranged to provide users with useful search capabilities, including the ability to browse lists of performers, audio titles, manuscript titles, and geographic locations in Florida where the fieldwork was completed. Savvy users can also employ the search engines to discover the recordings of specific fieldworkers. The chance to hear Zora Neale Hurston actually perform some of the work songs, blues tunes, and rhyming-game songs that she documented is an especially vibrant and popular feature of this website. This project is typical of other websites that predominantly make use of the expository mode in that it provides various links, including web pages for finding additional information about the collection and the Federal Writers' Project in Florida. Stetson Kennedy's essay, "A Florida Treasure Hunt," is an excellent feature on this site, as it provides his fascinating reflections on the efforts of the Works Progress Administration (WPA) in Florida. The site also includes as an extensive bibliography and information on using the collection for primary-source research.

The second major mode of public folklore programming in cyberspace is *observational*; websites that use this approach consist mainly of live webcasting of public folklore events, including performances at concerts, folklife festivals, and conferences. In contrast to the expository mode, the observational mode involves less mediation by the web designer, as it typically uses web cameras and digital sound-recording technology to position the site's viewer as another member of the audience. Folklorists who work within this mode tend to use one-camera shoots, with little editing and fairly limited production effects. The style, in fact, is influenced by cinema verité. As with the verité styles, producers in this mode use a direct form of production to depict events as they unfold, ideally with little intrusion from the camera operator and with no attempt to restructure the sequence of events within the performance (Sherman 1998, 21). As do many documentary film directors influenced by cinema verité, the creators of webcasts in the observational style often attempt to position their cameras directly within the audience, thereby blurring the boundary between the producer of the media event and those who are witnessing the performance. The overall feel for these websites is an increased sense of realism, fostering the idea that this mode of presentation is a more objective representation of an actual event, rather than a presentation that is sophisticatedly brokered through the site's producers. It is the folkloric equivalent of Jennicam, Jennifer Ringley's "reality show" in which she broadcast her life over the Internet in real time (Ringley 1998, 76).

Numerous public- and private-sector folklore organizations use the observational mode of presentation to webcast their events. The largest one recorded using this mode of presentation is the Smithsonian Folklife Festival. Produced by the Smithsonian's Center for Folklife and Cultural Heritage, this event regularly attracts audiences of over one million to a two-week event on the National Mall that is described as a "living museum without walls" (Kurin 1997, 125). Well over 16,000 individuals have participated as demonstrating artists, musical performers, story-tellers, raconteurs, and other carriers of tradition. The festival is orga-nized into three or four major program areas. Each one often consists of a presentation of the folklife and cultural heritage of a specific region or state in America, or the folklife of a nation or transnational ethnic group. Music and dance stages, craft demonstration areas, a performance space for demonstrations of foodways, and other showcases are designed to offer a range of folk cultures, and webcasts of the event are often trans-mitted from these specific areas. Thus viewers around the world can observe the festival's opening ceremony, musical performances, dem-onstrations of folk culture, and audience interactions as they unfold in real time. Most of these webcasts are displayed only once, but the Center for Folklife and Cultural Heritage and other sponsoring organizations sometimes include edited versions of these events on their websites. For example, the website devoted to the Smithsonian's 2002 festival pro-gram, "The Silk Road: Connecting Cultures, Creating Trust," includes excerpts from various presentations.

With the growing use of Internet technology, additional festivals and concerts are presented in real time on the Internet. These events frequently provide an entry point for Internet users to access other pre-sentations from additional public folklore research projects. The Western Folklife Center provides exemplary presentations of its fieldwork and programming, including its annual National Cowboy Poetry Gathering in Elko, Nevada. The Center creates webcasts of many of its events, but it also uses podcasts from previous events, thereby managing an online archival collection of cowboy poetry gatherings. Live webcasts as well as previously recorded podcasts include keynote addresses, poetry readings, interviews, and other features that employ the observational mode. These productions typically involve minimal editing and little or no voiceover, thereby allowing viewers a relatively less-mediated experience, witnessing the activity as if they were sitting in the audi-ence. Not only do these types of presentations compress space by cre-ating a performance area that connects visitors who are seated thou-sands of miles away with the actual audience, but these presentations also compress time. Recordings from events held during the Cowboy Poetry Gathering's quarter-century history are now available online, thereby bringing together early readings with contemporary activities. Combining current technology with previous analog recordings through ongoing cybercasts brings an aural and visual presence to the Western Folklife Center's fieldwork. This fieldwork becomes a living archive, with these resources available to specialized scholars as well as the public in ways that blur boundaries between academicians and laypeople.

The *interactive mode* often uses principles from the expository and observational modes, but its focus is on increasing the interaction between the website's user and the material's format. All Internet sites are interactive; computer users must make choices as they navigate the Web, and they must become actively engaged with a site's content and format to effectively use this technology. The interactive mode, however, foregrounds the choices that users make, and the users themselves create much of the educational experience offered through the site. The elements of interaction in cyberspace become clearer when this mode is contrasted with Sharon Sherman's (1998, 261–62) discussion of it in documentary films and videos. In interactive film, it is the filmmaker who negotiates the interaction. By positioning themselves into the scene, filmmakers using this mode to structure significant aspects of their production around the events precipitated by the filmmakers' involvement. Michael Moore is perhaps the most well-known practitioner of this style, but it also is evident in folklore documentaries produced by Barbara Kopple, Patricia Turner, and Les Blank when they call attention to new insights gleaned from their actual participation alongside the subjects who are featured in their production. On websites this mode may employ a great deal of interaction from the web designer, but interaction in cyberspace is focused primarily on the user. Because site visitors can interact to a far greater degree than viewers of documentaries, web designers have created new presentation formats that emphasize how viewers participate in the navigation and even creation of the website.

One of the oldest and most successful websites that focuses heavily on folklore and highlights interaction is Karen Ellis's "Educational CyberPlayGround." This massive, award-winning site is oriented to pre-kindergarten through high school teachers, but it also is accessed by college professors, scholars, and anyone with an interest in folkloric content on the Internet. The site contains well over 1,500 pages, and it has been accessed by two million visitors each year. Fortunately, ten quick links are available for easy navigation: music education, literacy, school directory, technology, transdisciplinary, teachers, linguistics, Internet, arts, and songs NCFR (National Children's Folksong Repository). These links take visitors to a wealth of material in the CyberPlayGround and provide connections to over 10,000 interdisciplinary links. Viewers can find directories, indexes, webcasts, and a myriad of resources for educational use.

While the CyberPlayGround uses the modes previously discussed, its NCFR is an excellent example of the interactive mode. Viewers using this resource are asked to first view a short video that explains the project. Images with a voiceover provide an overview of the importance of musical creativity within cultures; video vignettes of Grammy Award-winner Allan Slutsky and in-school video footage provide the rationale for the website. Essentially, the site is designed to identify, document, preserve, and interpret the traditional musical expressions of children. The NCFR involves teachers, students, parents, guardians, and other interested participants in the collection process, as they are encouraged to submit song texts and performances that they have documented. The process of collection often blurs the line between field-worker and performer, since new material can be submitted via e-mail messages, video footage, links to sites like YouTube, and even over the telephone. These collected materials are available through the website, and project's staff members continually develop new means of using children's folksongs as educational resources. The staff members pay special attention to ways in which their collection and documentation project can foster links between students, schools, and communities, and CyberPlayGround actively encourages the creation of vital online communities. In this respect, the interactive components of this site are much less controlled than those constructed by the designers who created the cultural interpretation in websites employing the expository mode. Because users are given greater opportunities to contribute to the site, the focus of CyberPlayGround is centered as much on the process of "doing folklore" as it is on the presentation and interpretation of traditional expressive culture.

As demonstrated in CyberPlayGround, the interactive mode is especially well suited to folklife-in-education programs. Another site that features a range of modes yet emphasizes interaction is the Wisconsin Arts Board's "Wisconsin Folks," which won the Dorothy Howard Folklife-in-Education Award. This website opens with a home page that welcomes visitors with a variety of attractive photo images and minimal text. Upon clicking past this introduction, visitors are given choices for navigating the site. They may search for information about folk artists and musicians through various options, including looking for artists from specific ethnic groups or locations in Wisconsin, or those employing diverse artistic forms and genres or various themes in their artwork. For example, a user may wish to identify artists and musicians from a particular area in southwestern Wisconsin listed as "CESA 4." This link provides the user with the names of individuals and groups from within this region who are featured on the website. Clicking on "Nodji Van Wychen," for example, takes the viewer to a series of pages about cranberry farming in the rural area near Warrens, Wisconsin. The introductory page contextualizes the hundred-year-old family tradition within Van Wychen's community by giving an overview of the essential aspects of her family's agricultural tradition. Hotlinks show digital photographs of cranberry-growing equipment, reflective questions are illustrated with relevant visual designs, and additional pages feature audio clips of interviews. After viewers work through the first few pages, they find two button links under the heading "Activities." The first one is entitled "What do you know?" and consists of an interactive quiz about the site's content. The second button is labeled "Work the Seasons" and takes viewers to another interactive locale. Viewers are invited to play a computer game in which they match the activities involved in growing cranberries with the specific season in which the work is completed. Cartoon-like graphics allow the user to spray the plants with water to protect the buds from freezing, flood the bogs to begin harvesting the berries, and learn about other activities associated with the occupational folklife of cranberry production. The interactive capabilities of this site also include opportunities for educators to move beyond the virtual world and directly interact with Van Wychen by contracting with her to come into their classrooms to speak directly with students. Scores of other tradition-bearers within the Wisconsin Folks website are also featured in similar ways, and viewers can hear audio samples of musical and storytelling performances, view virtual exhibits of folk arts, discover recipes and learn about foodways traditions, explore weather beliefs, and encounter a wealth of information about the state's traditional expressive culture.

Highly interactive modes often blend into the fourth major approach for presenting folklore on the Internet: the *reflexive mode*. Sherman explains that a reflexive documentary pushes the idea of interactive film into a further foray into the subjective qualities of cultural representation (1998, 262). In a reflexive documentary, the director calls attention to his or her own presence as a filmmaker or videographer and uses this unmasking to demonstrate how choices in using various production techniques shape the content of the cultural representation. Reflexive documentaries created by folklorists are made available through Tom Davenport's "Folkstreams." His own 2008 production, "Bodhidharma's Shoe," is a fine example of a reflexive ethnographic documentary, taking viewers through his own involvement in a Zen Buddhist "sesshin," a mediation retreat at a center in New Mexico. Typical techniques used in reflexive documentaries include first-person narration, inclusion of the filmmaker in the frame, sparse and simple editing, long-takes, relatively inexpensive cameras and audio-recording devices, and very little use of slick graphics in the editing. A unifying tenet in this mode of documentation is that the stylistic influences of cinema verité amplify a sense of reality in the piece, breaking Brecht's "fourth wall" to show that the "realism" of more objective modes of documentation is merely a style of production.

Designers of public folklore sites have adapted some of these ideas about reflexivity. Some use the first-person to navigate viewers through their websites, and most sites include links that allow users to interact directly with them, often through e-mail and sometimes by building links to various other sites. Reflexivity can be especially useful in interactive websites that encourage users to document and interpret their own folklore. One of the most successful sites to use the reflexive mode is Gail Matthews-DeNatale's "Keepsakes and Dreams." Matthews-DeNatale initiated this online writing forum as an educational resource for teaching language arts classes within the Urban Alternative, an educational project sponsored by George Mason University's Institute for Educational Transformation.

Student participants were asked to write about a range of topic relevant to their own life experiences by using any of the following questions to turn their memories into stories:

1.   What keepsakes do you value?

2.   What aspects of your cultural heritage do you hold dear?

3.   What are your dreams for the future?

4.   In what ways are your cultural keepsakes related to your dreams?

Responding to these questions, twenty participants collaboratively published fine pieces of writing that used their families' folklife as a resource for their own pieces. The writing in the Keepsakes and Dreams project reflects the multiethnic and international diversity of the Urban Alternative program. In the site, Matthews-DeNatale states that these accounts and stories were composed to show how new immigrants create cultural continuities in their new homes while also embracing change. She notes that immigrants who were writing about their dreams for the future might discover ways to realize their visions through this process. She also notes that the project was planned with a wider audience in mind. The website was built to blend cultural documentation with community education to foster intercultural dialogue and a richer understanding of local communities.

Cultural diversity is clearly evident as a positive resource within this site. Students were originally from Argentina, Bolivia, Cambodia, Guatemala, Hungary, Indonesia, Korea, Mexico, Pakistan, Panama, Peru, and Somalia. Each writer was given a web page on which to post his or her essays and reflections. Expressions of family folklore—especially in the form of mementos, heirlooms, poetry, and stories—are often central to the students' writing. Most of the participants included photographs of themselves, and many added other images that they had preserved from their home country. The photographs themselves often became central to the writer's reflections. Sokha Mob, a Cambodian student, writes about a keepsake that is depicted in a photograph on her web page:

> My necklace is the most valuable thing that I own because it represents my family and my heritage. [It] is a Buddha sculpture pendant that my mother gave to me on my wedding day. This is my most cherished and valued gift.
>
> After my grandmother died, my mother saved one of my grandmother's teeth for seven years. We believe that it is good to keep the teeth of our ancestors. My mother wanted to give the tooth to me, but first she took it to a craftsman in our town of Tani. The artist's name was Mr. Hang, and he was very old.
>
> Mr. Hang was a very knowledgeable and gifted ivory carver. There were not any people in our area who knew how to carve things as well as Mr. Hang. My mother thought that if he knew how to carve tusks, he would also be able to make a beautiful carving out of my grandmother's tooth. She asked Mr. Hang to make a Buddha pendant out of the tooth. Even though this was an unusual request, he said that he would do it.
>
> My mother didn't tell me about her surprise, she kept it a secret until my wedding day. On that important day, she gave me my necklace, and she also gave a second pendant to my husband. My husband's necklace had a pendant that was made out of my grandfather's tooth. But my special necklace was different from my husband's necklace, because only mine was carved into the shape of the Buddha. She told me that my necklace was special because she loved

me very much. She said that she loved her parents and she would
like us to keep them with us. She thought that if we wore our neck-
laces my ancestors would always live with us. It means so much to
me to know that every time we go to the temple to pray to God, we
also have our grandparents with us.

   I love my necklace very much. I wear it all the time because whenever I miss my mother and my country, I look at my pendant and it
makes me feel better.

   In these types of writing projects, the students' willingness to share
family histories and reveal personal memories and aspirations demands
important degrees of openness from the teacher. Matthews-DeNatale
includes her own reflections on the project within this website, and
the importance of incorporating reflexivity within the project becomes
clearer. She explains that the project involves collaborative learning, and
she suggests that this type of collaboration demands much more of her
own personal involvement in what became a learning community—
especially when compared to what typically is required of a teacher
within more conventional forms of classroom instruction. In sum, as a
form of collaborative education, "Keepsakes and Dreams" includes a
strong sense of Matthews-DeNatale's own subjective engagement with
her students' stories, because her role is defined as a co-creator of the
site, rather than simply as a teacher who is posting her students' work
on the Web. Those who read her introduction to the website and her own
journal will discover ways in which Matthews-DeNatale's self-disclo-
sure contributed to the project's development.

   The final mode of presentation is the *performative* mode. Sherman
(1998, 263) characterizes a folkloric documentary completed in the
performative mode as one that emphasizes the poetic, expressive, and
rhetorical aspects of the production over the more didactic elements of
historical and cultural contexts. A performative piece stresses the mul-
tivocality of symbolic expression and forces viewers to create the major
messages that are evoked in the juxtaposition of imagery, sound, and
text. A performative piece is artsy. Filmmakers and video producers
using this mode often avoid voiceover and other, more pedantic technical resources; they often rely heavily on editing, and particularly on cin-
ematic montage, to create a documentary that looks more like a performance piece than a scholarly representation. Sherman notes that there
are relatively few folkloric documentaries that employ this method, but
she suggests that Roberta Cantow's 1981 documentary "Clotheslines"
and Tony Silver and Henry Chalfant's 1983 film "Style Wars" represent
this mode of media production (1998, 264). Cantow's documentary, for

example, uses the juxtaposition of visual images associated with wash-day to evoke systems of associations about the values and meanings that emerge in gendered domestic culture. Silver and Chalfant's film pairs colorful images of graffiti-adorned subway cars with rap music to allow viewers to experience a sense of place, thereby contextualizing the interview content with seen and unseen graffiti taggers and painters of "pieces."

Folklife is the subject of video-like performative websites. Curiously, most of these productions are not created by professional folklorists. One of the best places to find these performative pieces is YouTube. The entries tend to be ephemeral, but it is well worth watching YouTube with an eye for folkloric content as seen through the lens of performative modes of production. A user named "Deathmaster66," for example, has a number of entries that are creative, interesting, and sometimes a bit mystifying. This self-identified 106-year-old "arsonist" has a min-ute-long piece entitled "He Rambled—Charlie Poole" that juxtaposes an eighty-year-old recording of Poole's old-time string band tune "He Rambled" with an early Popeye cartoon. The cartoon features a fight, a moment of conflict resolution, and, to complete the episode, Popeye and Olive Oyl dancing as a couple. The cryptic references, humor, and occa-sional brilliance of these types of YouTube videos certainly add some-thing to the dialogue on public folklore, but they are not the types of media productions that are created by public-sector folklorists—at least not while they are on company time. Public folklorists who have been trained through academic folklore programs, and are employed with state or federal agencies, have crafted few performative videos and even fewer websites that follow this mode of production. The Web provides creative individuals with great opportunities for using new technolo-gies in effective and artistically engaging ways, but artsy, irreverent, and perhaps even edgy uses of the Internet are not generally encouraged within governmental agencies. Still, there are a number of sites that uti-lize computer technology in ways that showcase the performative mode of expression.

One of the most interesting is the University of Central Florida's "Folkvine." Produced by the UCF's Cultural Heritage Alliance, much of the work is a collaboration between professors, students, and public folklorists from the Sunshine State. The site opens with a pastel image of a rural Florida road. A road sign reads "JCT 41—Explorin' Florida." The next image of another road, rendered in the same style, features the sign "Without a Guide?" By the time the next image rolls up, the view-ers understand the Burma-Shave-sign mode by seeing another image of a road with the sign "To See Great Art," which then dissolves into a fourth image of a roadside produce stand with the signpost "Just Come Inside." These visuals are all accompanied by a soundtrack that features the ambient sound of traffic noise mingled with seagulls screeching and other shorebirds calling, thereby evoking audio impressions of Florida's soundscape. Upon arriving at the exterior of the roadside produce stand, site visitors are then taken to a web page that invites them to come inside from the front porch. Viewers are then given options to click on various elements of the site, where they will discover that Folkvine is a showcase for Florida folk artists. The site presents information on folk art traditions from across the state, as well as "tour guides" exploring humanities concepts related to different aspects of these traditions. For example, viewers can mouse over and spin an image that represents a display stand for selling souvenir postcards, and then click on a specific card. The different postcards allow viewers to learn about artists such as the Jewish Ketubah (wedding contract) maker Eileen Brautman and "Diamond" Jim Parker's miniature model circus carvings. The theme of visiting with artists through the virtual world of a storefront is a creative entry point for the educational content. The site's designers employ the capabilities of the Web to use audio clips, images, text, games, and a variety of other presentations that move beyond the interactive mode into the performative. The Cultural Heritage Alliance is constantly expanding the site, and a major focus of its work is in continuing to explore the performative mode. Computerized images of folktales collected in Florida are now being made available on the site, and Folkvine is providing links to numerous other sites that feature sophisticated uses of technology.

These examples of websites that represent the work of public folklorists are intended to introduce readers to ways in which folklorists use the Internet to present folklore to the public. Virtually every public-folklore program has a website, and spatial constraints limit the number of sites that can be discussed in this chapter. Furthermore, the five modes of presentation that unify the overall design of these sites are not mutually exclusive. "Folkvine" is *performative, interactive, reflexive, observational,* and *expository* in various degrees, just as "Crossroads of the Heart" also includes elements of all five modes. Nor are website designs limited to these five modes of presentation, as the Internet can provide new opportunities for creating additional forms of representation. "Folkvine" and "Wisconsin Folks," for example, utilize what may be a sixth mode of presentation that is characteristic of computerized media: the *gaming* mode. In employing gaming as part of these sites' pedagogy, web designers are using familiar ways of interacting within cyberspace to further the goals of public folklore programming. Some of the games are perhaps of the "old-school" video-game style, but more folklorists are also looking at virtual reality games, such as Second Life, to further develop modes of cultural representation in cyberspace. Along with the gaming mode, some folklorists are using the *virtual exhibit* mode to present their work to the public. This seventh mode is evident in websites that accompany stationary exhibits. The Historical Museum of South Florida, for example, regularly features online exhibitions of folk culture. These have included presentations based on the traveling exhibit "Florida Folklife: Traditional Art in Contemporary Communities" and "At the Crossroads: Afro-Cuban Orisha Arts in Miami." These virtual displays are often beautifully presented and provide online visitors with opportunities to preview what they may see when they visit the museum or review what they have witnessed during a previous visit to the exhibit in the world of bricks and mortar. Adding the *gaming* mode and the *virtual exhibit* mode to the five other modes is but a starting point for identifying additional means of presenting folklore to the public in cyberspace.

Reflecting on the proliferation of public folklore in cyberspace over the past twenty years, numerous changes become clear, especially when contrasted with the use of the now-defunct Wang Corporation computers in the Kentucky Center for the Arts' "Patterns between the Rivers" exhibit. The computerized component of the Center's production was a novelty; now a digitized component is almost always expected in most major exhibits. In the Center's displays, the computer system was an add-on that came with the photographic and text panels; it was not linked to a worldwide network. Contemporary online exhibits currently connect thousands, even millions, of users. Computers' early search capabilities were simple and required lengthy waits for information to appear on a screen. Viewers' tolerance for these types of long waits would now be strained, as they are conditioned to faster CPUs and sophisticated search engines. But the biggest difference between then and now is related to McLuhan's emphasis on social changes created by the adoption of new media.

Whereas the early uses of computers in public folklore were designed to supplement real-world exhibits, many folklorists currently use computer technology as a primary resource for public programming. It is unlikely that all—or even most—public programming will be situated in cyberspace. Nevertheless, the use of computers has changed public folklorists' ideas about what constitutes "the public." Webcasts can attract larger audiences than concerts. Fieldwork data can easily be placed online, thereby creating a huge number of potential viewers, far greater than either folklorists or folk artists had ever anticipated. With the increased use of interactive and gaming modalities, users can simulate the folklore collection process, thereby emphasizing interaction in the virtual world, although possibly at the expense of direct interactions with those who carry forth folk traditions outside of cyberspace. This type of reliance on the virtual world and its simulations of actual processes, products, and people carries with it vast possibilities for increasing public understanding of the work of folklorists, just as it carries numerous problematic issues. As Burt Feintuch (1988) points out, part of the appeal of public folklore programming is its potential to encourage people within a community to interact directly with each other by witnessing displays of folk culture. Whether or not interactions in cyberspace carry the same sense of presence that is linked with fostering healthy and engaging conversations about culture conservation remains to be seen, as does whether its effects will be felt not only in real communities but also in cyberspace.

Appendix

Webography of Public Folklore Resources

COMPILED BY GREGORY HANSEN

This webography is designed to introduce readers to the variety of public folklore programs offered in the United States and its territories, as well as one Canadian site. Its primary focus is on public-sector agencies that are housed within federal, state, and local governments, but the webography also includes selected publicly and privately funded programs that are supported outside of public-sector budget allocations. This webography is designed to show the regional and ethnic diversity of public folklore programming, and especially interesting features on various websites are highlighted in the annotations. Although the focus is on *public* folklore, it is worth noting how many of these organizations are linked to various academic institutions. The webography is by no means comprehensive, but the links within the sites can expand this webography beyond the boundaries of the United States.

There are numerous challenges in compiling this type of resource. Users should be aware that organizations sometimes change their URL web addresses, shift their focus, lose their funding, or just become defunct. Even after they cease operating actively, some programs leave a web presence by creating an online archive. Consequently, although the listing here primarily consists of websites active at the time of publication and expected to remain active, it inevitably includes organizations and sites that are no longer in operation.

Alabama Center for Traditional Culture. Supported by the state's arts council, this site includes information on Alabama's traditional culture as well as downloadable essays on Alabama folklife, radio shows, and

information on the state's Heritage Award winners. http://www.arts.
state.al.us/actc/index-folkarts-actc.html.
Alabama Folklife Association. This website is a model one for a statewide folklore society. It includes information about folklore events in
Alabama, downloadable essays and articles, and information about var-
ious functions supported by the association. www.alabamafolklife.org/.
Alabama Folklife Program. This site is connected with the Alabama
Center for Traditional Culture, but it includes specific information
about the state's folklife program. http://www.arts.state.al.us/folklife/
folklife.htm.
Alaska Native Heritage Center. The "Education" and "Exhibits and
Collections" sections provide interesting information about a range of
cultural traditions in Alaska. http://www.alaskanative.net/.
Alaska State Council on the Arts. This site provides information on the
state's Traditional Native Arts Program (http://www.eed.state.ak.us/
aksca/native.htm) and on folk arts grants and opportunities in Alaska.
It also has good links to various arts organizations. http://www.educ.
state.ak.us/aksca/.
Albemarle/Charlottesville Historical Society. Although not specifically a
"folklife organization," this historical society has supported folklife and
oral history research projects. The site includes online exhibits on topics relevant to various aspects of folk culture in Virginia. http://www.
albemarlehistory.org/.
Alliance for California Traditional Arts. Online exhibits and descriptions of various projects are featured in the "Artists and Cultural
Heritage" section of the site. http://www.actaonline.org/index.htm.
American Folklife Center & Archive of Folk Culture. A premier website offered by the Library of Congress. Along with serving as a center
for finding out about folklife projects with a national and international
scope, this site also includes excellent online exhibits and digitized archival holdings. http://www.loc.gov/folklife/.
American Folklore Society. The website of the most prominent folklore
scholarly society in the world includes information about AFS as well as
online resources about specific topics in folklore and important folk artists and performers. http://www.afsnet.org/.
American Routes. This website supports the award-winning radio
show that is distributed and coproduced through American Public
Media. Radio shows and other resources are available online. http://
americanroutes.publicradio.org/
American Samoa Historic Preservation Office. This site has links to
photo galleries, videos, publications, and cultural organizations such as

the American Samoa Council on Culture, Arts, and Humanities. http://www.ashpo.org/

Anchorage Museum. This museum supports research and presentations on a range of cultural traditions from Alaska. The "Archives" and "Collections" components of this website are especially useful for folklore study. http://www.anchoragemuseum.org/.

Appalshop. A regional cultural center in Whitesburg, Kentucky, Appalshop supports media production, research, and other forms of cultural programming in Appalachia. The site's web broadcasts are especially relevant to folklife studies. http://www.appalshop.org/.

Arizona State Museum. The University of Arizona has supported numerous folklore projects. This site includes online presentations derived from the research of folklorists in the state. http://www.statemuseum.arizona.edu/exhibits/.

Arkansas Heritage. The state's Department of Arkansas Heritage supports this site. The educational resources on historic and vernacular architecture, as well as oral history, are especially well presented on this website. http://www.arkansasheritage.com/.

Artesanías y Artes Populares. This program is supported by Puerto Rico's Instituto de Cultural Puertorriqueña. "Artes Populares y Artesanías" and "Música" include information on scheduled events and exhibits that are relevant to various folk art traditions. http://www.icp.gobierno/pr/.

Arts Center of Cannon County. This local arts center supports research on Tennessee's folk culture. The website is especially strong in its presentations of material culture and folk arts. http://www.artscenterofcc.com/.

Arts Center of the Capital Region. Based in the west-central region of New York State, this arts center supports a variety of folklife programs. Their website includes online presentations of previous exhibits, including exhibits that feature folk traditions from New York State. http://www.artscenteronline.org/.

Arts and Cultural Council for Greater Rochester. This arts and cultural center supports a folk arts program within New York State. Folk artists are included within the onsite roster, and the website contains information about local folk arts programming. http://www.artsrochester.org/.

Asian Cultural Council. Based in New York City, this organization has an international scope to its programming and frequently showcases the traditional expressive culture of Asian ethnic and national groups. http://www.asianculturalcouncil.org/.

Atlanta History Center. This center frequently presents exhibits and programs on aspects of Georgia's history and culture that are relevant to folklife studies. The website's educational guides are especially useful for folklore study. http://www.atlantahistorycenter.com/.

Augusta Heritage Center. Davis and Elkins College in Elkins, West Virginia, support this folk heritage center. The website announces various programs, classes, and educational materials. http://www.augusta-heritage.com/.

Bayshore Discovery Project. This organization supports educational projects on the natural history and ecology of the New Jersey shore. The website includes information for learning about connections between the natural environment and local culture. http://www.ajmeerwald.org/.

Bishop Museum. Honolulu's premier museum on Hawai'ian history and culture includes numerous materials relevant to folk culture on their website. http://www.bishopmuseum.org/.

Blue Ridge Institute of Ferrum College. This historical and cultural center is devoted to research and programming on the regional heritage of the Appalachians. Materials on the website augment the institute's Center for Blue Ridge Folklore and include resources for educators and online exhibits. http://www.blueridgeinstitute.org/.

Brooklyn Arts Council. This arts council's folk arts program includes an online photo gallery from its archives and information about the council's folklife projects. http://www.brooklynartscouncil.org/.

California Academy of Sciences. This organization's Traditional Arts Program has been active in the greater San Francisco metropolitan area. http://www.calacademy.org/research/anthropology/tap/folkart.htm.

California Arts Council. The state arts council's site offers information on grants and opportunities for folk arts programming. http://www.cac.ca.gov/.

California Indian Basketweavers Association. This arts and advocacy group includes excellent online materials about basket-making traditions. The online photo gallery is especially well presented. http://www.ciba.org/.

California Traditional Music Society. Based in Encino, this organization supports folk music in California through a range of events. The site's biographies and its photo gallery are of particular interest to web-based researchers. http://www.ctmsfolkmusic.org/.

Center for Cultural Exchange. This Portland, Maine, organization is part of a network for intercultural education. Its website is particularly useful for finding organizations and materials for teaching about cultural diversity. http://www.centerforculturalexchange.org/.

Center for Documentary Studies. Duke University supports this North Carolina center. Its website includes online photographic exhibits, video presentations, and information about the programs and courses of study offered at the center. http://cds.aas.duke.edu/.

Center for Folklife, History, and Cultural Programs. Located in Glens Falls, New York, this center pays special attention to the folk culture of the Adirondacks. http://www.crandalllibrary.org/.

Center for Southern Folklore. Memphis, Tennessee's CSF offers a variety of programming on folk culture. The website provides information about the center's activities and has links to various partner organizations, some of which feature photos and streaming video/audio of various events supported by the center. http://www.southernfolklore. com/.

Center for the Study of Southern Culture. Housed in an old observatory at the University of Mississippi, this center has been an important contributor to studies of southern folk culture. Its attractive website includes online presentations of research done at the center as well as links to other organizations that support the study of southern culture. http://www.olemiss.edu/depts/south/.

Center for the Study of Upper Midwestern Cultures, University of Wisconsin–Madison. This regional studies center features excellent resources on folklife from this part of the U.S., and the site includes useful links to relevant projects. http://csumc.wisc.edu/.

Center for Traditional Music and Dance. This New York City organization supports a variety of programs about dance. Researchers will benefit from the website's information about its archival holdings and the site's links to related organizations. http://www.ctmd.org/.

Chattahoochee Folklife Project. This site includes useful information on folk traditions in Georgia. http://www.hcc-al-ga.org/folk_index.cfm.

Chesapeake Bay Maritime Museum. Folklorists have worked with this museum to document and interpret cultural traditions of the bay. The website is designed primarily to promote the museum, and it includes useful information in its educational section and a photo gallery. http:// www.cbmm.org/.

Cityfolk. Along with supporting a major music festival in Dayton, Ohio, Cityfolk also produces a variety of public folklore programs. Links from the home page to a Cityfolk blog on MySpace provide one of the few internet blog sites relevant to public folklore. http://www.cityfolk. org/.

City Lore, Inc. Based in New York City, this organization develops and promotes a wide variety of materials for teaching about folk culture.

The organization's virtual tours of the city and its "Cultural Catalog" are especially valuable resources. http://www.citylore.org/.

Club Passim. This organization is housed at the famous 47 Palmer Street address in Cambridge, Massachusetts. The site's "virtual mini-gallery" features artists who have been connected with this renowned folk club throughout the years. http://www.clubpassim.org/.

Commonwealth Council for Arts and Culture. The Commonwealth of the Northern Mariana Islands supports a folk arts program in this cluster of Pacific Islands. http://www.geocities.com/ccacarts/ccacwebfolkarts.html.

Country Music Foundation. Nashville supports this organization that features a museum and a hall of fame for country musicians. The website's online exhibit and audio links are especially interesting, and they provide a valuable resource for learning about the history of American country music. Along with satellite radio, the site also features archival recordings of early country music. http://www.countrymusichalloffame.com/.

Cultural Affairs Division of Arlington County. Arlington, Virginia, supports a Heritage Arts program within this division. The site includes online information about folk culture in the region. http://www.arlingtonarts.org/cultural_affairs/heritagearts.htm.

Cultural Resources Council. Syracuse, New York, cultural resources include a folk arts program that is featured in a section of this website. http://www.cspot.org/FolkArts.html.

Cultural Resources, Inc. Based in Rockport, Maine, this organization covers a wide range of folklife and cultural programming. The website provides an excellent overview of innovative projects completed by folklorists. http://www.cultural-resources.org/.

DC Commission on the Arts and Humanities. Washington, DC supports folk and traditional arts projects. The website includes information about various programs, including streaming video of festivals. http://dcarts.dc.gov/dcarts/site/default.asp.

Delaware Bayshores Program. Based in New Jersey, this organization focused on environmental education projects and ecotourism along the coast and includes folklife education within its programming. http://www.nature.org/newjersey/.

Delaware Folklife Program. This website provides information about the State of Delaware's folk arts programming. An online exhibit entitled "Delaware Folk Art Collection" provides a vibrant portrait of various traditional arts in the state. http://www.destateparks.com/folklife/index.asp.

Documentary Arts, Inc. Although based in Dallas, Texas, this organization conducts research on a great variety of traditional arts from across the nation. Highlights on this site include audio excerpts and an online photo gallery. http://www.docarts.com/.

Documentary Heritage Program. Based in Buffalo, this program offers good information from various archival holdings in New York State. http://www.archives.nysed.gov/a/records/mr_hrecords_dhp. shtml.

Down Jersey Folklife Center. This organization is part of regional folklife programming within New Jersey. The website includes online information about a variety of folk traditions in the state. http://www. wheatonarts.org/downjersey.

Educational CyberPlayGround. This award-winning website is a vast repository of resources on folklife, history, and expressive culture. It includes a wide range of presentations on folklife, from streaming video and audio feeds to interactive projects. The site is also an excellent resource for discovering links to folklife-related sites around the world. Although written for teachers as an educational resource, its scope is so vast and general than anyone interested in folklore will discover relevant topics on this site. http://www.edu-cyberpg.com/.

Florida Folklife Program. The State of Florida supports this website, which includes information about folklife projects in Florida, biographies of Florida folk artists, and audio clips from folklorists' research in the state. This site also has a fine section of links to other projects, including the Florida Memory Project (http://www.floridamemory.com/ Collections/folklife/), curated from the state's archives . One particularly interesting site focuses on folklore research in Florida during the WPA, and it includes audio excerpts of interviews completed by Zora Neale Hurston, John Lomax, and other prominent folklorists. http:// www.flheritage.com/preservation/folklife/.

Folk Alliance. Geared primarily to performers and producers, the Folk Alliance's website includes information about the organization's support for folk musicians. The site also allows users to download information about events supported by the alliance, and it includes resources for streaming video and audio. http://www.folkalliance.org/.

Folklife Program for New Jersey. This website provides information about the State of New Jersey's folk arts programming. http://www. co.middlesex.nj.us/culturalheritage/folklife.asp.

Folkstreams. This site is an excellent resource for viewing documentary films and videos about folklore. It includes early folklore documentaries as well as current productions. http://www.folkstreams.net/.

Fund for Folk Culture. This organization formerly provided support for programs that research, document, and present folklife. Links on this site connect users to a variety of folk arts organizations, and the site has downloadable articles and reports that are of particular value for arts advocacy. http://www.folkculture.org/.

Genesee-Orleans Regional Arts Council. This regional arts council within New York State includes a vibrant folk arts program. Their site provides information about its activities. A downloadable collection of traditional recipes was recently added to the site. http://www.goart.org/.

Georgia Traditional Arts Program. The website for Georgia's folk arts program provides information about its services and access to a roster of artists. http://www.gaarts.org/home.asp.

Great Lakes Center for Maritime Studies. Based out of Western Michigan University, this center focuses on studies of local history and culture. Its website includes an online photo gallery and links to relevant sites. http://www.wmich.edu/history/maritime/.

Guam Council on the Arts and Humanities Agency. This website provides information about the folk arts program in Guam. http://www.guamcaha.org/.

Hawai'i State Foundation on Culture and the Arts. Information about Hawai'i's statewide folk arts program is found on this website. Various online resources are available, including an e-version of "Our Arts, Our Land—A Young Reader's Guide to Selected Folk Artists of Hawai'i." http://www.hawaii.gov/sfca/.

Heritage Alliance/Zora Neale Hurston Institute. The University of Central Florida in Orlando supports this website. Much of the site has been built by students at the university. There is a strong focus on folklife and place-based education, and the alliance works in collaboration with numerous organizations in Florida. One of the university's web-based projects, "Folkvine" (http://www.folkvine.org), is one of the most creative applications of internet technology to folklife studies and is linked to this site. http://heritagealliance.ucf.edu/.

Historical Museum of Southern Florida. This museum in Miami has featured research by folklorists for over twenty-five years. The site has excellent online exhibits. http://www.hmsf.org/.

Idaho Commission on the Arts. This site leads users to Idaho's folk arts program. A special section of the website, "Focus on Folklife," features web-based resource information on events and folk artists in Idaho. http://www.arts.idaho.gov/grants/folkoverview.aspx.

Illinois Arts Council. This website includes information and links on folk arts programming in Illinois. http://www.state.il.us/agency/iac/.

Institute for Community Research. Based in Hartford, Connecticut, this organization coordinates numerous projects on folklife. The website includes photo essays and downloaded reports and summaries of various projects. http://www.incommunityresearch.org/.

Institute for Cultural Partnerships. Based in Harrisburg, this organization supports a range of cultural, historical, and folklife programming in Pennsylvania. The website includes biographies of folk artists living in Pennsylvania and a variety of educational resources and teachers' guides. http://culturalpartnerships.org/.

International Bluegrass Music Association. Based in Nashville, this organization promotes bluegrass music and provides a valuable educational program that integrates bluegrass music into classroom instruction. Lesson plans and other educational resources are available on the website. http://www.ibma.org/.

Iowa Arts Council. This website connects users to Iowa's folklife program. Among the numerous web-based resources is the online version of the awarding-winning multimedia presentation "Iowa Folklife: Our People, Communities, and Traditions." http://www.iowaartscouncil.org/.

Isla Center for the Arts. The University of Guam supports this website and cultural center. http://www.uog.edu/dynamicdata/CLASSIslaCenterArts.aspx.

John C. Campbell Folk School. Located in Brasstown, North Carolina, this organization offers classes that teach a variety of traditional artistic and musical forms. The school is currently collaborating with Western Carolina University to document the region's craft revival. Results from this research project are online. http://www.folkschool.org/.

John D. Calandra Italian American Institute. Along with its live programs, this City University of New York institute's website includes online presentations based on its programming. http://qcpages.qc.edu/calandra/.

Jubilee Community Arts & the Laurel Theater. Housed in an old church building in Knoxville, Tennessee, this arts organization features concerts and radio programs of folk music. The website includes links to Jubilee Community Arts shows available on internet radio. http://www.jubileearts.org/.

Julia de Burgos Latino Center. This center serves New York City's East Harlem community. The website includes information about various presentations of Latino traditional culture. http://www.juliadeburgos.org.

Kansas State Historical Society. Information on the state's folk arts program is presented on this website. The site also includes an online presentation of oral histories and personal-experience narratives garnered during field research. http://www.kshs.org/.

Kentucky Historical Society. The Kentucky Folklife Program is part of this website. Educational resources can be downloaded from the site, and the historical society also showcases online presentations from its oral history program. http://history.ky.gov/.

Long Island Traditions. Based in Port Washington, New York, this organization develops folklife programming on Long Island. The website includes information on the organization, copies of newsletters, educational materials, and online versions of photographic exhibits. http://www.longislandtraditions.org/.

Louisiana Division of the Arts. Information about Louisiana's folklife program is available on this website. A good place to begin exploring is the online presentation "Folklife in Louisiana." The site is also linked to the "Louisiana Voices Folklife in Education Project" (http://www.louisianavoices.org). This award-winning online resource has become a model for similar projects and is available from the site. http://www.louisianafolklife.org.

Louisiana Folklife Center. The folklife center, in Natchitoches, is supported by Northwestern State University. This website includes numerous online features such as biographies of folk artists and musicians, educational resources, and links to other websites that support folklife research and programming. http://www.nsula.edu/folklife/.

Maine Arts Commission. This website provides information on projects offered through the state's folk arts program. http://mainearts.maine.gov/.

Maine Folklife Center & Northeast Archive of Folklore and Oral History. Based at the University of Maine, this website includes online resources developed from archival materials. http://www.umaine.edu/folklife/.

Maryland Historical Trust. This organization supports folklife programming within its projects on cultural conservation and historic preservation. The folklife links will connect users to museums that include folklife programming, and the site provides video support as well as downloadable newsletters, articles, and educational resources. http://www.marylandhistoricaltrust.net/.

Maryland State Arts Council. This site supports the state's folk arts program. http://www.msac.org/.

Massachusetts Cultural Council. The Massachusetts folklife program is included on this website. Audio samples of recordings from the state's apprenticeship program are an especially interesting online feature. http://www.massculturalcouncil.org/.

McKissick Museum. This museum focuses on the history and culture of South Carolina. It devotes special attention to southern folk culture, and the website's folklife section includes an excellent online component, "Digital Traditions" (http://www.digitaltraditions.net), that includes material from exhibits of folklife. http://www.cas.sc.edu/mcks/index.html.

Michigan Traditional Arts Program. This site spotlights resources from Michigan's folklife projects. The website provides excellent materials, including online exhibits and educational resources. The materials linked from the "Folkpatterns" section are useful for teachers across the country. http://museum.cl.msu.edu/s-program/MTAP/.

Micronesian Area Research Center. Information on folk arts programming in Micronesia is available on this site. http://www.uog.edu/dynamicdata/MicroAreaResearchCenter.aspx.

Mid Atlantic Arts Foundation. This regional folklife center includes a searchable database of folk artists, an events calendar, and contact information for various northeastern folk arts programs.The emphasis is on New Jersey, Pennsylvania, and Delaware. http://www.midatlanticarts.org/.

Milwaukee County Historical Society. The society's museum has folk collections related to the city and county, and their website includes online exhibits that are relevant to folklife and oral history. http://www.milwaukeehistory.net/.

Mind-Builders Creative Arts Center. The Dr. Beverly Robinson Community Folk Culture Program at this center teaches young people how to document and interpret cultural traditions in their families and neighborhoods. Various projects are placed online through this website. http://www.mind-builders.org/.

Mississippi Arts Commission Heritage Program. This site presents information on Mississippi's folk arts program. One section of the website (http://www.arts.state.ms.us/crossroads/) features the innovative and beautifully presented multimedia website "Crossroads of the Heart." http://www.arts.state.ms.us/.

Mississippi Band of Choctaw Indians. This website contains excellent resources on American Indian traditional culture. http://www.choctaw.org/.

Mississippi Cultural Crossroads. This local arts agency site includes research and presentations of folk culture, primarily in Port Gibson and Claiborne County, Mississippi. http://www.msculturalcrossroads.org/.

Missouri Folk Arts Program. The website of this folk arts program includes online presentations of research and excellent digital archival material. http://museum.research.missouri.edu/mfap/.

Missouri Historical Society. Based in St. Louis, this historical society has online presentations about folklife. http://www.mohistory.org/.

Montana Arts Council. Montana's folklife program is supported through the state arts council. Well-written essays on various aspects of Montana folklife can be downloaded from this site, which also contains good resources for teaching about folklore. http://art.mt.gov/.

Mountain West Center for Regional Studies. The website presents good information about Utah State University's archives and folklife programming. http://www.usu.edu/mountainwest/.

Museum of International Folk Art. Santa Fe is the site for the largest folk arts museum in the world, where over 130,000 objects from 100 nations are curated. Their website includes a photo gallery of aspects of the museum's collections and programming. http://www.moifa.org/.

National Council for the Traditional Arts. This organization is mainly known for producing the National Folk Festival. Their site includes an excellent audio archive of numerous performances and information about its wide range of programming. http://www.ncta.net/.

National Endowment for the Arts. The NEA supplies the financial lifeline for most public folk arts programming, and it also has vivid presentations of folk arts on its site. The information on the National Heritage Fellowship Award winners is especially vibrant. http://www.arts.endow.gov/.

National Museum of the American Indian. This world-class museum features a special emphasis on the traditional culture of American Indians that is reflected in its website. http://www.si.edu/nmai/.

National Network for Folk Arts in Education. This site serves as a center for folklorists and educators working within elementary and secondary schools by providing links to educational resources, a schedule of folklife education events and workshops, and a newsletter. http://www.carts.org/.

Nebraska Folklife Network. This site provides information on an organization that brings together research on Nebraska's folk culture. http://www.nefolklife.org/.

Nevada Arts Council. Information about the activities of Nevada's folklife program are available on this website. http://dmla.clan.lib.nv.us/docs/arts/.

New England Foundation for the Arts. Online and downloadable information about folk arts programming in the New England states and the foundation's own projects are available on this website. http://www.tapnet.org/www.nefa.org/.

New Hampshire State Council on the Arts. This website connects users to the council's New Hampshire Folklife Program. Online resources include information about traditional and ethnic musicians in the state, and downloadable versions of festival guides and exhibit catalogs. http://www.nh.gov/folklife/index.htm.

New Jersey Historical Society. This organization's ethnic history program is especially useful to folklorists. http://www.jerseyhistory.org/.

New Jersey State Council on the Arts. This site connects computer users to New Jersey's folk arts programs. The network of links within the state is especially useful. http://www.njartscouncil.org/.

New Mexico Arts Division. This website provides an entry to the state's folk arts program. The site include online exhibits on folklife in New Mexico. http://www.nmarts.org/.

New Orleans Jazz & Heritage Festival. This site includes online presentations about the festival's folklife area. The online galleries and webcasts are especially interesting features. http://www.nojazzfest.com/.

New York Folklore Society. This folklore society promotes numerous research projects and published the journal *Voices*. The online "Gallery of New York Folk Art" is an interesting feature on this site. http://www.nyfolklore.org/.

New York State Council on the Arts. New York's folk arts program is supported through the state's arts council. This site includes information about various programs that fund folklife research and presentations of folk arts. http://www.nysca.org/.

North Carolina Arts Council. The state's folklife program can be accessed through this website. Online photo galleries, a digital slideshow, and downloadable resources provides site visitors with good information on a variety of folk traditions in the state. http://www.ncarts.org/.

North Carolina Folklife Institute. This site provides interesting presentations of folklife from various projects completed by institute staff. The online photo galleries, essays, and streaming audio programs are especially effective. http://www.ncfolk.org/.

North Dakota Council on the Arts. Information on North Dakota's folk arts program is available on this site. The online artists' profiles include good feature stories on traditional arts from the state. http://www.state.nd.us/arts/.

Northwest Folklife. Seattle's folklife center produces numerous events, including a prestigious festival each year. The website has streaming audio of past performances from this event. http://www.nwfolklife. org/.

Northwest Heritage Resources. Based in Olympia, Washington, this organization showcases regional folklife through a variety of programs and services. The site includes educational resources that can be downloaded and printed as well as a multimedia presentation that introduces viewers to the region's folk culture. http://www.northwestheritageresources.org/.

Northwest Native American Basketweavers Association. This site provides information on basketweaving traditions. An online photo exhibit focuses on designs and motifs in various basket-making traditions. http://www.nnaba.org/.

Nunavut Arts and Crafts Association. This organization supports First Nations' artists in northern Canada. The site includes biographies of artists from numerous communities, including the Arviat, Iqaluit, Kugluktuk, Okpik, Pangnirtung, and Serapio. http://www.nacaarts. org/home.html.

Old Town School of Folk Music. Chicago's famous institution for teaching and supporting folk music built this website. It contains information about various programs, and includes online resources and links for hearing musicians who have been featured in various events at the school. http://www.oldtownschool.org/.

Oregon Folklife Program. The Oregon Historical Society's website includes information about the state's folklife program. http://www. ohs.org/education/folklife.

Ozark Studies Institute. Located in southwest Missouri, this organization develops research projects and presentations about folklife of the Ozarks. The online exhibits and resource information on Jewish communities in the Ozarks are especially interesting features of this site. http:// ozarksstudies.missouristate.edu/programs.htm.

Philadelphia Folklore Project. Along with supplying information about events and activities offered through this organization, this website includes a "Virtual Tour" (http://www.folkloreproject.org/programs/ exhibits/index.cfm) of some of the art traditions in the city's neighborhoods. http://www.folkloreproject.org/.

Philadelphia Folksong Society. In addition to producing the Philadelphia Folk Festival, this organization also coordinates other events that serve the greater metropolitan area. The website includes downloadable recordings of past festival performances. http://www.pfs.org/.

Pine Hills Culture Program. This project is housed within the Center for Oral History and Cultural Heritage at the University of Southern

Mississippi. Online information includes photographs from research and essays about various aspects of Mississippi folklife as well as portraits of folk artists. http://www.usm.edu/oralhistory/gen_info.html.

Rangeley Lakes Region Logging Museum. This site can be found through Margaret R. Yocum's home page. The online photographs and descriptions of woodcraft from Maine are well worth a visit to this site. http://mason.gmu.edu/~myocom/.

Rhode Island Historical Preservation & Heritage Commission. This site includes information on various programs and resources about folklife in Rhode Island. http://www.ri.gov/.

Rhode Island State Council on the Arts. The council supports the state's folk and traditional arts program. Along with information about services provided by the arts council, this site also includes a web log about folklife topics. http://www.arts.ri.gov/folkarts/.

Rivers of Steel National Heritage Area. The Steel Industry Heritage Corporation of western Pennsylvania supports this organization. The website features research on the occupational folklife of the steel industry as well as information about regional folklife in Pennsylvania. The site includes information about oral histories and ethnographic studies completed by the organization and useful resources for educators. http://www.riversofsteel.com/.

Rose Center and Council for the Arts. Based in Morristown, Tennessee, this center has a focus on the traditional arts of Appalachia. The website contains an online photo gallery and newsletters. http://www.rosecenter.org/.

Sealaska Heritage Foundation. This organization features the culture of the Tlingit, Haida, and Tsimshian people of the coastal Northwest in this colorful website. http://www.sealaskaheritage.org/.

Smithsonian Institution. The museum's Center for Folklife and Cultural Heritage can be accessed at http://www.folklife.si.edu/, and Folkways Recordings is at http://www.folkways.si.edu/. There is a wealth of information on both sites, including streaming video of the Smithsonian Folklife Festival and downloadable recordings from Folkways. The site is also filled with articles and feature stories about various Smithsonian programs, educational resource guides, and numerous ways and opportunities for learning about folk culture.

South Carolina Arts Commission. The home page for this state's folklife and traditional arts program includes grant guidelines and information useful for supporting folklife studies in South Carolina. http://www.southcarolinaarts.com/.

South Dakota Arts Council. Along with providing administrative information about South Dakota's folk arts program, this website includes an online presentation about the state's apprenticeship program, featuring master artists from the northern Great Plains. http://www.sdarts.org/.

Southern Arts Federation. This regional arts center supports folklife program in the southeastern states. The website includes information about various programs as well as online resources that are relevant to the study of folklore. http://www.southarts.org/folklorist.htm.

South Georgia Folklife Project. Based out of Valdosta State University, this regional folklife program has an impressive website. It includes essays on folklife in Georgia, photo galleries, radio shows, and video archives about various traditions in the Deep South. http://www.valdosta.edu/library/find/arch/folklife/index.html.

Southwest Center. The website for this center, based at the University of Arizona, includes online resources from the university's archives as well as past fieldwork projects. http://www.uasouthwestcenter.org/.

SPACES. An acronym for "Saving and Preserving Arts and Cultural Environments," SPACES is dedicated to the preservation and advocacy of large-scale art projects. The site includes a photo gallery of various projects from the southwestern United States. http://www.spacesarchives.org/.

State Arts Council of Oklahoma. This arts council website includes information about its own folk arts programs, as well as other community arts program resources. http://www.oklaosf.state.ok.us/~arts/.

StoryCorps. Sound Portrait Productions formed a partnership with the Library of Congress, National Public Radio (NPR), and public radio stations nationwide to create this innovative and rewarding project. Along with listening to stories on NPR programs, those interested in StoryCorps' work can access other tales on this interactive website and even enter their own narratives. http://www.storycorps.org/.

Talking Across the Lines. This project is based in southern Maryland. Along with describing the organization's fieldwork-based projects, the website includes sound bytes on various topics that are relevant to folklife and cultural diversity. http://www.folktalk.org/.

Tennessee Arts Commission. Information about the state's folklife program is included on this website, which describes the program and contains a calendar of events that are relevant to folklife programs in Tennessee. http://www.arts.state.tn.us/.

Texas Folklife Resources. Information about the state's folk arts program is available on this website. Online curriculum guides on a range of topics relevant to folk culture in the Lone Star State are especially useful features. http://www.texasfolklife.org/.

Totem Heritage Center. A vivid feature of the website for this Ketchikan, Alaska, museum is the photo gallery of traditional arts from the coastal Northwest. http://www.city.ketchikan.ak.us/departments/museums/totem.html.

Traditional Arts Indiana. Indiana's folklife program is based out of Indiana University. The website includes an interactive map, slides shows of folk artists, and reports on projects. http://www.indiana.edu/~tradarts/.

Traditional Arts in Upstate New York. The "North Country Folklore Online" section of this site (http://northcountryfolklore.org/) features streaming audio and strong photographic essays on various aspects of folklore in New York State's North Country, which includes the Adirondack Mountains and the St. Lawrence River Valley. http://www.tauny.org/.

Tuckerton Seaport. This organization supports the Jersey Shore Folklife Center (http://www.tuckertonseaport.org/jerseyshorefolklifecenter.html), which provides programming for regional folklife projects within New Jersey's Pinelands and the Jersey Shore. Good information about participating folk artists is available through the folklife center's link. http://www.tuckertonseaport.org/.

Utah Arts Council. The arts council supports the Utah Folk Arts Program. This site includes information about grant writing and events supported by the folklife program. http://www.arts.utah.gov/folkarts/.

Vermont Folklife Center. Multimedia presentations and online radio shows are strong features on this site. The center's guide to recording equipment provides a useful service for folklorists, oral historians, radio show producers, and other researchers. http://www.vermontfolklifecenter.org/.

Virginia Folklife Program. This site includes information about folklife programming in the state. Features include videos from fieldwork and links to relevant YouTube videos. http://www.virginiafolklife.org/.

Ward Museum of Wildfowl Art. Located in Salisbury, Maryland, this museum preserves and presents the history of decoy carving and waterfowl art in America. Online photographs from gallery shows are prominently featured on this website. http://www.wardmuseum.org/.

Warren E. Roberts Virtual Museum of Early Indiana Life. Indiana University students, faculty, and staff created this website in response to

Warren Roberts' dream of creating an open-air museum of pioneer life in southern Indiana. The site presents research conducted and coordinated by Roberts and has especially strong presentations of vernacular architecture and other forms of material culture. http://www.indiana.edu/~wer.

Washington State Arts Commission. The site for accessing information about Washington's folklife program, this resource includes downloadable essays on folk artists and interesting articles on cultural traditions practiced in the state. http://www.arts.wa.gov/.

Western Folklife Center. This regional folklife center hosts a site with a wide range of presentations, such as podcasts, cybercasts, and online videos of various events, including the National Cowboy Poetry Gathering. http://www.westernfolklife.org/.

Western Kentucky University. The university's website includes photo galleries and resource information that is useful for learning about professional training for public folklorists. http://www.wku.edu/folkstudies/.

Western States Arts Federation. The federation is a regional arts center that features folklife programming. The "Annotated Arts Link" on its website leads user to relevant public folklore sites. http://www.westaf.org/.

Wisconsin Arts Board. This website provides information about Wisconsin's folk arts program. The links to the online resource "Wisconsin Folks" (http://www.arts.state.wi.us/static/folkdir/index.htm) is particularly interesting. This interactive feature is an innovative way to explore the people and traditions of the state. http://artsboard.wisconsin.gov/.

World Music Institute. Based in New York City, this site includes audio samples and information about artists and programs supported by this organization. http://www.heartheworld.org/.

Wyoming Arts Council. This site links users to the state's folk arts program and to other resource agencies that focus on the folk culture of Wyoming. http://wyoarts.state.wy.us/Folk/index.asp.

References

Abrahams, Roger D. 1983. *The Man-of-Words in the West Indies*. Baltimore: The Johns Hopkins University Press.

Abramowitz, Rachel. 2007. "Urp! Step Back From the Media Buffet." *Los Angeles Times*, March 18. http://www.sptimes.com/2007/03/18/Floridian/Urp_Step_back_from_th.shtml (accessed 29 March 2007).

Adest, Abbi. 2006. "Rupert Murdoch Comments on Fox Interactive's Growth." http://seekingalpha.com/article/15237-rupert-murdoch-comments-on-fox-interactive-s-growth.

American Folklife Center. "Florida Folklife from the WPA Collections: 1937–1942." http://www.memory.loc.gov/ammem/collections/florida/.

"Association of Inclusionist Wikipedians." Wikimedia. http://meta.wikimedia.org/wiki/Association_of_Inclusionist_Wikipedians (accessed 9 May 2008).

Anderson, Benedict. 1991. *Imagined Communities: Reflections on the Origins and Spread of Nationalism*. New York: Verso Press.

Anderson, Chris. 2008. "The End of Theory." *Wired*, July. 108–9.

Anvari.org. 2005. "Chain Letters—To Forward or Not." http://www.anvari.org/fun/Misc/Chain_Letters_-_To_Forward_or_Not.html.

Appadurai, Arjun. 1986. *The Social Life of Things: Commodities in Cultural Perspective*. Cambridge: Cambridge University Press.

Aranza, Jacob. 1983. *Backward Masking Unmasked: Backward Satanic Messages of Rock and Roll Exposed*. Lafayette, LA: Vital Issues Press.

Augusto, David. 1970. "Network Analysis: A Contribution to the Theory of Folklore Transmission." *Folklore Forum* 3: 78–90.

Baker, Ronald L., and Simon J. Bronner. 2005. "'Letting Out Jack': Sex and Aggression in Manly Recitations." In *Manly Traditions: The Folk Roots of American Masculinities*, ed. Simon J. Bronner, 315–50. Bloomington: Indiana University Press.

Bargh, John A., Katelyn Y. A. McKenna, and Grainne M. Fitzsimons. 2002. "Can You See the Real Me? Activation and Expression of the 'True Self' on the Internet." *Journal of Social Issues* 58: 33–48.

Baron, Robert and Nick Spitzer, eds. 2007. *Public Folklore*. Jackson: University Press of Mississippi.

Barrick, Mac. 1982. "Celebrity Sick Jokes." *Maledicta: International Journal of Verbal Aggression* 6: 57–62.

———. 1987. Correspondence to Simon Bronner (8 October).

Barry, Dave. 2007. "You've Got Trouble." *New York Times Book Review*, May 6.

Bartis, Peter. 2002. "Folklife and Fieldwork: An Introduction to Field Tech-
      niques." Washington, DC: American Folklife Center/Library of Congress.
Bauman, Richard. 1972. "Differential Identity and the Social Base of Folklore."
      In *Toward New Perspectives in Folklore*, ed. Américo Paredes and Richard
      Bauman, 31–41. Austin: University of Texas Press.
———. 1983. "Folklore and the Forces of Modernity." *Folklore Forum* 16: 153–58.
———, ed. 1992. *Folklore, Cultural Performances, and Popular Entertainments: A
      Communications-Centered Handbook*. New York: Oxford University Press.
Bauman, Richard, and Charles L. Briggs. 2003. *Voices of Modernity: Language
      Ideologies and the Politics of Inequality*. Cambridge: Cambridge University
      Press.
Baym, Nancy K. 1993. "Interpreting Soap Operas and Creating Community:
      Inside a Computer-Mediated Fan Culture." *Journal of Folklore Research* 30:
      143–77.
Beatty, Roger Dean. 1976. "Computerlore: The Bit Bucket." *New York Folklore* 2:
      223–24.
Ben-Amos, Dan. 1971. "Toward a Definition of Folklore in Context." *Journal of
      American Folklore* 84: 3–15.
———. 1972. "Toward a Definition of Folklore in Context." In *Toward New
      Perspectives in Folklore*, ed. Américo Paredes and Richard Bauman, 3–15.
      Austin: University of Texas Press.
Bendix, Regina. 1997. *In Search of Authenticity: The Formation of Folklore Studies*.
      Madison: University of Wisconsin Press.
———. 1998. "Of Names, Professional Identities, and Disciplinary Futures."
      Journal of American Folklore 111: 235–46.
Benjamin, Walter. [1936] 2007. "The Work of Art in the Age of Mechanical
      Reproduction." In *Illuminations: Essays and Reflections*, ed. Hannah Arendt,
      217–52. New York: Schocken.
Bennett, Gillian. 1988. *Traditions of Belief*. London: Penguin.
Bennett, Sue, Karl Maton, and Lisa Kervin. 2008. "The 'Digital Natives' Debate:
      A Critical View of the Evidence." *British Journal of Educational Technology* 39:
      775–86.
Berger, Asa, and Peter Burke. 2005. *A Social History of the Media*. 2nd ed. Malden,
      MA: Polity Press.
Berger, John. 1977. *Ways of Seeing*. London: Penguin.
Bermejo, Fernando. 2007. *The Internet Audience: Constitution & Measurement*.
      New York: Peter Lang.
Bernstein, Richard J. 1971. *Praxis and Action: Contemporary Philosophies of Human
      Activity*. Philadelphia: University of Pennsylvania Press.
Binary Jokes. 2008. englishforums.com. http://www.englishforums.com/Eng-
      lish/BinaryJoke/2/kvbc/Post.htm (accessed 13 June 2008).
Bird, Allyson. 2006. "Teens Immortalize Friends on MySpace." *Miami Herald*,
      October 9.
Blank, Trevor J. 2007. "Examining the Transmission of Urban Legends: Mak-
      ing the Case for Folklore Fieldwork on the Internet." *Folklore Forum* 37:
      15–26.
"Blogs for Natalee." 2005. http://blogsfornatalee.com (accessed February 2007
      to February 2008).

Blumenreich, Beth, and Bari Lynn Polonsky. 1974. "Re-evaluating the Concept of Group: ICEN as an Alternative." *Folklore Forum,* Bibliographic and Special Series, 12: 12–18.

Brafman, Ori, and Rod A. Beckstrom. 2006. *The Starfish and the Spider: The Unstoppable Power of Leaderless Organizations.* New York: Penguin Portfolio.

Bronner, Simon J. 1986. *American Folklore Studies: An Intellectual History.* Lawrence: University Press of Kansas.

———. [1986] 2004. *Grasping Things: Folk Material Culture and Mass Society in America.* Lexington: University Press of Kentucky.

———. 1988a. "Art, Performance, and Praxis: The Rhetoric of Contemporary Folklore Studies." *Western Folklore* 47: 75–101.

———. 1988b. "Political Suicide: The Budd Dwyer Joke Cycle and the Humor of Disaster." *Midwestern Folklore* 14: 81–90.

———. 1995. *Piled Higher and Deeper: The Folklore of Student Life.* Little Rock: August House.

———. 1998. *Following Tradition: Folklore in the Discourse of American Culture.* Logan: Utah State University Press.

———. 2000. "The Meaning of Tradition: An Introduction." *Western Folklore* 59: 87–104.

———. 2002. *Folk Nation: Folklore in the Creation of American Tradition.* Wilmington, DE: Scholarly Resources.

———. 2006. "Folk Logic: Interpretation and Explanation in Folkloristics." *Western Folklore* 65: 401–34.

———. 2007. "The Analytics of Alan Dundes." In *The Meaning of Folklore: The Analytical Essays of Alan Dundes,* ed. Simon J. Bronner, 1–50. Logan: Utah State University Press.

Brooks, Pat. 1973. *Using Your Spiritual Authority.* Monroeville, PA: Banner.

Brunvand, Jan H. 1981. *The Vanishing Hitchhiker.* New York: W. W. Norton.

———. 1984. *The Choking Doberman.* New York: W. W. Norton.

———. 1990. *Curses! Broiled Again!: The Hottest Urban Legends Going.* New York: W. W. Norton.

———. 2001. "Folklore in the News (and on the Net)." *Western Folklore* 60: 47–76.

"Budd Dwyer." 2008. Urban Dictionary. http://www.urbandictionary.com/define.php?term=Budd+Dwyer&defid=2397819 (accessed 22 September 2008).

"Budd Dwyer." 2008. Uncyclopedia.org. Wiki, July 24. http://uncyclopedia.org/wiki/Budd_Dwyer (accessed 26 July 2008).

Carlson, David. 2005. "Online Timeline." *Nieman Reports* 59: 45–83.

Carter, Denise. 2005. "Living in Virtual Communities: An Ethnography of Human Relationships in Cyberspace." *Information, Communication, & Society* 8: 148–67.

"Casio F91W." Wikipedia. http://en.wikipedia.org/wiki/Casio_F91W (accessed on 18 April 2008).

"Category: User En-N." Wikipedia. http://en.wikipedia.org/w/index.php?title=Category:User_en-N&oldid=11649069 (version of 29 March 2005).

Centers for Disease Control and Prevention. 2007. "Teen Drivers: Fact Sheet." http://www.cdc.gov/ncipc/factsheets/teenmvh.htm.

Chernev, Alexander. 2003. "When More Is Less and Less Is More: The Role of Ideal Point Availability and Assortment in Consumer Choice." *Journal of Consumer Research* 30: 170–83.

Choe, Stan. 2001. "What is Photoshopping? A New Sport on the Web." Knight Ridder newspapers, printed in *Centre Daily Times*, March 10.

Christy. 2008. "Spiritual Warfare." Christy's Christian Collage. http://www.ccpoet.com/warfare.html (accessed 15 April 2008).

Clark, Lynn Schofield. 1999. "Popular Culture: Replacing Religion for Today's Teens?" http://www.biblesociety.org.uk/exploratory/articles/clark99.pdf.

Clark, Wesley M. 2008. "The Premise Of Spiritual Warfare in Relation to Alien Abductions." CE 4. http://www.angelfire.com/on2/ce4/premise.html (accessed 15 April 2008).

Cocchiara, Giuseppe. 1981. *The History of Folklore in Europe*, trans. John N. McDaniel. Philadelphia: Institute for the Study of Human Issues.

Cohen, Rosalie A. 1969. "Conceptual Styles, Cultural Conflict, and Nonverbal Tests of Intelligence." *American Anthropologist* 5: 828–56.

"Commons: Babel." Wikimedia Commons. http://commons.wikimedia.org/w/index.php?title=Commons:Babel&oldid=150100 (version of 9 April 2005).

Cooper, Marc. 2004. "Among the NASCAR Dads." *Nation*, March 22. Posted March 4, http://www.thenation.com/doc/20040322/cooper2 (accessed 17 January 2006).

Cusick, Frederick, Dan Meyers, and Walter F. Roche, Jr. 1987. "Treasurer Dwyer Kills Self: Suicide at News Session." *Philadelphia Inquirer*, January 23, 1, 16A.

Dance, Daryl Cumber, ed. 2002. *From My People: 400 Years of African American Folklore*. New York: W. W. Norton.

Daniel. 2008. MySpace. Blog, February 18. http://blog.myspace.com (accessed 26 September 2008).

Danielson, Larry. 1986. "Religious Folklore." In *Folk Groups and Folklore Genres: An Introduction*, ed. Elliott Oring, 45–65. Logan: Utah State University Press.

Dardel, Eric. [1954] 1984. "The Mythic." In *Sacred Narrative: Readings in the Theory of Myth*, ed. Alan Dundes, 225–43. Berkeley: University of California Press.

Davenport, Tom. "Folkstreams." http://www.folkstreams.net/.

Davies, Christie. 2003. "Jokes That Follow Mass-Mediated Disasters in a Global Electronic Age." In *Of Corpse: Death and Humor in Folklore and Popular Culture*, ed. Peter Narváez, 35–82. Logan: Utah State University Press.

Davidson, Cathy N. 2007. "We Can't Ignore the Influence of Digital Technologies." *Chronicle Review* 53 (March 23), B20. http://chronicle.com/weekly/v53/i29/29b02001.htm (accessed 1 July 2008).

Dawkins, Richard. 1976. *The Selfish Gene*. New York: Oxford University Press.

DeAngelis, Tori. 2004. "Too Many Choices?" *Monitor on Psychology* 35: 56.

Dean and Susan. 5 October 1999. Personal interview with the author.

Dégh, Linda. 1993. "The Legend Conduit." In *Creativity and Tradition: New Directions*, ed. Simon J. Bronner, 105–26. Logan: Utah State University Press.

———. 1994. *American Folklore and the Mass Media*. Bloomington: Indiana University Press.

———. 1997. "Conduit Theory/Multiconduit Theory." In *Folklore: An Encyclopedia of Beliefs, Customs, Tales, Music, and Art,* ed. Thomas A. Green, 142–44. Santa Barbara, CA: ABC-CLIO.

Dégh, Linda, and Andrew Vázsonyi. 1973. *The Dialectics of the Legend.* Folklore Preprint Series 6. Bloomington: Indiana University Folklore Institute.

———. 1975. "The Hypothesis of Multi-Conduit Transmission of Folklore." In *Folklore: Performance and Communication,* ed. Dan Ben-Amos and Kenneth Goldstein, 207–52. The Hague: Mouton.

Dennett, Daniel C. 1990. "Memes and the Exploitation of Imagination." *Journal of Aesthetics and Art Criticism* 48: 127–35.

Dew, Diana S. 2008. "Spiritual Warfare." A Love I Could Not Deny. http://dianedew.com/spirwar.htm (accessed 15 April 2008).

"Diagnosing Missing White Woman Syndrome." 2006. CNN, March 14. http://www.cnn.com/CNN/Programs/anderson.cooper.360/blog/2006/03/diagnosing-missing-white-woman.html (accessed 12 August 2006).

Doctorow, Cory. 2006. "On 'Digital Maoism: The Hazards of the New Online Collectivism,' by Jaron Lanier." Edge: The Reality Club, June. http://www.edge.org/discourse/digital_maoism.html (accessed 31 May 2009).

Domi, Loser. 2008. The Wonderful World of Loser Domi. Blog, June 26. http://wwold.blogspot.com/2008_06_01_archive.html (accessed 25 September 2008).

Dorson, Richard M. 1970. "Is There a Folk in the City?" *Journal of American Folklore* 83: 185–216.

———. 1972. "Introduction: Concepts of Folklore and Folklife Studies." In *Folklore and Folklife: An Introduction,* ed. Richard M. Dorson, 1–50. Chicago: University of Chicago Press.

Dorst, John. 1990. "Tags and Burners, Cycles and Networks: Folklore in the Telectronic Age." *Journal of Folklore Research* 27: 179–90.

Douglas, Mary. 1991. "Jokes." In *Rethinking Popular Culture,* ed. C. Nukerji and M. Schudson, 291–310. Berkeley and Los Angeles: University of California Press.

Douglas, Nick. 2008. "90 Day Jane Not Killing Herself, Not as Hot as You Hoped." Gawker, February 13. http://gawker.com/356131/90-day-jane-not-killing-herself-not-as-hot-as-you-hoped (accessed 22 September 2008).

Drout, Michael D. C. 2006. "A Meme-Based Approach to Oral Traditional Theory." *Oral Tradition* 21: 269–94.

Dundes, Alan. [1962] 2007. "On the Psychology of Collecting Folklore." In *The Meaning of Folklore: The Analytical Essays of Alan Dundes,* ed. Simon J. Bronner, 414–21. Logan: Utah State University Press.

———. 1965a. "On Computers and Folktales." *Western Folklore* 24: 185–89.

———. 1965b. "What is Folklore?" In *The Study of Folklore,* ed. Alan Dundes, 1–3. Englewood Cliffs, NJ: Prentice-Hall.

———. [1966] 2007a. "Here I Sit: A Study of American Latrinalia." In *The Meaning of Folklore: The Analytical Essays of Alan Dundes,* ed. Simon J. Bronner, 360–74. Logan: Utah State University Press.

———. [1966] 2007b. "Metafolklore and Oral Literary Criticism." In *The Meaning of Folklore: The Analytical Essays of Alan Dundes,* ed. Simon J. Bronner, 80–87. Logan: Utah State University Press.

————. 1973. *Mother Wit from the Laughing Barrel: Readings in the Interpretation of Afro-American Folklore.* Englewood Cliffs, NJ: Prentice-Hall.

————. 1979. "The Dead Baby Joke Cycle." *Western Folklore* 38: 145–57

————. 1980. "Who are the Folk?" In *Interpreting Folklore* by Alan Dundes. Bloomington: Indiana University Press.

————. 1980. *Interpreting Folklore.* Bloomington: Indiana University Press.

————. 1981. "Many Hands Make Light Work or Caught in the Act of Screwing In Light Bulbs." *Western Folklore* 40: 261–66. Also in Dundes, Alan. 1987. *Cracking Jokes: Studies of Sick Humor Cycles & Stereotypes,* 143–49. Berkeley, CA: Ten Speed Press.

————. 1982. "*Volkskunde, Völkerkunde* and the Study of German National Character." In *Europäische Ethnologie,* eds. Heide Nixdorff and Thomas Hauschild, 257–65. Berlin: Dietrich Reimer Verlag.

————, ed. 1999. *International Folkloristics: Classic Contributions by the Founders of Folklore.* Lanham, MD: Rowman & Littlefield.

————. 2004. "As the Crow Flies: A Straightforward Study of Lineal Worldview in American Folk Speech." In *What Goes Around Comes Around: The Circulation of Proverbs in Contemporary Life,* eds. Kimberly J. Lau, Peter Tokofsky, and Stephen D. Winick, 171–87. Logan: Utah State University Press.

————. 2005. "Folkloristics in the Twenty-First Century (AFS Invited Presidential Plenary Address, 2004)." *Journal of American Folklore* 118: 385–408.

Dundes, Alan, and Carl R. Pagter. 1975. *Urban Folklore from the Paperwork Empire.* Austin, TX: American Folklore Society.

————. [1978] 1992. *Work Hard and You Shall Be Rewarded: Urban Folklore from the Paperwork Empire.* Bloomington: Indiana University Press.

————. 1987. *When You're Up to Your Ass in Alligators: More Urban Folklore from the Paperwork Empire.* Detroit: Wayne State University Press.

————. 1991a. "The Mobile SCUD Missile Launcher and Other Persian Gulf Warlore: An American Folk Image of Saddam Hussein's Iraq." *Western Folklore* 50: 303–322.

————. 1991b. *Never Try to Teach a Pig to Sing: Still More Urban Folklore from the Paperwork Empire.* Detroit: Wayne State University Press.

————. 1996. *Sometimes the Dragon Wins: Yet More Urban Folklore from the paperwork Empire.* Syracuse: Syracuse University Press.

Dundes, Alan, and Paul Renteln. 2005. "Foolproof: A Sampling of Mathematical Folk Humor." *Notices of the American Mathematical Society* 52: 24–34.

Durkheim, Emile. 1951. *Suicide: A Study in Sociology,* trans. John A. Spaulding and George Simpson. New York: Free Press.

E-GuestBooks.com. 2008. "Vancouver Missing." January 10. http://www.e-guestbooks.com/cgi-bin/e-guestbooks/guestbook.cgi?action=view&user=Renegade98 (accessed 15 January 2008).

Eichhorn, Kate. 2001. "Sites Unseen: Ethnographic Research in a Textual Community." *Qualitative Studies in Education* 14: 565–78.

Eisenthal, David. 2007. "A Strange Case—R. Budd Dwyer." Eisenthal Report. Blog, January 19, 2007. http://davideisenthal.typepad.com/the_eisenthal_report/2007/01/a_strange_case.html (accessed 22 September 2008).

Ellis, Bill. 2000. *Raising the Devil: Satanism, New Religions, and the Media.* Lexington: University Press of Kentucky.

———. 2001. "A Model for Collecting and Interpreting World Trade Center Disaster Jokes." *Newfolk: New Directions in Folklore* 5. http://www.temple.edu/isllc/newfolk/wtchumor.html.

———. 2003. "Making a Big Apple Crumble: The Role of Humor in Constructing a Global Response to Disaster." In *Of Corpse: Death and Humor in Folklore and Popular Culture*, ed. Peter Narváez, 35–79. Logan: Utah State University Press.

———. 2006. "Internet." In *Encyclopedia of American Folklife*, ed. Simon J. Bronner, 627–30. Armonk, NY: M.E. Sharpe.

Ellis, Karen. "Educational CyberPlayGround." http://www.edu-cyberpg.com/.

Ellwood, Robert. 1988. "Contemporary Religion as Folk Religion." In *History and Future of Faith: Religion Past, Present, and To Come*, 118–30. New York: Crossroad.

"End Time Deliverance Ministry." 2008. Demon Buster.com. http://www.demonbuster.com/daily.html (accessed 15 April 2008).

"Entering Contests: What Cannot Be Used in an Entry?" http://www.worth1000.com/popup.asp?faq=3.

"Ephesians 6:12 in Relation to UFO Aliens." 2008. Alien Resistance.org. http://www.alienresistance.org/powers.htm (accessed 15 April 2008).

Everett, Holly. 2002. *Roadside Crosses in Contemporary Memorial Culture.* Denton: University of North Texas Press.

Feintuch, Burt, ed. 1988. *The Conservation of Culture: Folklorists and the Public Sector*. Lexington: University Press of Kentucky.

Fernback, Jan. 2003. "Legends on the Net: An Examination of Computer-Mediated Communication as a Locus of Oral Culture." *New Media & Society* 5: 29–45.

Feyerabend, Paul. 1988. *Against Method*. Rev. ed. London: Verso.

Fichter, Darlene. 2006. "Web 2.0, Library 2.0 and Radical Trust: A First Take." *Blog on the Side*, April 2. http://library2.usask.ca/~fichter/blog_on_the_side/2006/04/web-2.html (accessed 1 July 2008).

Fine, Gary Alan. 1979. "Folklore Diffusion through Interactive Social Networks: Conduits in a Preadolescent Community." *New York Folklore* 5: 87–126.

———. 1980. "Multi-Conduit Transmission and Social Structure: Expanding a Folklore Classic." In *Folklore on Two Continents: Essays in Honor of Linda Dégh,* ed. Nikolai Burlakoff and Carl Lindahl, 300–9. Bloomington, IN: Trickster Press.

———. 1983. "Network and Meaning: An Interactionist Approach to Structure." *Symbolic Interaction* 6: 97–110.

Fine, Gary Alan, and Bruce Noel Johnson. 1980. "The Promiscuous Cheerleader: An Adolescent Male Belief Legend." *Western Folklore* 39: 120–29.

Fineman, Mia. 2004. "Photography, Vernacular." In *Encyclopedia of American Folk Art*, ed. Gerard C. Wertkin, 384–87. New York: Routledge.

Fleece, Jeffery A. 1946. "Words in -FU." *American Speech* 21: 70–72.

Foote, Monica. 2007. "Userpicks: Cyber Folk Art in the Early 21st Century." *Folklore Forum* 37: 27-38.

Fox, William. 1983. "Computerized Creation and Diffusion of Folkloric Materials." *Folklore Forum* 16: 5–20.

Frand, Jason. 2000. "The Information-Age Mindset: Changes in Students and Implications for Higher Education." *EDUCAUSE Review* 35: 14–24.

Frank, Russell. 2004. "When the Going Gets Tough, the Tough Go Photoshopping: September 11 and the Newslore of Vengeance and Victimization." *New Media & Society* 6: 633–58.

———. 2006. "Absent of Chores, Days Slip Away." *Centre Daily Times*, February 12, Living section.

Frasure, Basil. 2008. "When the Enemy Comes." Whole Person Counseling. http://www.wholeperson-counseling.org/revival/w-enemy.html (accessed 15 April 2008).

Fuller, Steve. 2002. *Social Epistemology*. Bloomington: Indiana University Press.

Georges, Robert A. 1969. "Toward an Understanding of Storytelling Events." *Journal of American Folklore* 82: 313–28.

Georges, Robert A., and Michael Owen Jones. 1995. *Folkloristics: An Introduction*. Bloomington: Indiana University Press.

Gill, Sam. 1994. "The Academic Study of Religion." *Journal of the American Academy of Religion* 64: 965–75.

Glassie, Henry. 1999. *Material Culture*. Bloomington: Indiana University Press.

Goethals, Gregor. 2003. "Myth and Ritual in Cyberspace." In *Mediating Religion: Conversations in Media, Religion and Culture*, ed. Jolyon Mitchell and Sophia Marriage, 257–70. London: T& T Clark.

Golbeck, Jennifer, Bijan Parsia, and James Hendler. 2003. "Trust Networks on the Semantic Web." In *Proceedings of Cooperative Intelligent Agents 2003, August 27–29, Helsinki, Finland*. http://www.mindswap.org/papers/CIA03.pdf.

Goldstein, Diane. 2004. *Once Upon a Virus: AIDS Legends and Vernacular Risk Perception*. Logan: Utah State University Press.

Gonos, George, Virginia Mulkern, and Nicholas Poushinsky. 1976. "Anonymous Expression: A Structural View of Graffiti." *Journal of American Folklore* 89: 40–48.

Good, A. J. 2008. "Spiritual Warfare." Apocalyptic Hope. http://www.cyber-time.net/~ajgood/little.html (accessed 15 April 2008).

Goodenough, Ward H. 1964. "Cultural Anthropology." In *Language in Culture and Society*, ed. Dell Hymes, 36–39. Bombay, India: Allied Publishers.

Goodman, Ellen. 2004. "Forgetting the 'Dad' in NASCAR Pitch." *Boston Globe*, February 19. http://www.boston.com/news/globe/editorial_opinion/oped/articles/2004/02/19/forgetting_the_dad_in_nascar_pitch/ (accessed 17 January 2006).

Govier, Trudy. 1997. *Social Trust and Human Communities*. Montreal: McGill–Queen's University Press.

Green, Thomas A., ed. 2006. *The Greenwood Library of American Folktales*, 4 volumes. Westport, CT: Greenwood.

Greenberg, Andrea. 1973. "Drugged and Seduced: A Contemporary Legend." *New York Folklore Quarterly* 29: 131–58.

Gregory, R. L. 1970. *The Intelligent Eye*. New York: McGraw-Hill.

Grider, Sylvia. 2001. "Spontaneous Shrines: A Modern Response to Tragedy and Disaster." http://www.temple.edu/isllc/newfolk/shrines.html.

Grimes, William. 1992. "Computer As a Cultural Tool: Chatter Mounts on Every Topic." *New York Times*, December 1, section C, 13–14.

Guare, John. 1990. *Six Degrees of Separation*. New York: Vintage.

Guice, Jon. 1998. "Looking Backward and Forward at the Internet." *Information Society* 14: 201–11.

Hafner, Katie, and Matthew Lyon. 1998. *Where Wizards Stay Up Late: The Origins of the Internet*. New York: Simon & Schuster.

Hammond, Frank, and Ida Mae Hammond. 1973. *Pigs in the Parlor: A Practical Guide to Deliverance*. Kirkwood, MO: Impact Books.

Hardy, Quentin. 2006. "On 'Digital Maoism: The Hazards of the New Online Collectivism' by Jaron Lanier." Edge: The Reality Club, June. http://www.edge.org/discourse/digital_maoism.html (accessed 31 May 2009).

Healy, David. 1997. "Cyberspace and Place: The Internet As Middle Landscape on the Electronic Frontier." In *Internet Culture*, ed. David Porter, 55-69. New York: Routledge.

Herskowitz, Linda. 1987. "Psychiatrists: An Act of Rage, Despair." *Philadelphia Inquirer*, January 23, 16a.

Hine, Christine. 2000. *Virtual Ethnography*. London: Sage.

———. 2009. "Question One: How Can Qualitative Internet Researchers Define the Boundaries of Their Projects?" *Internet Inquiry: Conversations about Method*, ed. Annette N. Markham and Nancy K. Baym, 1–29. Los Angeles: Sage Publications.

Historical Museum of South Florida. http://www.hmsf.org/.

"History of Wikipedia." Wikipedia. http://en.wikipedia.org/wiki/History_of_Wikipedia (accessed 18 April 2008).

"History of Wikis." Wikipedia. http://en.wikipedia.org/wiki/History_of_wikis (accessed 6 April 2008).

Holbek, Bengt. 1969. "Computer Classification of Proverbs: Report on a Small Scale Experiment." *Proverbium* 14: 372–76.

Holloway, Beth. 2007. *Loving Natalee*. New York: Harper Collins.

Howard, Robert Glenn. 1997. "Apocalypse in Your In-Box: End Times Communication on the Internet." *Western Folklore* 56: 295–315.

———. 2000. "On-Line Ethnography of Dispensationalist Discourse: Revealed versus Negotiated Truth." In *Religion on the Internet*, ed. Douglas Cowan and Jeffery K. Hadden, 225–46. New York: Elsevier.

———. 2001. "Passages Divinely Lit: Revelatory Vernacular Rhetoric on the Internet." PhD diss., University of Oregon.

———. 2005. "Toward a Theory of the World Wide Web: The Case for Pet Cloning." *Journal of Folklore Research* 42: 323–60.

———. 2006. "Sustainability and Narrative Plasticity in Online Apocalyptic Discourse after September 11, 2001." *Journal of Media and Religion* 5: 25–47.

———. 2008a. "Electronic Hybridity: The Persistent Processes of the Vernacular Web." *Journal of American Folklore* 121: 192–218.

———. 2008b. "The Vernacular Web of Participatory Media." *Critical Studies in Media Communication* 25: 490–512.

———. Forthcoming a. "Enacting a Virtual 'Ekklesia': Online Christian Fundamentalism as Vernacular Religion." *New Media & Society*.

———. Forthcoming b. "Vernacular Media, Vernacular Belief: Locating Christian Fundamentalism in the Vernacular Web." *Western Folklore*.

"House Rule." Wikipedia. http://en.wikipedia.org/wiki/House_rules (accessed 10 May 2008).

Hufford, David J. 1982. *The Terror that Comes in the Night: An Experience-Centered Study of Supernatural Assault Traditions*. Philadelphia: University of Pennsylvania Press.

———. 1983. "The Supernatural and the Sociology of Knowledge: Explaining Academic Belief." *New York Folklore* 9: 21–30.

———. 1995a. "Beings without Bodies: An Experience-Centered Theory of the Belief in Spirits." *Out of the Ordinary: Folklore and the Supernatural*, ed. Barbara Walker, 11–45. Logan: Utah State University Press.

———. 1995b. "Introduction." *Western Folklore* 54: 1–11.

———. 1995c. "The Scholarly Voice and the Personal Voice: Reflexivity in Belief Studies." *Western Folklore* 54: 57-76.

———. 1998. "Folklore Studies Applied To Health." *Journal of Folklore Research* 35: 295–313.

Hufford, Mary. 1991. *American Folklife: A Commonwealth of Cultures*. Washington, DC: American Folklife Center, Library of Congress.

———, ed. 1994. *Conserving Culture: A New Discourse on Heritage*. A Publication of the American Folklore Society, Published for the American Folklife Center at the Library of Congress. Urbana and Chicago: University of Illinois Press.

HurricanEAJW2. 2008. "Bud Dwyer—Extended Version." YouTube, August 27. http://www.youtube.com/watch?v=0Y8ebVhlnBo (accessed 22 September 2008).

Hutchings, Tim. 2007. "Creating Church Online: A Case-Study Approach to Religious Experience." *Studies in World Christianity* 13: 243–60.

Hymes, Dell. 1975. "Folklore's Nature and the Sun's Myth." *Journal of American Folklore* 88: 345–69.

"I Did it for the Lulz." 2008. Encyclopaedia Dramatica. http://www.encyclopediadramatica.com/I_did_it_for_the_lulz#Budd_Dwyer (accessed 22 September 2008).

Information Today. 2007. "Social Networking Timeline." *Searcher* 15: 38.

"ILoo." 2007. Snopes.com: Rumor Has It. Urban Legend Reference Pages, August 11. http://www.snopes.com/computer/internet/iloo.asp (accessed 3 October 2008).

International Safe Travels Foundation. 2007. http://www.internationalsafetravels.org/ (accessed 1 February 2008).

"Internet Timeline." 2000. *Teacher Librarian* 27: 68.

Iyengar, Sheena, and Mark Lepper. 2000. "When Choice Is Demotivating: Can One Desire Too Much of a Good Thing?" *Journal of Personality and Social Psychology* 79: 995–1006.

Jackson, Timothy Allen. 2001. "Towards a New Media Aesthetic." In *Reading Digital Culture*, ed. David Trend, 347–53. Malden, MA: Blackwell.

Jeffreys, Mark. 2000. "The Meme Metaphor." *Perspectives in Biology and Medicine* 43: 227–42.

Johnson, Steven. 1999. *Interface Culture: How New Technology Transforms the Way We Create and Communicate*. New York: Basic Books.

Jennings, Karla. 1990. *The Devouring Fungus: Tales of the Computer Age*. New York: W.W. Norton.

Jones, Ernest. [1912] 1961. *Papers on Psycho-Analysis*. Boston: Beacon Press.

Jones, Michael Owen. 1971. "(PC + CB) x SD (R + I + E) = Hero." *New York Folklore Quarterly* 27: 243–60.

Jordan, Rosan Augusta. 1997. "Computer-Mediated Folklore." In *Folklore: An Encyclopedia of Beliefs, Customs, Tales, Music, and Art*, ed. Thomas A. Green, 140–42. Santa Barbara, CA: ABC-CLIO.

Keisling, William, and Richard Kearns. 1988. *The Sins of Our Fathers: A Profile of Pennsylvania Attorney Leroy S. Zimmerman and a Historical Explanation of the Suicide of State Treasurer R. Budd Dwyer*. Harrisburg: Privately Printed.

Kelly, Ansgar. 1968. *The Devil, Demonology, and Witchcraft: The Development of Christian Beliefs in Evil Spirits*. New York: Doubleday.

Ketner, Kennth Laine. 1976. "Identity and Existence in the Study of Human Traditions." *Folklore* 87: 192–200.

Keys, Dave. 2008. "What Does All This Mean to Us?" Welcome! to Hillbillie Dave's. http://members.tripod.com/~dwkeys/mission.html (accessed 15 April 2008).

Kibby, Marjorie. 2005. "Email Forwardables: Folklore in the Age of the Internet." *New Media & Society* 7: 770–90.

Kirshenblatt-Gimblett, Barbara. 1983. "The Future of Folklore Studies in America: The Urban Frontier." *Folklore Forum* 16: 175–234.

———. 1995. "From the Paperwork Empire to the Paperless Office: Testing the Limits of the 'Science of Tradition.'" In *Folklore Interpreted: Essays in Honor of Alan Dundes*, ed. Regina Bendix and Rosemary Levy Zumwalt, 69–92. New York: Garland.

———. 1996. "The Electronic Vernacular." In *Connected: Engagements with Media*, ed. George E. Marcus, 21-66. Chicago: University of Chicago Press.

———. 1998. "Folklore's Crisis." *Journal of American Folklore* 111: 281–327.

Kõiva, Mare. 2003. "Folkloristics Online: The Estonian Experience." *Folklore: An Electronic Journal of Folklore* 25: 7–34.

Knapp, Mary, and Herbert Knapp. 1976. *One Potato, Two Potato . . . The Secret Education of American Children*. New York: W. W. Norton.

Kobayashi, Toshiyuki, Wilfried Schmid, and Jae-Hyun Yang, eds. 2008. *Representation Theory and Automorphic Forms*. Boston: Birhäuser.

Kornblut, Anne. 2006. "Cheney Shoots Fellow Hunter in Accident on a Texas Ranch." *New York Times*, February 13.

Köstlin, Konrad, and Scott M. Shrake. 1997. "The Passion for the Whole: Interpreted Modernity or Modernity as Interpretation." *Journal of American Folklore* 110: 260–76.

Koven, Mikel J. 2000. "'Have I Got a Monster for You!': Some Thoughts on the Golem, 'The X-Files' and the Jewish Horror Movie." *Folklore* 111: 217–30.

Krauss, Daniel. 2000. "The Morbid Urge." Gadfly Online. http://www.gadflyonline.com/archive/JulyAugust00/archive-morbid.html (accessed 26 September 2008).

Krawczyk-Wasilewska, Violetta. 2006. "E-Folklore in the Age of Globalization." *Fabula* 47: 248– 54.

Kuntsman, Adi. 2004. "Cyberethnography as Home-Work." *Anthropology Matters Journal* 6: 1–10.

Kurin, Richard. 1997. *Reflections of a Culture Broker: A View from the Smithsonian.* Washington, DC: Smithsonian Institution Press.

Labbo, Linda D. 1996. "A Semiotic Analysis of Young Children's Symbol Making in a Classroom Computer Center." *Reading Research Quarterly* 31: 356–85.

Laineste, Liisi. 2003. "Researching Humor on the Internet." *Folklore: An Electronic Journal of Folklore* 25. http://www.folklore.ee/folklore/vol25/humor.pdf.

Lamb, Brian. 2005. "Q & A: Jimmy Wales." C-SPAN, September 25. http://qanda.org/Transcript/?ProgramID=1042 (accessed 6 April 2008).

Lanham, Richard. 1993. *The Electronic Word: Democracy, Technology, and the Arts.* Chicago: University of Chicago Press.

Lanier, Jaron. 2006. "Digital Maoism: The Hazards of the New Online Collectivism." Edge: The Third Culture, May 30. http://www.edge.org/3rd_culture/lanier06/lanier06_index.html (accessed 18 April 2008).

Larson, Bob. 1982. *Bob Larson's Book of Cults.* Wheaton, IL: Tyndale House.

———. 1988. *Talk Back with Bob Larson: Mormonism and Magic.* Sandy, UT: Mormon Miscellaneous.

———. 1989. *Bob Larson's New Book of Cults.* Wheaton, IL: Tyndale House.

———. 1997. *UFOs and the Alien Agenda.* Nashville, TN: T. Nelson.

———. 1999. *Larson's Book of Spiritual Warfare.* Nashville, TN: T. Nelson.

Laske, Otto. 1990. "The Computer as the Artist's Alter Ego." *Leonardo* 23: 53–66.

Laurel, Brenda. 1991. *Computers as Theatre.* Reading, MA: Addison-Wesley.

Laurelei. 2008. MySpace.com. Blog. http://profile.myspace.com (accessed 26 September 2008).

Lavazzi, Tom. 2001. "Communication On(the)line." *South Atlantic Review* 66: 126–44.

Lawless, Elaine J. 1998. "*Ars Rhetorica en Communitas*: Reclaiming the Voice of Passionate Expression in Electronic Writing." *Rhetoric Review* 16: 310–27.

Lederman, Rena. 2004. "Towards an Anthropology of Disciplinarity." *Critical Matrix* 15: 60–69.

Lee, Dorothy. [1950] 1968. "Codifications of Reality: Lineal and Nonlineal." In *Every Man His Way: Readings in Cultural Anthropology,* ed. Alan Dundes, 329–43. Englewood Cliffs, NJ: Prentice-Hall.

Lee, O-Young. 1992. *The Compact Culture: The Japanese Tradition of "Smaller is Better,"* trans. Robert N. Huey. Tokyo: Kodansha International.

Levine, Daniel H. 1990. "Popular Groups, Popular Culture, and Popular Religion." *Comparative Studies in Society and History* 32: 718–64.

Lewis, Jim. 1987. "Need Cited to Discuss Dwyer Death." *Patriot-News* (Harrisburg, PA), February 6, C1.

Lieber, Andrea. 2009. "Domesticity and the Home/Page: Blogging and the Blurring of Public and Private among Orthodox Jewish Women." In *Jews at Home: The Domestication of Identity,* ed. Simon J. Bronner. Oxford, UK: Littman.

Lipartito, Kenneth. 2003. "Picturephone and the Information Age: The Social Meaning of Failure." *Technology and Culture* 44: 50–81.

"List of Chat Acronyms & Text Message Shorthand." Netlingo. http://www.netlingo.com/emailsh.cfm (accessed 14 November 2008).

"List of Guantánamo Bay Detainees." Wikipedia. http://en.wikipedia.org/wiki/List_of_Guantanamo_detainees (accessed 18 April 2008).

"List of Wikipedias." Wikimedia. http://meta.wikimedia.org/w/index.php?title=List_of_Wikipedias&oldid=941360 (version of 2 April 2008, accessed 7 May 2008).

Longenecker, Gregory J. 1977. "Sequential Parody Graffiti." *Western Folklore* 36: 354–64.

Loomis, Grant C. 1958. "Mary Had a Parody: A Rhyme of Childhood in Folk Tradition." *Western Folklore* 17: 45–51.

Lord, Albert B. 1960. *The Singer of Tales*. Cambridge, MA: Harvard University Press.

Lowe, Donald M. 1982. *History of Bourgeois Perception*. Chicago: University of Chicago Press.

Lynch, Dainne. 1998. "A Place on the Web for Self-Restraint." *Christian Science Monitor* website, March 9. http://www.csmonitor.com/atcsmonitor/cyber-coverage/media/media0309.shtml (accessed 25 September 2008).

"Lynn Moran, 24: Missing in Portland, Maine." 2005. October 16. http://www.missingabducted.com/200510/lynn_moran_24_m.html (accessed 2 February 2008).

Malone, Guy. 2008. "Roswell NM—Alien Resistance HQ, UFO Bible Stop Alien Abduction Info." Alien Resistance.org. http://www.alienresistance.org/ (accessed 15 April 2008).

Mannheim, Karl. [1925] 1952. "The Problem of a Sociology of Knowledge." In *Essays on the Sociology of Knowledge*, trans. Paul Kecskemeti, 134–54. London: Routledge and Kegan Paul.

Maranda, Pierre. 1967. "Computers in the Bush: Tools for the Automatic Analysis of Myths." In *Essays on the Verbal and Visual Arts*, ed. June Helm, 77–83. Seattle: University of Washington Press.

Martin, Terry, and Kenneth J. Doka. 2000. *Men Don't Cry, Women Do: Transcending Gender Stereotypes of Grief*. Philadelphia: Brunner-Mazel.

Marvin, Lee-Ellen. 1995. "Spoof, Spam, Lurk, and Lag: The Aesthetics of Text-Based Virtual Realities." *Journal of Computer-Mediated Communication* 1. http://jcmc.indiana.edu/vol1/issue2/marvin.html.

Mason, Bruce L. 1996. "Moving toward Virtual Ethnography." *American Folklore Society News* 25: 4–6.

Matthews-DeNatale, Gail. "Keepsakes & Dreams." http://www.gailonline.org/keepsakes/.

McCarl, Robert McCarl. 1986. "Occupational Folklore." In *Folk Groups and Folklore Genres: An Introduction*, ed. Elliott Oring, 71–89. Logan: Utah State University Press.

McCaullum, E. L. 2001. "The Timezone Endgame." *CR: The New Centennial Review* 1: 141–73.

McClelland, Bruce. 2000. "Online Orality: The Internet, Folklore, and Culture in Russia." In *Culture and Technology in New Europe: Civic Discourse in Transformation in Post-Communist Nations*, ed. Laura B. Lengel, 179–91. Stamford, CT: Ablex.

McLuhan, Marshall. [1964] 1994. *Understanding Media: The Extensions of Man*. Cambridge, MA: MIT Press.

Mechling, Jay. 1993. "On Sharing Folklore and American Identity in a Multicultural Society." *Western Folklore* 52: 271–89.
———. 2004. "Picturing Hunting." *Western Folklore,* 63(1–2): 51–78.
———. 2005. "Found Photographs and Children's Folklore." *Children's Folklore
   Review* 27: 7–31.
———. 2006. "Solo Folklore." *Western Folklore* 65: 435–54.
Mencia, Carlos. 2008. "Re: The Biggest Tragedy in the World of Justice Will Soon
   Be a Movie." Vindy.com. Discussion Groups: Talk of the Valley, August 29.
   http://forums.vindy.com (accessed 25 September 2008).
Mertyl, Steve. 2006. "Tough Wolfe Was Downtown Eastside Guardian Angel
   before She Vanished." Vancouver Eastside Missing Women. http://www.
   missingpeople.net/vancouver_missing_women.htm (accessed 10 February
   2007).
Mika, Peter. 2007. *Social Networks and the Semantic Web.* New York: Springer.
Mikkelson, Barbara, and David P. Mikkelson. 2008. Snopes.com: Rumor Has It.
   http://snopes.com (accessed 16 June 2008).
"Milestones." 1987. *Time,* February 2, 68.
"Milestones in the Evolution of Today's Internet." 2007. *Congressional Digest* 86:
   38.
Millard, William B. 1997. "I Flamed Freud: A Case Study in Telextual
   Incendiarism." In *Internet Culture,* ed. David Porter, 145–60. New York:
   Routledge.
Miller, Laura. 2001. "Women and Children First: Gender and the Settling of the
   Electronic Frontier." In *Reading Digital Culture,* ed. David Trend, 214–20.
   Malden, MA: Blackwell.
Miller, Montana. 2007. "'It Wouldn't Be Heaven Without MySpace': Teenagers,
   Death, and Emerging Frames of Immortality." Unpublished paper, Depart-
   ment of Popular Culture, Bowling Green State University.
"Missing Child: Penny Brown." 2007. http://urbanlegends.about.com/library/
   blmiss7.htm (accessed 1 February 2008).
"Missing White Woman Syndrome." Wikipedia. http://en.wikipedia.org/
   wiki/Missing_white_woman_syndrome/ (accessed 27 January 2008).
Mississippi Arts Commission. "Crossroads of the Heart." http://www.arts.
   state.ms.us/crossroads/.
Monger, George. 1997. "Modern Wayside Shrines." *Folklore* 108: 113–14.
Montaldo, Charles. 2008. "Natalee Holloway: Missing in Aruba." http://crime.
   about.com/od/current/a/natalee.htm (accessed 2 February 2008).
———. 2009. "The Murder of Jessie Davis." http://crime.about.com/od/
   current/a/Jessie_davis.htm (accessed 29 May 2009).
Mullen, Patrick B. 2000. "Belief and the American Folk." *Journal of American
   Folklore* 113: 119–43.
Nakamura, Hajime. 1964. *Ways of Thinking of Eastern Peoples: India-China-Tibet-
   Japan.* Honolulu: East-West Center Press, 1964.
Newell, William Wells. 1883. *Games and Songs of American Children.* New York:
   Harper and Brothers.
"News and Current Events: Natalee Holloway." 2005. November 7. http://
   forums.about.com/n/pfx/forum.aspx?tsn=1&nav=messages&webpage
   =ab-gosoamerica&tid=810 (accessed 4 January 2007).

Nickerson, Bruce e. 1974. "Is There a Folk in the Factory?" *Journal of American Folklore* 87: 133–39.

"'90 Day Jane' A Hoax, Takes Down Site." 2008. Flumesday.com. Blog, February 13. http://www.flumesday.com/2008/02/13/90-day-jane-a-hoax-takes-down-site/ (accessed 28 September 2008).

Noyes, Dorothy. 1995. "Group." *Journal of American Folklore* 108: 449–78.

———. 2006. "The Judgment of Solomon: Global Protections for Tradition and the Problem of Community Ownership." *Cultural Analysis* 5: 27–56.

OCLC. 2003. *2003 Environmental Scan: A Report to the OCLC Membership.* http://www.oclc.org/reports/escan/introduction/default.htm (accessed 29 March 2007).

O'Connor, Bonnie Blair. 1995. *Healing Traditions.* Philadelphia: University of Pennsylvania Press.

Okin, J. R. 2005. *The Internet Revolution: The Not-for-Dummies Guide to the History, Technology, and Use of the Internet.* Winter Harbor, ME: Ironbound Press.

Origgi, Gloria. 2004. "Is Trust an Epistemological Notion?" *Episteme* 1: 1–12.

Oring, Elliott. 1978. "Transmission and Degeneration." *Fabula* 19: 193–210.

———. 1986. "Folk Narratives." In *Folk Groups and Folklore Genres: An Introduction*, ed. Elliott Oring, 121–46. Logan: Utah State University Press.

———. 1987. "Jokes and the Discourse on Disaster." *Journal of American Folklore* 100: 276–86.

———. 1992. *Jokes and Their Relations.* Lexington: University Press of Kentucky.

———. 1994. "The Arts, Artifacts, and Artifices of Identity." *Journal of American Folklore* 107: 211–47.

———. 1998. "Anti Anti-'Folklore.'" *Journal of American Folklore* 111: 328–38.

———. 2003. *Engaging Humor.* Urbana: University of Illinois Press.

———. 2008. "Legendry and the Rhetoric of Truth." *Journal of American Folklore* 121: 127–66.

Paredes, Américo, and Richard Bauman, eds. 1972. *Toward New Perspectives in Folklore.* Austin: University of Texas Press for the American Folklore Society.

Park, Michael Y. 2002. "Online Art Form Gains Popularity." FOXNews.com, March 18. http://www.foxnews.com/story/0,2933,48116,00.html

Parsons, Patrick R., and William E. Smith. 1988. "R. Budd Dwyer: A Case Study in Newsroom Decision Making." *Journal of Mass Media Ethics* 3: 84–94.

Patiris, Phillip D. 1999. "The Budd Dwyer Suicide Clip: Communication Ethics . . . and a Change of Mind." Modern Television. Blog, November 20. http://www.moderntv.com/modtvweb/qtclips/buddintro.htm (accessed 24 September 2008).

Petöfi, János S. and Eva Szöllösy. 1969. "Computers in Folklore Research." *Computational Linguistics* 8: 65–70.

"Photoshop Tutorials." http://www.worth1000.com/tutorials.asp.

Porter, Mark. 2001. "Cyberdemocracy: The Internet and the Public Sphere." In *Reading Digital Culture*, ed. David Trend, 259–71. Malden, MA: Blackwell.

Powell, Chris, and George E. C. Paton, eds. 1988. *Humour in Society.* London: MacMillan.

Prensky, Marc. 2001a. "Digital Natives, Digital Immigrants." *On the Horizon* 9(5): 1–6.

————. 2001b. "Digital Natives, Digital Immigrants, Part II: Do They Really *Think* Differently?" *On the Horizon* 9(6): 1–6.

Preston, Michael J. 1994. "Traditional Humor from the Fax Machine: 'All of a Kind.'" *Western Folklore* 53: 147–69.

————. 1996. "Computer Folklore." In *American Folklore: An Encyclopedia*, ed. Jan Harold Brunvand, 154–55. New York: Garland.

Primiano, Leonard Norman. 1995. "Vernacular Religion and the Search for Method in Religious Folklife." *Western Folklore* 54: 37–56.

"Pseudonymity." Wikipedia. http://en.wikipedia.org/wiki/Pseudonymity (accessed 6 April 2008).

Putnam, Robert D. 2000. *Bowling Alone: The Collapse and Revival of American Community*. New York: Simon & Schuster.

Randall, Lisa. 2002. "Extra Dimensions and Warped Geometries." *Science* 296: 1422–27.

Read, Allen Walker. 1935. *Lexical Evidence from Folk Epigraphy in Western North America: A Glossarial Study of the Low Element in the English Vocabulary*. Paris: Privately Printed.

"Revision History of Kurt Andersen." Wikipedia. http://en.wikipedia.org/w/index.php?title=Kurt_Andersen&action=history (accessed 6 April 2008).

"Revision History of Simon J. Bronner." Wikipedia. http://en.wikipedia.org/w/index.php?title=Simon_J._Bronner&action=history (accessed 6 April 2008).

Rheingold, Howard. 2000. *The Virtual Community: Homesteading on the Electronic Frontier*. Cambridge, MA: MIT Press. Electronic version (1993) available at http://www.rheingold.com/vc/book/2.html.

————. 2001. "The Virtual Community.' In *Reading Digital Culture*, ed. David Trend, 272–80. Malden, MA: Blackwell.

Ringley, Jennifer. 1999. "Why I Star in My Own Truman Show: Jennicam's Jennifer Ringley on Why She Broadcasts Her Life Online." *Cosmopolitan*, October, 76.

Robinson, Eugene. 2005. "(White) Women We Love." *Washington Post*, June 10. http://www.washingtonpost.com/wp-dyn/content/article/2005/06/09/AR2005060901729.html (accessed 11 October 2006).

Rodríguez, Rubén Rosario. 2007. "Liberating Epistemology: Wikipedia and the Social Construction of Knowledge." *Religious Studies and Theology* 26: 173–201.

Roemer, Danielle. 1994. "Photocopy Lore and the Naturalization of the Corporate Body." *Journal of American Folklore* 107: 121–38.

Ronnell, Avital. 2001. "A Disappearance of Community.' In *Reading Digital Culture*, ed. David Trend, 287–93. Malden, MA: Blackwell.

Rosen, Jonathan. 2000. *The Talmud and the Internet: A Journey Between Worlds*. New York: Farrar, Straus and Giroux.

Ross, Andrew. 2001. "The New Smartness." In *Reading Digital Culture*, ed. David Trend, 354–63. Malden, MA: Blackwell.

Roush, Jan. 1997. "Folklore Fieldwork on the Internet: Some Ethical and Practical Considerations." In *Between the Cracks of History: Essays on Teaching and Illustrating Folklore*, eds. Francis Edward Abernathy and Carolyn Fiedler, 42-53. Publications of the Texas Folklore Society 55. Nacogdoches, TX: Texas Folklore Society.

Russell, Don. 1998. "Dwyer Suicide Lives On: Sex Isn't All That Parents Should Monitor on the Web." *Philadelphia Daily News* website, February 16. http://www.moderntv.com/modtvweb/budd/buddpress/budd16b.htm (accessed 25 September 2008).

Saint Claire, Marie. 2005. "Natalee Holloway Missing in Aruba: A Psychic Investigation." Underworld Tales. http://www.underworldtales.com/aruba.htm.

Salamon, Hagar. 2001. "Political Bumper Stickers in Contemporary Israel: Folklore as an Emotional Battleground." *Journal of American Folklore* 114: 277–308.

Santino, Jack. 2006. "Spontaneous Shrines, Performative Commemoratives, and the Public Memorialization of Death." In *Spontaneous Shrines and the Public Memorialization of Death*, ed. Jack Santino, 5–16. New York: Palgrave Macmillan.

"Scared Monkeys Missing Persons Site, 2005–2008." http://missingexploited.com/ (accessed January 2007 to February 2008).

Sebeok, Thomas A. 1965. "The Computer as a Tool in Folklore Research.' In *The Use of Computers in Anthropology*, ed. Dell Hymes, 255–72. The Hague: Mouton.

Shapin, Steven. 1995. *A Social History of Truth: Civility and Science in Seventeenth-Century England*. Chicago: University of Chicago Press.

Shatzer, Milton J., and Thomas R. Lindlof. 1998. "Media Ethnography in Virtual Space: Strategies, Limits, and Possibilities." *Journal of Broadcasting and Electronic Media* 42: 170–89.

Shopes, Linda. 2003. "Commentary: Sharing Authority." *Oral History Review* 30: 103–10.

Shea, Virginia. 1994. *Netiquette*. San Francisco: Albian.

Sherman, Sharon R. 1998. *Documenting Ourselves: Film, Video, and Culture*. Lexington: University Press of Kentucky.

Shipley, David, and Will Schwalbe. 2007. *Send: The Essential Guide to Email for Home and Office*. New York: Alfred A. Knopf.

"SikhiWiki Homepage." SikhiWiki. http://www.sikhiwiki.org (accessed 7 May 2008).

"SikhiWiki: Introduction." SikhiWiki. http://www.sikhiwiki.org/index.php/SikhiWiki:Introduction (accessed 10 May 2008).

Silver, David, Adrienne Massanari, and Steve Jones, eds. 2006. *Critical Cyberculture Studies*. New York: New York University Press.

Simmel, Georg. 1906. "The Sociology of Secrecy and of Secret Societies." *American Journal of Sociology* 11: 441–98.

Simons, Elizabeth Radin. 1986. "The NASA Joke Cycle: The Astronauts and the Teacher." *Western Folklore* 45: 261–77.

Simpson, George. 1951. "Editor's Introduction." In *Suicide: A Study in Sociology* by Emile Durkheim, edited by George Simpson, 13–32. New York: Free Press.

Sims, Robert S. 2008. "Battle Focused." Battle Focused Ministries. http://www.battlefocused.org/ (accessed 15 April 2008).

Smith, Michael R. 1987. "Newsroom Dilemma." *Editor & Publisher*, January 31, 9–11.

Smith, Robert James. 1999. "Roadside Memorials: Some Australian Examples." *Folklore* 110: 103–05.

Smithsonian Institution. "Silk Road: Connecting Cultures, Creating Trust." http://www.silkroadproject.org/.

———. "Smithsonian Folklife Festival." http://www.festival.si.edu/.

Smyth, Willie. 1986. "Challenger Jokes and the Humor of Disaster." *Western Folklore* 45: 243–60.

"Special: Statistics." Wikipedia. http://en.wikipedia.org/wiki/Special:Statistics (accessed 6 April 2008).

"Spiritual Aggression." 2003. Alternative Counseling. http://www.wcc. net/~bfrasure/spr-agr.html (accessed 15 April 2008).

"Spiritual Mapping for Effective Spiritual Warfare." 2008. Battle Axe Brigade. http://www.battleaxe.org/map.html (accessed 15 April 2008).

"Spiritual Warfare: Battle—Spiritual Warfare." 2008. Aaron's Bible University. http://www.aaronsbibleuniversity.com/Documents/Spiritual_Warfare/ Battle_Spiritual_Warfare.htm (accessed 15 April 2008).

"Spiritual Warfare: Cares, Worries, Pleasures." 2008. Aaron's Bible University. http://www.parentalguide.com/Documents/Spiritual_Warfare/cares_ worries_pleasures1.htm (accessed 15 April 2008).

Sproull, Lee, and Sara Kiesler. 1992. *Connections: New Ways of Working in the Networked World*. Cambridge, MA: MIT Press.

"Sockpuppet (Internet)." Wikipedia. http://en.wikipedia.org/wiki/Sockpup- pet_(Internet) (accessed 6 April 2008).

Sommerer, Christa, and Laurent Mignonneau. 1999. "Art as a Living System: Interactive Computer Artworks." *Leonardo* 32: 165–73.

Stelter, Brian. 2008. "Charging by the Byte to Curb Internet Traffic." *New York Times*, June 15, 1, 21.

Stewart, Edward C., and Milton J. Bennett. 1991. *American Cultural Patterns*. Revised Edition. Yarmouth, ME: Intercultural Press.

Stivale, Charles J. 1997. "Spam: Heteroglossia and Harassment in Cyber- space." In *Internet Culture*, ed. David Porter, 133–44. New York: Routledge.

Stratton, Jon. 1997. "Cyberspace and the Globalization of Culture." In *Internet Culture*, ed. David Porter, 253–76. New York: Routledge.

"Suicide Video Link." 2007. MetaTalk, April 28. Discussion Thread. http:// metatalk.metafilter.com/14104/suicide-video-link (accessed 26 Septem- ber 2008).

Sullivan, Bob. 2005. "Kids, Blogs and Too Much Information." MSNBC web- site. http://www.msnbc.msn.com/id/7668788/ (accessed 15 June 2008).

Swiss, Thomas. 2004. "Electronic Literature: Discourses, Communities, Tradi- tions." In *Memory Bytes: History, Technology, and Digital Culture*, eds. Lau- ren Rabinovitz and Abraham Geil, 283–304. Durham: Duke University Press.

Tabbi, Joseph. 1997. "Reading, Writing, Hypertext: Democratic Politics in the Virtual Classroom." In *Internet Culturei,* ed. David Porter, 233–52. New York: Routledge.

"Talkback: 'Missing in Paradise' (Natalee Holloway)." 2007. June 20. http:// www.carlabaron.net/forum/showthread.php?p=7166.

Tancer, Bill. 2006. "MySpace Moves into #1 Position for All Internet Sites." http://weblogs.hitwise.com/bill-tancer/2006/07/myspace_moves_into_1_position.html.

Tangherlini, Timothy R. 1990. "'It Happened Not too Far from Here . . .': A Survey of Legend Theory and Characterization." *Western Folklore* 49: 371–90.

Templeton, Brad. "RHF Submission Guidelines." Rec.Humor.Funny. http://www.netfunny.com/rhf/submit.html.

Thomas, Jeannie Banks. 2006. "Communicative Commemoration and Graveside Shrines: Princess Diana, Jim Morrison, My 'Bro' Max, and Boogs the Cat." In Santino, *Spontaneous Shrines*, 7–40.

———. 2007a. "The Usefulness of Ghost Stories." In *Haunting Experiences: Ghosts in Contemporary Folklore*, by Diane E. Goldstein, Sylvia Ann Grider, and Jeannie Banks Thomas, 25–59. Logan: Utah State University Press.

———. 2007b. "Gender and Ghosts." In *Haunting Experiences: Ghosts in Contemporary Folklore*, Diane E. Goldstein, Sylvia Ann Grider, and Jeannie Banks Thomas, ___. Logan: Utah State University Press.

Thompson, Stith, ed. 1968. *One Hundred Favorite Folktales*. Bloomington, IN: Indiana University Press.

Toffler, Alvin. 1980. *The Third Wave*. New York: Morrow.

TripAdvisor. 2005. "Aruba Forum: Alert." June 3. http://www.tripadvisor.com/ShowTopic-g147247-i144-k158081-o120-Aruba.htm (accessed 17 February 2007).

Truscello, Michael. 2003. "The Architecture of Information: Open Source Software and Tactical Postructuralist Anarchism." *Postmodern Culture* 13, May. http://muse.jhu.edu/journals/postmodern_culture/toc/pmc13.3.html (accessed 12 June 2008).

Tucker, Elizabeth. 2005. *Campus Legends*. Westport, CT: Greenwood.

———. 2007. *Haunted Halls: Ghostlore of American College Campuses*. Jackson: University Press of Mississippi.

Tumulty, Karen. 2008. "Can Obama Shred the Rumors?" *Time*, June 23, 40–41.

Turkle, Sherry. 1995. *Life on the Screen: Identity in the Age of the Internet*. New York: Simon and Schuster.

"2012: The Year the Internet Ends." 2008. ScrewAttack.com. Blog. http://www.screwattack.com/node/4003 (accessed 14 November 2008).

Underberg, Natalie. 2006. "Virtual and Reciprocal Ethnography on the Internet: The East Mims Oral History Project Website." *Journal of American Folklore* 119: 301–11.

University of Central Florida. "Folkvine." http://www.folkvine.org/.

"USA Congressional Staff Edits to Wikipedia." Wikipedia. http://en.wikipedia.org/wiki/USA_Congressional_staff_edits_to_Wikipedia (accessed 6 April 2008).

"User contributions" [User:68.83.74.246]. Wikipedia. http://en.wikipedia.org/wiki/Special:Contributions/68.83.74.246 (accessed 6 April 2008).

"User: Darwinek." Wikipedia. http://en.wikipedia.org/w/index.php?title=User:Darwinek&direction=prev&oldid=165819959 (version of 6 October 2007).

"User: Ezhiki." Wikipedia. http://en.wikipedia.org/wiki/User:Ezhiki (accessed 17 December 2008).

"User: Larix." Wikipedia. http://en.wikipedia.org/wiki/User:Larix (accessed 9 May 2008).

"User: Mailer Diablo/The Mailer Diablo Deletion Project/Userbox Wars." Wikipedia. http://en.wikipedia.org/wiki/User:Mailer_diablo/The_Mailer_Diablo_Deletion_Project/Userbox_Wars (accessed 10 May 2008).

"User: Mtmelendez/Userboxes/Maltese Falcon." Wikipedia. http://en.wikipedia.org/wiki/User:Mtmelendez/Userboxes/Maltese_Falcon (accessed 7 April 2008).

"User: Rhanyeia, 10 March 2008." In "Wikipedia Talk: Userboxes." Wikipedia. http://en.wikipedia.org/wiki/Wikipedia_talk:Userboxes (accessed 18 April 2008).

"User Talk: Ian[13]." Wikipedia. http://en.wikipedia.org/w/index.php?title=User_talk:Ian13&oldid=33380400 (version of 31 December 2005).

"User Talk: Ilmari Karonen/archive2." Wikipedia. http://en.wikipedia.org/wiki/User_talk:Ilmari_Karonen/archive2 (accessed 18 April 2008).

"User Talk: Tony Sidaway." Wikipedia. http://en.wikipedia.org/w/index.php?title=User_talk:Tony_Sidaway&diff=33714517&oldid=33714334#Userboxes_.28again.29 (version of 3 January 2006).

"Vancouver Eastside Missing Women." http://www.missingpeople.net/Vancouver_missing_women.htm (accessed 21 January 2007).

"Vancouver Missing, Guestbook ." 2007. January 22. http://www.missingpeople.net/Vancouver_missing.htm (accessed 2 March 2007).

Victor, Jeffrey S. 1993. *Satanic Panic: The Creation of a Contemporary Legend*. Chicago: Open Court.

Virilio, Paul. 2001. "Speed and Information: Cyberspace Alarm!" In *Reading Digital Culture*, ed. David Trend, 23–27. Malden, MA: Blackwell.

"Virus Hoaxes & Realities." 2008. Snopes.com: Rumor Has It. Urban Legends References Pages. http://snopes.com/computer/virus/virus.asp (accessed 3 October 2008).

Waldrop, M. Mitchell. 1985. "String as a Theory of Everything." *Science* 229: 1251–53.

Wales, Jimmy. 2006. "Post to [WikiEN-l] Jimbo and his strategy." February 20. http://lists.wikimedia.org/pipermail/wikien-l/2006-February/040148.html (accessed 18 April 2008).

Wallace, Patricia. 1999. *The Psychology of the Internet*. Cambridge, UK: Cambridge University Press.

Webb, Mark. 2004. "Can Epistemology Help? The Problem of the Kentucky-Fried Rats." *Social Epistemology* 18: 51–58.

Weber, Steven. 2004. *The Success of Open Source*. Cambridge, MA: Harvard University Press.

Weber, Sandra, and Shanly Dixon. 2007. *Growing Up Online: Young People and Digital Technologies*. New York: Palgrave Macmillan.

Webster, Frank. 2005. "Network." In *New Keywords: A Revised Vocabulary of Culture and Society*, eds. Tony Bennett, Lawrence Grossberg, and Meaghan Morris, 239–41. Malden, MA: Blackwell.

Welsch, Roger. 1974. "Bigger'n Life: The Tall Tale Postcard." *Southern Folklore Quarterly* 38: 311–23.

Weingard, Robert. 1988. "A Philosopher Looks at String Theory." *PSA: Proceedings of the Biennial Meeting of the Philosophy of Science Association* 2: 95–106.

Westerman, William. 2006. "Folkloristics and the Wikipedia: A Call for Submissions, of Sorts." *American Folklore Society News* 35: 7.

Western Folklife Center. http://www.westernfolklife.org/site1/index.php.

"What is a Demon?" 2003. Bob Larson Ministries. http://www.boblarson.org/materials/what_is_a_demon/what_is_a_demon.html (accessed April 15, 2004).

White, Merry. 1994. *The Material Child: Coming of Age in Japan and America.* Berkeley: University of California Press.

Whisnant, David E. 1983. *All That is Native and Fine: The Politics of Culture in an American Region.* Chapel Hill: University of North Carolina Press.

White, Thomas B. 1990. *The Believer's Guide to Spiritual Warfare.* Ann Arbor, MI: Servant.

Wilbur, Shawn P. 1997. "An Archaeology of Cyberspaces: Virtuality, Community, Identity." In *Internet Culture*, ed. David Porter, 5–22. New York: Routledge.

Will. 2005. Response to "Ray Gricar Missing." StateCollege.com. Discussion thread on Townhall Forum, April 21. http://www.statecollege.com/townhall (accessed 26 September 2008).

Williams, Susan. 2001. "Folklore Documents the 'Full Complexity of the Human Condition.'" IU Home Pages. http://www.homepages.indiana.edu/041301/text/folklore.html (accessed 15 November 2008).

"Wiki." Wikipedia. http://en.wikipedia.org/wiki/Wiki (accessed 6 April 2008).

"Wikiculture." Wikimedia. http://meta.wikimedia.org/wiki/Wikiculture (accessed 9 May 2008).

"Wikimania 2008 Main Page." Wikimania. http://wikimania2008.wikimedia.org/wiki/Main_Page (accessed 10 May 2008).

"Wikipedia." Wikipedia. http://en.wikipedia.org/wiki/Wikipedia (accessed 5 April2008).

"Wikipedia: Administrators." Wikipedia. http://en.wikipedia.org/wiki/Wikipedia:Administrators (accessed 6 April 2008).

"Wikipedia Article Traffic Statistics: Most Viewed Articles in February." http://stats.grok.se/en/top (accessed 6 April 2008).

"Wikipedia: Bot Policy." Wikipedia. http://en.wikipedia.org/wiki/Wikipedia:Bot_policy (accessed 18 April 2008).

"Wikipedia: Etiquette." Wikipedia. http://en.wikipedia.org/wiki/Wikipedia:Etiquette (accessed 6 April 2008).

"Wikipedia: Five Pillars." Wikipedia. http://en.wikipedia.org/wiki/Wikipedia:5P (accessed 6 April 2008).

"Wikipedia: List of Wikipedians by Number of Edits." Wikipedia. http://en.wikipedia.org/wiki/Wikipedia:List_of_Wikipedians_by_number_of_edits (accessed 7 May 2008).

"Wikipedia: Neutral Point of View." Wikipedia. http://en.wikipedia.org/wiki/Wikipedia:Neutral_point_of_view (accessed 6 April 2008).

"Wikipedia: Neutral Point of View/FAQ." Wikipedia. http://en.wikipedia.org/wiki/Wikipedia:Neutral_point_of_view/FAQ (accessed 6 April 2008)

"Wikipedia: Policies and Guidelines." Wikipedia. http://en.wikipedia.org/wiki/Wikipedia:Policies_and_guidelines (accessed 6 April 2008).

"Wikipedia: Replies to Common Objections." Wikipedia. http://en.wikipedia.org/wiki/Wikipedia:Replies_to_common_objections (accessed 6 April 2008).

"Wikipedia Statistics: Active Wikipedians." Wikimedia. http://stats.wikimedia.org/EN/TablesWikipediansEditsGt5.htm (accessed 6 April 2008).

"Wikipedia Talk: Esperanza." Wikipedia. http://en.wikipedia.org/wiki/Wikipedia_talk:Esperanza (accessed 18 April 2008).

"Wikipedia Talk: Proposed Policy on Userboxes." Wikipedia. http://en.wikipedia.org/wiki/Wikipedia_talk:Proposed_policy_on_userboxes (accessed 9 May 2008).

"Wikipedia Talk: T1 and T2 Debates." Wikipedia. http://en.wikipedia.org/wiki/Wikipedia_talk:T1_and_T2_debates#The_German_solution (accessed 18 April 2008).

"Wikipedia Talk: Userboxes/Archive 4." Wikipedia. http://en.wikipedia.org/wiki/Wikipedia_talk:Userboxes/Archive_4 (accessed 18 April 2008).

"Wikipedia Talk: Userboxes/New Userboxes." Wikipedia. http://en.wikipedia.org/wiki/Wikipedia:Userboxes/New_Userboxes (accessed 7 April 2008).

"Wikipedia: Templates for Deletion." Wikipedia. http://en.wikipedia.org/w/index.php?title=Wikipedia:Templates_for_deletion&oldid=33343409#Template:User_NoSanta (version of 31 December 2005).

"Wikipedia: Transclusion." Wikipedia. http://en.wikipedia.org/wiki/Wikipedia:Transclusion (accessed 6 April 2008).

"Wikipedia: Userboxes." Wikipedia. http://en.wikipedia.org/w/index.php?title=Wikipedia:Userboxes&oldid=28698767 (version of 18 November 2005).

"Wikipedia: Userboxes." Wikipedia. http://en.wikipedia.org/wiki/Wikipedia:Userboxes (accessed 7 April 2008).

"Wikipedia: Userboxes/Politics." Wikipedia. http://en.wikipedia.org/w/index.php?title=Wikipedia:Userboxes/Politics&direction=next&oldid=249421900 (version of 4 November 2008).

"Wikipedia: Userboxes/Userboxes." Wikipedia. http://en.wikipedia.org/wiki/Wikipedia:Userboxes/Userboxes (accessed 7 April 2008).

"Wikipedia: User Page." Wikipedia. http://en.wikipedia.org/wiki/Wikipedia:User_page (accessed 6 April 2008).

"Wikipedia: What Wikipedia Is Not." Wikipedia. http://en.wikipedia.org/wiki/Wikipedia:NOT (accessed 6 April 2008).

"Wikipedia: Wikipediholic." Wikipedia. http://en.wikipedia.org/wiki/Wikipedia:Wikipediholic (accessed 7 May 2008).

"Wikipedia: Wikipediholism Test." Wikipedia. http://en.wikipedia.org/wiki/Wikipedia:Wikipediholism_test (accessed 7 May 2008).

"Wikipedia: WikiProject." Wikipedia. http://en.wikipedia.org/wiki/Wikipedia:WikiProject (accessed 18 April 2008).

"Wikipedia: WikiProject Council/Directory/Culture." Wikipedia. http://en.wikipedia.org/wiki/Wikipedia:WikiProject_Council/Directory/Culture (accessed 10 May 2008).

"Wikipedia: WikiProject Council/Directory/Geographical/Americas." Wikipedia. http://en.wikipedia.org/wiki/Wikipedia:WikiProject_Council/Directory/Geographical/Americas (accessed 10 May 2008).

"Wikipedia: WikiProject Userboxes." Wikipedia. http://en.wikipedia.org/wiki/Wikipedia:WikiProject_Userboxes (accessed 10 May 2008).

Winchester, Simon. 2003. *The Meaning of Everything*. Oxford: Oxford University Press, 2003.

Wisconsin Arts Board. "Wisconsin Folks." http://www.arts.state.wi.us/static/folkdir/index.htm.

Wodehouse, P. G. 1919. *A Damsel in Distress*. New York: George H. Doran.

Wojcik, Daniel. 1996. "Polaroids from Heaven." *Journal of American Folklore* 109: 129–48.

———. 1997. *The End of the World As We Know It: Faith, Fatalism, and Apocalypse in America*. New York: New York University Press.

Wood, Andrew F., and Matthew J. Smith. 2005. *Online Communication: Linking Technology, Identity, and Culture*. Mahwah, NJ: Lawrence Erlbaum.

Yoder, Don. 1974. "Toward a Definition of Folk Religion." *Western Folklore* 33: 2–15.

Yoshida, Mitsukuni, Tanaka Ikko, and Sesoko Tsune, eds. 1982. *The Compact Culture: The Ethos of Japanese Life*. Hiroshima: Toyo Kogyo.

Žižek, Slavoj. 2001. "From Virtual Reality to the Virtualization of Reality." In *Reading Digital Culture*, ed. David Trend, 17–22. Malden, MA: Blackwell.

Zuckerman, M., J. Porac, D. Lathin, R. Smith, and E. L. Deci. 1978. "On the Importance of Self-Determination for Intrinsically Motivated Behavior." *Personality and Social Psychology Bulletin* 4: 443–46.

Zukin, Sharon. 2004. *Point of Purchase: How Shopping Changed American Culture*. New York: Routledge.

About the Contributors

TREVOR J. BLANK is a doctoral student in American studies at the Pennsylvania State University, Harrisburg. He earned his master's degree at Indiana University's Folklore Institute in 2007. He has presented research at over a dozen conferences nationwide and has published articles in such journals as *Folklore Forum, Pioneer America Society Transactions, The Folklore Historian,* and *Material Culture.* He recently coauthored *Spring Grove State Hospital* (with David S. Helsel), which examines the history of the second oldest continuously operating psychiatric facility in America.

SIMON J. BRONNER is the Distinguished University Professor of American Studies and Folklore at the Pennsylvania State University, Harrisburg. He has also taught at Harvard University, the University of California at Davis, Osaka University (Japan), and Leiden University (The Netherlands). He is the author and editor of over twenty-five books, including *Encyclopedia of American Folklife, Following Tradition: Folklore in the Discourse of American Culture, Manly Traditions: The Folk Roots of American Masculinities,* and *Piled Higher and Deeper: The Folklore of Student Life.* His awards for scholarship include the John Ben Snow Foundation Prize, Peter and Iona Opie Prize, and Wayland D. Hand Prize for folklore and history.

ROBERT DOBLER is a graduate student in the Folklore Department at the University of Oregon. He has a B.A. in English from the Pennsylvania State University. His research interests include contemporary vernacular memorialization processes, roadside attractions, neosideshow groups, and millennial religious movements. He has published on topics including bohemianism, graffiti, and the religious comics of Jack Chick. He was recently awarded the Don Yoder Prize for the Best Student Paper in Folk Belief or Religious Folklife, and the Alma Johnson Graduate Folklore Award.

RUSSELL FRANK is a folklorist by training and a journalist by trade. He worked at newspapers for thirteen years before joining the journalism faculty at the Pennsylvania State University, where he is now an associate professor of communications. His research interests include journalism ethics, literary journalism, and the study of what he calls newslore: folklore in the news and the news in folklore.

GREGORY HANSEN is an associate professor of folklore and English at Arkansas State University. He has worked as a public folklorist for a variety of organizations, including the Kentucky Center for the Arts, Danish Immigrant Museum, Smithsonian Institution, and Florida Folklife Program. His creative and scholarly works include documentary video productions, photographic exhibits, and the coordination of festivals, concerts, and educational programs on folklife studies. He recently published *A Florida Fiddler: The Life and Times of Richard Seaman*.

ROBERT GLENN HOWARD is associate director of the Folklore Program and an assistant professor in the Communication Arts Department at the University of Wisconsin, where he teaches courses on folklore, religion, and rhetoric. His research focuses on everyday expressive communication in network technologies and has appeared in such journals as the *Journal of American Folklore, Critical Studies in Media Communication, Journal of the American Society for Information Science and Technology*, and *New Media & Society*. He currently serves as the editor of the journal *Western Folklore*.

LYNNE S. MCNEILL is a lecturer in folklore and English at Utah State University and is a doctoral candidate in folklore at Memorial University of Newfoundland. Her research interests include legend and belief, narrative, emerging contexts for tradition, space and place, ethnography, and globalization. Her favorite tale type is AT313C.

ELIZABETH TUCKER teaches folklore at Binghamton University. Her publications include *Campus Legends* (2005), *Haunted Halls: Ghostlore of American College Campuses* (2007), and *Children's Folklore: A Handbook* (2008). She edits the journal *Children's Folklore Review*. During her free time, she enjoys surfing the Web and e-mailing with folklorists around the world.

WILLIAM WESTERMAN is a lecturer in the Writing Program at Princeton University, where he teaches courses on migration and social justice. Prior to that, he was the director of the Cambodian American Heritage Museum and Killing Fields Memorial in Chicago, Illinois; the founder and director of the Program for Immigrant Traditional Artists at the International Institute of New Jersey; and staff folklorist for the Philadelphia Folklore Project. He has taught at Rutgers, Villanova, and the University of Pennsylvania, from which he received his Ph.D. in folklore and folklife.

Index